Students
as
Tutors
and
Mentors

In memory of

Alec Dickson

founder of Voluntary Service Overseas and of

Community Service Volunteers

whose boundless faith in young people
was the inspiration for many people now involved
in organising student tutoring and mentoring

and in respect for, and gratitude to, the thousands of

students

who are giving generously of their time
to help other people.

Students as Tutors and Mentors

EDITED BY

Sinclair Goodlad

published in association with BP

KOGAN PAGE

London • Philadelphia

First published in 1995.

Apart from any fair dealing for the purposes of research or private study, or criticism or review, as permitted under the Copyright, Designs and Patents Act, 1988, this publication may only be reproduced, stored or transmitted, in any form or by any means, with the prior permission in writing of the publishers, or in the case of reprographic reproduction in accordance with the terms of licences issued by the Copyright Licensing Agency. Enquiries concerning reproduction outside those terms should be sent to the publishers at the undermentioned address:

Kogan Page Limited
120 Pentonville Road
London N1 9JN

© Sinclair Goodlad, 1995

British Library Cataloguing in Publication Data

A CIP record for this book is available from the British Library

ISBN 0 7494 1792 7

Typeset by Photoprint, Torquay
Printed and bound in Great Britain by
Biddles Ltd, Guildford and King's Lynn

CONTENTS

v

Contents

PART E: THE WIDER SCENE

PREFACE AND ACKNOWLEDGEMENTS

This is not a book of conference proceedings; however, it was stimulated by a conference planned by John C Hughes, formerly BP Fellow in Student Tutoring at Imperial College, and currently manager of the British Petroleum International Mentoring and Tutoring Project. Without his work, and that of his colleagues Roger Banfield, Nancy John and Julie Nicholls, and without the financial support of BP, the conference would not have happened and the book would not have been written. It is fitting that Russell Seal, a managing director of BP, should have written the foreword to the book.

The BP team was assisted by a planning group consisting of Brian Gay, Sinclair Goodlad, Meenal Gupta, John Mohan, Lorraine Price and Danny Saunders. This steering group was supported by an international advisory group consisting of Nathan Avani, Toni Beardon, Amos Carmeli, Christopher Cole, Russell Elsegood, Carol FitzGibbon, Allen Flinn, Audrey Gartner, Joe Hogan, John Jones, Alison Lockwood, Rob Northcott, Glenn Odenbrett, Judy Porter, John Potter, Barry Rowswell, Margaret Rutherford, Ron Sims, Jay Smink, Carol Stoel, Joe Tierney, Keith Topping, Jan Torres, Jenni Wallace and Jerald Wilbur. These people undertook (anonymous) refereeing of papers in their special fields. Caroline Gatenby did heroic work in typing. Clare Andrews, Dolores Black and Liz Roberts of Kogan Page have seen the book through the process of production. To all I am most grateful.

The European Commission made a grant towards the production of the book which has made possible the lowering of the cover price to a figure that (it is hoped) people can afford. Support for the BP conference was also given by the British Council, British Airways, the UK Department for Education and the UK Department of Employment.

Preface and acknowledgements

One of the keynote speakers at the conference was to have been Alec Dickson, founder of Voluntary Service Overseas and of Community Service Volunteers, whose boundless faith in young people was the inspiration for many people now involved in organising student tutoring and mentoring. Alec died shortly before the conference took place. This book is dedicated to his memory, and it is written in respect for, and gratitude to, the thousands of students who are giving generously of their time to help other people. If this book stimulates others to emulate them, it will have served its purpose.

Sinclair Goodlad
Imperial College
London June 1995

FOREWORD

Russell Seal

Having opened the BP International Conference, *Students as Tutors and Mentors* early in 1995, it is a pleasure for me to provide the Foreword to this book.

As a managing director of a major international company which believes that sharing best practice across 70 countries where it operates is the way to grow and learn, I am pleased to see evidence of experience from so many countries in this book – the conference itself had delegates from 34 countries. The rich diversity of international cultures provided a unique opportunity to listen and learn from each other and now this book helps to spread the experiences to communities across the globe.

BP believes it is the company's duty to be a good neighbour and to earn the trust of the community by being a responsible corporate citizen. We therefore stress to our employees the importance of working in partnership with the communities around our business sites. In so doing we aim to maintain and enhance our valued good reputation, and thus our own ability to perform – a win-win for all parties.

With continuous change and uncertainty about the future nature of work, the need for an educated society and business to work closely together is greater now than at any time. Students who act as tutors and mentors are provided with the opportunity to develop their transferable skills, which helps them find rewarding and challenging careers. School pupils who have student tutors or mentors are provided with positive role models to raise their aspirations to continue with education and training and also get added assistance with their learning.

BP is committed to supporting programmes like this because working with people in education is about interdependence. BP needs a thriving economy in which to operate. Society needs a thriving economy in which to live. The key to this for both BP and society is education.

Foreword

This is the fifth year of BP support for the International Mentoring and Tutoring Project, a project we run in a valued partnership with Imperial College, University of London. Since 1990 and as a result of this project, more than 200 universities and colleges around the world plus thousands of schools have benefited from the project's expertise and that of our educational and business partners. Some 200,000 young people around the world this year will benefit from a student tutor and over the five years more than half a million young people have been helped.

As well as providing free consultancies to universities in many countries we have given direct grants for pilot projects to more than 85 universities in 15 countries. We have also published resources including a 'how to' pack, a training video and more than 100,000 background booklets for schools, colleges and universities.

We put the secret of the project's success down to a simple proverb:

Tell me and I forget
Show me and I remember
Involve me and I understand.

I am sure this book will contribute to our levels of understanding.

For more information on the resources published by BP please contact BP Educational Service, PO Box 934, Poole, BH17 7BR, UK. Tel: +44 (0)1202 669940, Fax: +44 (0)1202 661999.

CONTRIBUTORS

Sir Christopher Ball is Director of Learning at the Royal Society of Arts, Manufactures and Commerce (RSA). President of the Association of Colleges for Further and Higher Education (1990–92), he was formerly Warden of Keble College, Oxford (1980–88), and Chairman of the Board of the National Advisory Body for Public Sector Higher Education (1982–88). He is the author of a number of books and reports on learning, including *Fitness for Purpose* (SRHE, 1985), *Aim Higher* (RSA, 1989), *More Means Different* (RSA, 1990), *Learning Pays* (RSA, 1991), *Sharks and Splashes: The future of education and employment* (New Zealand Institute of Policy Studies, 1991) and *Profitable Learning* (RSA, 1992). His latest RSA report on early learning, entitled *Start Right*, was published in March 1994.

Toni Beardon taught in secondary schools for many years and now lectures in mathematics education in the Department of Education of the University of Cambridge, England, where she works on research and initial teacher training and runs the STIMULUS tutoring programme. As an OFSTED Inspector she is experienced in evaluating standards of teaching and learning. She has written an undergraduate mathematics text and software and teachers' manuals for teaching mathematics and statistics, and papers on mathematics teaching and on student profiling. She has also written training materials for peer tutors and she co-authored the BP handbook on peer tutoring. As a primary school governor, she is closely in touch with the management of primary schools and particularly the provision for children with special educational needs. She takes an active role in professional associations, especially in popularising and promoting public understanding of mathematics. She was president of the Cambridge branch, and serves on national committees, of the Mathematical Association and she chairs the committee organising the Royal Institution Masterclasses in Cambridge.

Ian Campbell works at East Birmingham College, England, were he is Course Team Leader for Intermediate GNVQ Business, and lectures on Information Technology and Teacher Training. Previously he worked for 13 years in secondary and special schools in London and Birmingham as a teacher of mathematics. In 1993 he was appointed to a CSV/British Telecom Research Fellowship at the University of Birmingham. His chapter contains the first published results of a study of student tutoring and pupil aspirations which will eventually be submitted as an MPhil dissertation.

Val Clulow is a lecturer in the Syme Department of Marketing, Faculty of Business and Economics, at Monash University, Australia. She is the Course Director for the Bachelor of Business (Retail Management) which is an off-campus undergraduate programme undertaken by retail managers from all over Australia. She began her career as a teacher, but had an early interest and involvement in her family's business. She then worked in the retail industry in Australia for many years in the field of management training and development. She conducted a private consulting business in the management training field before joining Monash University in 1990. She has recently started work on her PhD which will build on her previous study of mentoring as a link between business and higher education.

Peter Fisher is Head of Communication Studies and Chair of the Faculty of Arts, Manukau Polytechnic, Auckland, New Zealand. Holder of an MA (Hons) and a Diploma in Teaching, he has been responsible for establishing and managing a wide range of programmes up to degree level, and various educational services. His particular interests are leadership, management styles, and educational services for students.

Marc Freedman is Vice President at Public/Private Ventures, a not-for-profit research organisation in the United States focused on education and social policy. He is author of *The Kindness of Strangers: Adult mentors, urban youth, and the new voluntarism* (Jossey-Bass/Macmillan, 1993), as well as numerous other studies about mentoring, national service programmes, intergenerational relations and productive ageing. At present, he is an adviser to various private foundations and federal agencies, including the Corporation for National Service and the US

Department of Health and Human Services, and is at work on a new book, *The Age of Renewal*, which argues that the ageing of American society will be a source of social rejuvenation. A graduate of Swarthmore College and Yale University, Freedman was selected by the British government in 1995 to serve as one of the first Atlantic Fellows in Public Policy.

Levina Furstenberg has, since 1988, been a lecturer in the Faculty of Education at the University of Port Elizabeth, South Africa. She has a BSc from the University of Pretoria, a BEd from the University of South Africa, and MEd and PhD degrees from the University of Port Elizabeth. She taught biological subjects in secondary schools and has lectured at the Port Elizabeth Technikon. She is involved in several research programmes developing teaching strategies and supporting systems.

Sinclair Goodlad, who is Director of the Humanities Programme at the Imperial College of Science, Technology & Medicine, University of London, studied at Cambridge and took his PhD at the London School of Economics. He has taught in India and at MIT in the USA and has been visiting associate at the University of California, Berkeley. His books concerned with peer tutoring include *Learning by Teaching* (CSV, 1979) and (with Beverley Hirst) *Peer Tutoring* (Kogan Page, 1989) and *Explorations in Peer Tutoring* (editor, Blackwell, 1990). His most recent book, *The Quest for Quality: Sixteen forms of heresy in higher education* (SRHE & Open University Press, 1995), locates tutoring in the wider context of a systematic philosophy of higher education.

Sharon H. Harwell is Research Assistant Professor of Education and Associate for Education Reform (K-8) in the Institute for Science Education at the University of Alabama in Huntsville, Alabama in the USA. She received her doctorate in education from Vanderbilt University and a Master of Education degree and a Specialist in Education degree from the University of Georgia. She teaches pre-service teachers and nursing students in human growth and development and supervises the Student Buddy Tutoring Program in the Department of Education. She conducts research and staff development activities in hands-on activity-based science for inservice teacher educators at the elementary and middle school level.

Shirley Hill is a Research Psychologist in the Centre for Paired Learning at the University of Dundee in Scotland. She is currently conducting two evaluation studies of student tutoring, funded by British Telecom and the Community Service Volunteers Learning Together initiative, as well as two studies of dyadic within-year peer tutoring with university students in economics and mathematics, funded by the Scottish Higher Education Funding Council through the Higher Education Effective Learning Project. She is also involved in a longitudinal study of early literacy development funded by the ESRC.

Robert Frank Hofmeyr took a BA and a University Education Diploma at the University of Natal. He taught classics (1965–81) before entering university administration, principally in the field of academic personnel administration, being promoted in 1990 to the post he now holds – that of Deputy Registrar and coordinator and adviser in the office of the Vice-Chancellor of the University of Witwatersrand, Johannesburg. His research interests include educational technology and language teaching, and tertiary education in South Africa.

Jo Howse is Manager of the Learning Centre at Manukau Polytechnic, Auckland, New Zealand. With a Master's degree in Educational Administration and a Diploma in Teaching, she has had experience as Assistant Director, Kohia Teachers Centre, Auckland and Head of Department in Secondary Education. Her interests include multicultural education, effective leadership, education management, professional development and teaching styles. She is currently National President of the New Zealand Education Administration Society and was the 1994 NZEAS Conference Convenor.

Carol Johnston is a lecturer in the Department of Education at the University of Melbourne, Australia, Deputy Chairperson of the Center for Economics Education, and a board member of the Faculty of Education. Having graduated from the University of Melbourne in 1968, she has worked as an economist and teacher in Canada and Australia. She is Chief Examiner for Economics for Victoria and has been instrumental in the design of the economics curriculum for secondary schools in the state. She has published a number of secondary school economics textbooks and teaching aids. Her work in recent years has led her to explore peer tutoring as an avenue for improvement in undergraduate learning.

John Jones is Head of the Educational Development Unit at Hong Kong Polytechnic University, having taken up the position in late 1994. Prior to

Education Research Office. In 1993, Dr Jones organised a Peer Tutoring Conference in Auckland, with support from BP, that attracted more than 100 participants from throughout Australia and other parts of the world. Earlier in his career, John Jones taught physics at the University of Malawi, and worked as an educational researcher at the University of Papua New Guinea.

Stephanie McIvor graduated in 1990 with a degree in chemistry from the University of York. As a student and in the four years since graduating, she has worked in the field of human resource management: managing a carvery restaurant in York, managing farm workers and fruit pickers in Scotland, and since 1991 managing the Explainers of the Science Museum – the professional science communicators and demonstrators of the interactive galleries. Since February 1994, she has been Research Assistant for the Nuffield Funded Science Interpretation Project. She is also studying part-time for a Master's degree in science communication at Imperial College.

John Potter is the Manager of CSV Education, a division of Community Service Volunteers. CSV Education works with schools, colleges and universities in the UK to involve young people in learning through positive community action. John was educated at Lancing College and New College Oxford where he took a BA in Politics, Philosophy and Economics. After national service, he trained for the Church of England ministry at Wells Theological College, was a curate at Wyken, Coventry, and then warden of the hall of residence and senior lecturer at the then Lanchester Polytechnic (now Coventry University). After service as vicar of Writtle (1970–78) and Canon of Derby Cathedral (1978–85), he became successively Development Officer, National Development Coordinator, and Education Manager with CSV, including special responsibility for developing student tutoring through CSV Learning Together and a wide range of service learning projects in schools, including peer education and social action programmes.

Margaret Rutherford was born and educated in the UK, taking her first degree in aeronautical engineering at Imperial College, London. Her research interests moved to physics and then to physics education (for PhD studies). She is currently Director of the College of Science, University of the Witwatersrand, South Africa, and involved in programmes for increasing access with success for educationally disadvantaged students. Her major research activities are in language and communication in science for second-language students and in relevant

University of the Witwatersrand, South Africa, and involved in programmes for increasing access with success for educationally disadvantaged students. Her major research activities are in language and communication in science for second-language students and in relevant explanations in science.

Heidi Schwarzwalder was born in Madagascar of German parents and lived in several African countries and four and a half years in West Berlin. Having always attended French schools in Africa, she went to France to study economics, political science and Arabic language and civilisation, graduating in 1995. Her professional aim is to work in international organisations in developing countries, and especially in the Middle East.

Margaret Shore is Manager, Community Services and Health Business Unit, at the Cooloola Institute, Queensland, Australia. Before taking up this appointment in 1989, she was director of an extended services children's centre (0–5 year olds) in South Australia providing a variety of care and educational programmes for children and their parents. Present courses for which she is responsible include welfare, nursing, early childhood and diversional therapy. Her chapter is part of the study undertaken for the award of a PhD through the University of Queensland under Professor John Elkins, Dean of the Graduate School of Education.

Carol Taylor, who took her BA in Toronto and her CEd in Nottingham, is a senior tutor in the Department of Social Anthropology at the University of the Witwatersrand, Johannesburg, South Africa. She has been a member of the department since 1991, with special responsibility for academic development. Her area of special interest is multicultural education.

Keith Topping is Director of the Centre for Paired Learning in the Department of Psychology at the University of Dundee, Scotland. He develops and researches the effectiveness of methods for non-professionals (such as parents or peers) to tutor others in fundamental skills (eg, reading, spelling, writing) and higher order learning (science, maths, etc.), for use across a wide age and ability range and in many different contexts. He is also Director of a postgraduate educational psychology training programme and Director of the Higher Education Effective Learning Project.

PART A: INTRODUCTION

Chapter 1

STUDENTS AS TUTORS AND MENTORS

Sinclair Goodlad

This chapter sets the scene for the rest of the book by locating student tutoring and mentoring as forms of study service. A key emerging issue is that of the management of complex systems. Each of the necessary actions is compared to a link in a chain. A fruitful approach to the promotion of student tutoring and mentoring is to look for the weakest link(s) in one's chain and take remedial action. The chapter concludes by outlining the structure of the book.

This book is about an idea of awesome power – that of people helping one another with their learning.

An idea is, however, only as strong as the structures that carry it. The object of this book is, therefore, to explore, by case studies and research, some of the settings and processes that are most conducive to the efficient and effective deployment of students as tutors and mentors. Although the basic process of one person helping another is simple, the organisation of a system is not. Money is needed to pay for organisers and facilitators: that money would be wasted if due thought were not given to the purposes the activity may serve and the procedures most likely to serve those purposes.

This first chapter defines student tutoring and mentoring; establishes *study service* as a conceptual framework; identifies key actions (comparing them to links in a chain); and describes the structure of the book.

1.1 Definitions

The basic ideas are very old and very fruitful: the very word 'mentor' derives from the name of the guide and friend of Telemakhos in Homer's *Odyssey*, while the process of tutoring was independently promoted by Andrew Bell (1797) and Joseph Lancaster (1805) who wrote engagingly of its virtues:

> 'The tutors enable their pupils to keep pace with their classes.'
> Andrew Bell, *Experiment in Education*, 1797.

> '(It) establishes such habits of industry, morality and religion, as have a tendency to form good scholars, good men, good subjects, and good Christians.'
> Andrew Bell, *Experiment in Education*, 1797.

> 'Lively, active-tempered boys are the most frequent transgressors of good order, and the most difficult to reduce to reason; the best way to form them is by making monitors of them.'
> Joseph Lancaster, *Improvements in Education*, 1805.

In modern usage, student tutoring and mentoring involve

students from colleges and universities. . .
helping pupils in local schools. . .
on a sustained and systematic basis. . .
under the direction and supervision of teachers.

The differences may be represented thus:

	Tutoring	**Mentoring**
Focus	Academic learning	Life skills
Location	Usually in classroom	Often outside classroom
Mode	1 to several	1 to 1
Duration	A few weeks	Several months/years

As Keith Topping and Shirley Hill show (in Chapter 2), many permutations and combinations are possible. It is not profitable to dwell too

2

long on the differences, but rather to see how the basic ideas can best be put to use.

1.2 Student Tutoring and Mentoring as Solutions to Specific Problems

The one key suggestion I wish to urge is: always see student tutoring and mentoring as solutions to specific problems – rather than adopt them just for the sake of it. Student tutoring and mentoring are spreading fast. The contributors to this book would not have become involved with the subject unless they believed the idea had potential; but they are realistic about what is possible. Our collective object is not to dampen enthusiasm but rather to give it focus. All the examples here assembled show student tutoring and mentoring as considered responses to identifiable needs.

One over-arching need in formal education is to bring together the needs of theory and practice, of society and of the individual. It is through study service that this can be achieved.

A not uncommon phenomenon in higher education, particularly perhaps that of scientists and engineers, is for the main ingredients of professional formation to exist as separate spheres of activity. The situation may be represented diagrammatically as in Figure 1.1.

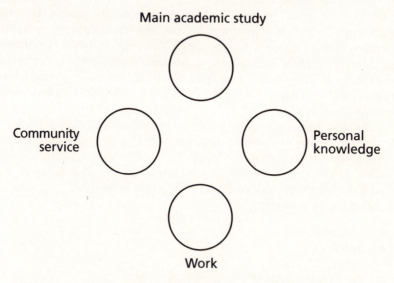

Figure 1.1 The separation of the elements of professional formation

1.3 Student Tutoring and Mentoring as Forms of Study Service

The intention of study service is to bring about a fruitful merging of these concerns by devising activities through which students can learn and simultaneously serve the needs of other people.

If study service is effective, it brings about a merging of concerns, as shown in Figure 1.2. Each sphere is crucial: the problem is how best to achieve the benefits from each sphere without doing damage to the others.

Students' *main academic study* involves the focusing power of disciplines, the systematic limiting of fields of discourse in the interests of precision and economy, and thereby an acceleration of learning.

Complementary to this is the need for *personal knowledge*: for opportunities for reflection about matters of wider concern. Sometimes this is attempted by 'lateral enrichment' – through the provision in a specialised degree course of separate courses in commentating disciplines.

Induction into the realities of *work* is usually sought through vacation training/internships/co-op. However, students are often only marginally involved in the main work of the agencies to which they are attached, and there may be little interweaving of the work with academic reflection and analysis.

Community service, especially student community action, is usually work outside the curriculum: with the elderly (cleaning, decorating, shopping); the homeless (soup runs); the educationally handicapped (groupwork); immigrants (language tuition); young people (youth clubs, adventure playgrounds); hospitals (visiting, musical performances); welfare rights (stalls and neighbourhood centres); or fund-raising through 'rags'.

Admirable although each of these dimensions of education may be, they derive great force when brought together through study service. These ideas are developed at length in *The Quest for Quality* (Goodlad, 1995b). Suffice it here to say that student tutoring and mentoring are ideal forms of study service because, if properly handled, they can offer students the opportunity for:

- commitment
- initiative
- cooperation
- the development of communication skills
- knowledge of the organisation of knowledge

Main academic study

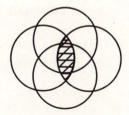

Community
service

Personal
knowledge

Work

Figure 1.2 The merging of the elements of professional formation

- responsibility to a definable client
- direct contact with an ultimate beneficiary
- concentration on work that could not otherwise be done.

The case studies in Chapters 3 to 10 of this book, and the research they report, give specific examples of what has been achieved. Appendix B offers brief notes on a number of schemes described at the BP conference (though space does not permit inclusion of many of the others).

Two crucial ingredients of study service of any sort are *reciprocity* and *competence of service* (see Goodlad, 1982).

Reciprocity is needed to avoid the exploitation of students. That is to say, students must have something to gain from the experience; they are not there as cheap substitutes for professionals, but rather as people doing work that extends and deepens the range of services that professionals already provide.

The competence of students is needed to avoid the exploitation of clients: the service clients receive must not be in any way inferior to that which they would receive in other circumstances.

These two objects are best achieved through the interweaving of study and service (rather than through the service being rendered in large blocks of time separate from the study), and through the opportunity for adequate supervision of the students by their teachers as well as by the professionals with whom they work.

Chapters 11 to 14 of this book examine some of the benefits accruing through tutoring and mentoring to students and those whom they seek to serve. Chapters 15 and 16 describe ways in which tutoring and mentoring have been built into the curricula of the students to achieve the closest possible integration of study and service.

1.4 Benefits To Be Drawn From Student Tutoring and Mentoring

The chapters in this book indicate not only the great range of uses to which student tutoring and mentoring can be put but also the considerable difficulty of measuring the effects of the activity. Measurement of attitude change is notoriously difficult – not least because it is hard to disentangle the effects of the tutoring and mentoring from everything else that is going on (see, for example, Chapter 4 of Goodlad & Hirst, 1989).

Imperial College's first experiments in student tutoring, funded in 1975 by a grant from the Leverhulme Trust, were within the framework of socio-technical group projects in which the students not only did the tutoring but also carried out a detailed evaluation. The school in which the tutoring took place was The Pimlico School, London, whence the name of the scheme, 'The Pimlico Connection' – the name being a deliberate invocation of two famous film titles, *Passport to Pimlico* and *The French Connection* that made people think that they must have heard of the scheme before! In 'The Pimlico Connection', evaluation was:

- originally by psychometric tests,
- then by in-depth interviews, plus
- open-ended questionnaires, and
- ultimately by a combination of specific questions and open-ended replies.

The principal benefits to participants (in findings replicated frequently since) were as follows:

Pupils:

- lessons more interesting
- lessons easier to follow
- lessons more enjoyable
- seemed to learn more

Students:

- practice in communication skills
- feeling of doing something useful with what they had already learned
- getting to know about people from social backgrounds different from their own
- gaining insight into how other people saw their subjects
- increased self-confidence
- reinforcing knowledge of their subjects
- no great interference with college studies

Teachers:

- lessons were easier to handle
- teaching was more enjoyable
- pupils seemed to learn more.

(Numerical values on these items are recorded in, for example, Chapter 5 of *Peer Tutoring* by Goodlad & Hirst, 1989).

One detail that may be useful to people starting new schemes: having had a warm response to circulating copies of the students' group project reports, we have in every year since 1975 produced an annual report on 'The Pimlico Connection'. These reports (the production of which is one of the main costs of the tutoring) have been useful in many ways, including:

- in giving local visibility to the scheme
- for informing teachers and tutors new to the idea
- valuable for fund raising
- a tangible reward to students for their efforts.

From these remarks you will see that student tutoring and mentoring are ideal as a form of study service, which is in turn ideal as a focus for education, particularly education for the professions (see Goodlad, 1984).

As always, our own developments continue to be stimulated by needs. Imperial College and the Science Museum (the UK national museum for science and technology) are on adjacent sites. In 1975, the first band of 'Pimlico Connection' tutors took their tutees to the museum, and attempts were made to make better use of this amazing resource on our doorstep. The time turned out not then to be ripe for further developments; but happily they are now taking place through our Science

7

Interpretation Project (SIP), funded by the Nuffield Foundation. Stephanie McIvor has been appointed Project Officer to develop a scheme of students as interpreters of science, and to develop a wider scheme of museum volunteers to draw upon the talents of the many people who would like to be involved in science communication.

Two important needs (among many others) are being addressed through this extension of the tutoring: first, Imperial College's continuing need to offer students demanding practice in communicating scientific ideas – a primary personal and professional skill whatever work they subsequently do; second, the need for the museum to make its fine collection more accessible to schoolchildren and the wider public by the outreach activities of volunteers. (Stephanie McIvor's Chapter, 4, gives more details.)

Our experience at Imperial College has probably been similar to that of many other people, if shaped by our peculiar character as an institution specialising in science, technology and (since 1988) medicine. The one key idea we hold onto is that:

> student tutoring and mentoring must be seen as the solution to a problem.

1.5 Searching for Weak Links in the Chain

The fact that people came from 34 countries to discuss at the conference the possibilities of student tutoring and mentoring is abundant testimony to the attraction of the idea. We could all, no doubt, have had a congenial time confirming our beliefs. However, our primary task was to look for weak links in our systems. If this book helps others in that process, then it will have served its purpose.

One way of doing this could be (following, for example, Kotler, 1994) through a traditional SWOT analysis – identifying Strengths, Weaknesses, Opportunities, and Threats. An initial listing might look something like this:

Strength:	fundamental simplicity of the ideas
Weakness:	complexity (and cost) of systems of delivery
Opportunity:	huge range of activities possible
Threats:	expecting too much – or too little. Perceived danger of substitution.

Somewhat simpler is to see the components of a scheme as a chain – and to look for the weakest links with a view to strengthening them.

Appendix A offers a check-list of matters that require attention. In brief they are:

- define aims
- structure the content
- define roles and logistics
- get secure finance
- train the tutors/mentors
- support the tutors/mentors
- evaluate the scheme.

All schemes of student tutoring and mentoring need attention to all of these items. Although the idea of tutoring and mentoring is simple, the process of managing schemes is complex. Indeed, as a scheme grows in either conceptual or administrative complexity, so emerges the need for a paid coordinator – which may be the most difficult part of a scheme to sustain! Figure 1.3 (the axes of which deliberately bear no quantities) illustrates the process.

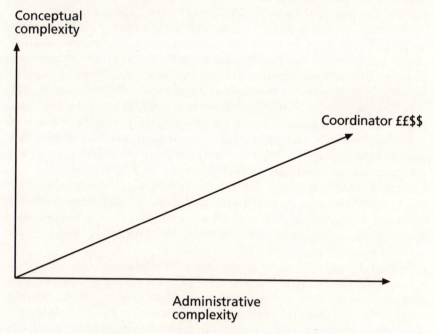

Figure 1.3 When is a coordinator of a scheme needed?

For many schemes, the need for funding for a coordinator may be the weakest link. However, there are many other complexities in running an effective scheme. The chapters that follow illustrate some of them.

1.6 The Structure of the Book

Each chapter examines in its own way the strengths and weaknesses of particular forms of tutoring or mentoring, many of them referring to the (now abundant if variable) research literature. There are, however, differences of emphasis between the sections that readers may find useful.

Section B, after an overview by Keith Topping and Shirley Hill, offers a number of case studies of tutoring or mentoring – in economics (3), in science interpretation in museums (4), as a service to prisoners (5), in anthropology (6), as an opportunity for underqualified science teachers to improve their qualifications (7), as a support system for adult students (8), and as a method for raising standards (9). In Chapter 10, John Potter sketches the range of activities being undertaken through the Learning Together initiative of Community Service Volunteers (CSV) which has become the principal focus for initiatives in the United Kingdom.

Section C consists primarily of research studies examining the benefits to participants. It is relatively straightforward to show how tutoring offers cognitive and transferable skill gains for tutors (11); it is, however, proving difficult to demonstrate one of the most hoped-for outcomes of tutoring – an increase in the aspirations of those who are tutored (12). Two detailed studies conclude Section C – one (13) from the USA that shows how tutoring can be useful for changing the personal constructs of intending teachers, the other (14) a cautionary tale that shows (not surprisingly, but significantly) that tutors without proper training do not communicate as effectively as professionals.

Section D consists of two chapters (15 and 16) that show how tutoring can be integrated into the curriculum of the tutors – and, importantly for a hugely expanded higher education sector in many countries, how students can help each other through the facilitating aegis of an institution's learning centre (16).

Section E, on the wider scene, contains three chapters that look towards the future. Marc Freedman (17) offers a survey of opportunities and constraints in the development of mentoring schemes, offering cautionary tales from previous social experiments in the USA. Margaret Rutherford and Robert Hofmeyr (18) suggest that schemes involving university students visiting local schools may have limited applications in developing countries. As with all situations in which tutoring and mentoring are being considered as possible approaches, the need is shown to be for methods finely tuned to local needs rather than for application of a formula. Finally, Sir Christopher Ball (19) gives a wide-ranging analysis of the changing nature of learning in modern societies and the many opportunities for student tutoring and mentoring in the emerging scene. Sir Christopher's chapter offers a vigorous call for action for an idea whose time has clearly come.

Address for correspondence: Dr Sinclair Goodlad, Director of the Humanities Programme, Room 440 MED, Imperial College of Science, Technology & Medicine, Exhibition Road, London SW7 2BX. Tel. 0171 594 8752. Fax 0171 594 8759. email s.goodlad@ic.ac.uk

PART B: USES OF STUDENT TUTORING AND MENTORING: CASE STUDIES

Chapter 2

UNIVERSITY AND COLLEGE STUDENTS AS TUTORS FOR SCHOOLCHILDREN:
A Typology and Review of Evaluation Research

Keith Topping and Shirley Hill

Student tutoring programmes vary according to tutor and tutee characteristics, the curriculum tutored, contact arrangements and goals, and outcomes and rewards for tutors and tutees. In the UK, such tutoring usually occurs in school classrooms, supervised by the classteacher. Programmes have generated a substantial body of evaluation research of very various quality. Subjective feedback is usually very positive, especially from the tutors. More substantial evidence of cognitive gains for tutors is limited. Structured programmes designed to improve basic skills in tutees have shown some significant success, but evidence of improved tutee aspirations is slight. It is concluded that programmes should specify clear, realistic, achievable and measurable objectives and be structured, operated and quality controlled to maximise the probability that objectives will be achieved.

Peer tutoring can be defined as 'people from similar social groupings who are not professional teachers helping each other to learn and learning themselves by teaching'. It should not be confused with other kinds of 'cooperative learning' or 'mentoring'.

Peer tutoring occurs within schools (Topping, 1988) and within higher education institutions (Topping, 1995), but also between centres of learning. One example of cross-institution or cross-sector tutoring involves students in universities and colleges tutoring schoolchildren (ERIC, 1988). However, there are many very different ways in which this type of tutoring can be arranged. A further complication is that in North America the term 'student' is used for all learners in schools and college/university, while in Europe it is used only for learners in college/university.

Reviewing the evaluation literature is thus complex. Even where positive outcomes have been demonstrated in one study, it cannot be assumed that these will be found in all replications, and still less that gains from one type of tutoring will automatically result from different types of tutoring. A typology of various practices is essential to ensure that like is compared with like.

2.1 A Typology of Student Tutoring

Studies and descriptions in the international literature show differences on a number of dimensions: (1) tutee characteristics, (2) tutor characteristics, (3) curriculum, (4) contact constellation, (5) time, (6) place, (7) style, (8) goals and outcomes for tutees, (9) goals and outcomes for tutors and (10) explicit reward for tutors.

Tutee characteristics can be further discriminated into sub-categories: learning disabled (eg, Flippo *et al.*, 1993), learning delayed (eg, Sandler *et al.*, 1970), socio-economically disadvantaged (eg, Eisenberg *et al.*, 1980 a and b), English as second language (eg, Fischetti *et al.*, 1989), ethnic minorities (eg, Rhodes & Garibaldi, 1990), drop-out risk (eg, Fasko & Flint, 1990), other 'at-risk' tutees, gender groups and the gifted (eg, Prillaman & Richardson, 1989).

Categories of tutor characteristics have included the academically competent, the academically under-prepared, pre-service teachers (eg, Rhodes & Garibaldi 1990; Bacon, 1992), ethnic minorities (eg, Sandler *et al.*, 1970) and student athletes (eg, Juel, 1991).

The curriculum of tutoring has included reading, other literacy skills, maths, science, information technology (eg, Ross *et al.*, 1989), other school curricular areas, specific homework (eg, Cloward, 1967), vocational skills, sports skills, recreational skills and cultural activities (eg, Eisenberg *et al.*, 1980 a and b).

Contact constellations have varied greatly. Tutoring has occurred in one-to-one situations, tutors dealing with a single tutee or several consecutively. Groups of between two and 30 are frequently found to be tutored by one tutor.

From an international perspective, tutoring occurs at many different times, including class time, break or recess time, after school, in the evening, at weekends and during school holidays. It has occurred in many different places, including in class, elsewhere in school, at a community centre, on the university or college campus, at the tutee's home and in various community activity settings.

The style and aims of tutoring have also varied – some programmes are intended to be remedial, some compensatory and some are targeted at enrichment.

Goals and outcomes for tutees are of course important. Outcomes for tutees have included raised aspirations (eg, Sandler *et al.*, 1970), improved basic skills, deeper learning, improved motivation (eg, Sandler *et al.*, 1970), affective and attitudinal gains (eg, Flippo *et al.*, 1993), a reduction in tutee drop-out from school, generalised gains in achievement (eg, Ross *et al.*, 1989), improved attendance at school (eg, Huisman *et al.*, 1992) and gains in various transferable skills.

Goals and outcomes for tutors have included under the general heading of cognitive and transferable skills: better communication skills, deeper understanding, practice in applying knowledge, improved retention and greater commitment to the area of tutoring. Under the general heading of affective and social gains, improved motivation, self-esteem, self-understanding, and self-confidence have all been reported, together with greater empathy with others and a greater sense of achievement. More tangible and observable gains for tutors have included reduced drop-out rates, course accreditation or credit, and payment.

2.2 Outcomes for Tutors

Research in the UK

In the United Kingdom, 'student tutoring' is the name usually given to the practice of having students from universities and colleges tutor children in primary (elementary) and high school classrooms under the guidance of the classteacher. The UK 'model' of student tutoring is unusually internally consistent, reflecting rapid growth in this particular type of venture in the UK in recent years as a result of funding and promotion by a national coordinator.

Goodland (1985) and Goodlad *et al.* (1979) reported on four years of subjective feedback in the 'Pimlico Connection' at Imperial College, University of London. Questionnaire returns from 273 tutors were analysed (response rate 83%). Forty per cent considered their knowledge of some aspect of their subject had been improved to some extent, 95% felt they benefited from practice in the communication of scientific ideas, 84% felt they had gained insight into how other people perceived their subject, 76% reported increased self-confidence, 82% reported improved understanding of people with a social background different from their own, 88% felt they were doing something useful with what they had learned and only 26% felt that the time commitment to tutoring interfered with their college studies.

The similar Cambridge STIMULUS Project (Beardon, 1990) also reported subjective feedback, although with a lower response rate (less than 50% for tutors). Of the tutors, 19% reported reinforced knowledge, 100% benefits from practising communication, 79% improved insight into others, 79% increased self-confidence, 65% benefits from wider cultural contact, 85% from a sense of doing something useful and 77% reported student tutoring helped them to make a decision about their future career. However, 40% reported an interference effect with their studies.

A study in Birmingham involved all the members of a university architecture course tutoring schoolchildren in design projects, on a non-voluntary basis (Gadsby, 1993). Unfortunately, response rates are not given. Sixty per cent of the tutors reported knowledge reinforcement, 92% communication practice, 80% greater insight into others' learning, 82% increased self-confidence, 86% improved awareness of others, and 89% a feeling of usefulness.

Similar results continued to be generated in the UK. The annual reports of the Pimlico Connection (eg, Hughes, 1993a) document positive subjective feedback from tutors. In 1992/93 the response rate from tutors was 83%, 99% of the respondents reported having benefited in communication, 46% in reinforcement of knowledge, 76% in gaining insight into others, 84% in increased self-confidence, 90% in learning about other cultures, 95% in useful applications of knowledge, and 31% in helping make an informed career choice. Twenty-four per cent reported interference with college studies. Sixty-six per cent of tutors felt they had acted as a positive role model to the tutees and 53% felt that the school-children now knew more about college and university life.

In a Scottish study (MacDougall, 1993) all 19 responding tutors (response rate 68%) felt that they were welcomed and supported by the school and had found their experience enjoyable. However, 68% of the respondents felt they had not had sufficient time to talk to pupils about life in higher education. Unsurprisingly, 75% of tutees reported they had learnt nothing about life in higher education. Presumably their aspirations were therefore unlikely to have changed. Curiously, 63% of responding teachers reported they felt the student tutor had improved their pupils' interest in higher education.

Subsequently, student tutoring was promoted throughout the UK under the auspices of the Community Service Volunteers Learning Together project. Subjective feedback from a number of initiatives were gathered together in an annual report (Community Service Volunteers, 1994a), but unfortunately relatively few area initiatives report response rates. However, the London South West Connection reported a 61% response rate from tutors, associated with 99% reporting improved communication, 58% reinforced knowledge, 70% greater insight into others, 95% increased self-confidence, 89% increased knowledge about other cultures and 95% useful application of knowledge. Seventy-eight per cent felt they had acted as positive role models and 25% felt that tutoring interfered with college studies (CSV, 1994a). CSV has also been involved in student tutoring in the area of financial literacy, but the report on this topic (CSV, 1994b) gives insufficient evaluative details to enable conclusions to be drawn.

Research in North America

Two major surveys of programmes involving college and university students as tutors or mentors for elementary and high school students were completed by Cahalan & Farris (1990) and Reisner *et al.* (1990). Although both of these reports gave an excellent overview of practice, fine detail of the evaluation of specific projects was not included.

Cahalan and Farris (1990) noted that students most frequently participated as volunteers in 40% of programmes, as paid tutors in 29%, as a course requirement in 28% and as a graduation requirement in 3%. (In the UK model, the vast majority of tutors are volunteers and receive only travelling expenses.) Whilst 17% of tutors were members of a racial or ethnic minority, 75% of tutees were. Likewise, 15% of tutors but 69% of tutees were socio-economically disadvantaged. Thirty per cent of tutors were male but 50% of tutees were female. Of the tutees, 40% were in elementary school, 27% in middle or junior high schools, 27% in senior high schools, while 5% were pre-school and 2% were school drop-outs.

In 46% of cases, tutoring mostly took place on campus, in 39% at the school, in 8% of cases mainly at a community centre or agency, and in 1% at the tutee's home. Where transport was provided, in 66% of cases this was by the tutor and in 26% by the college or university. In 61% of cases the tutoring was mostly one-to-one, in 22% in a small group of three or less, and in 17% in a larger group. Tutors generally spent three hours per week tutoring, 37% two or fewer hours, 30% three to four hours, and 18% 10 or more hours per week.

The average amount of time allocated during tutoring to basic skills remediation was 59%, a further 28% being allocated to homework assistance; 8% was allocated to recreation or cultural activities.

Programme managers were asked to rate their self-perceived success in meeting the programme goals. Regarding outcomes for the tutors, 86% of programmes claimed success in providing practical experience in a professional field, 84% success in providing exposure to a non-campus experience, 77% success in developing commitment to public service. However, no supportive evidence was given.

The Reisner *et al.* (1990) survey indicated that 77% of tutoring programmes in the US targeted improvements in basic skills in the tutees, and a further 9% targeted improved tutee self-esteem. Although a small number of programmes aimed to 'expose participants to college' and 'provide role models', aspirations were not specifically mentioned. For the tutors, in 57% of cases the primary goal was to provide them with practical experience, in 29% of cases to develop a public service commitment. Some of these goals clearly represent processes rather than products, and some are more readily capable of evaluation than others.

Forty-six per cent of tutees were in elementary schools and 47% in junior or senior high schools. Seventy per cent of tutees were from racial or ethnic minority groups, 66% were socio-economically disadvantaged and 70% academically disadvantaged. Programmes served equal numbers of boys and girls. Thirty-five per cent of tutors were volunteers, 29% were paid and 32% participated as a course requirement. Forty-nine per cent of tutoring programmes cited the school campus as the most frequent place for tutoring to occur, 37% the college or university campus, 9% a community centre or agency and 2% the tutee's home. These figures are very similar to those of Cahalan & Farris (1990).

Sixty per cent of tutoring programmes reported that they conducted evaluation. High levels of attainment of programme goals were typically reported, again without evidence. Subjective goal attainment scaling by those with an emotional investment in perceiving successful outcomes cannot be considered adequate data.

Fresko & Chen (1989) employed path analysis to examine the effects of tutoring on the satisfaction of 425 college student tutors of disadvantaged elementary school children in Grades 4–9. Subsidiary analyses considered the effects of tutor/tutee ethnic similarity, degree of tutor expertise and the extent of perceived goal attainment by the tutors. The major factor related to tutor satisfaction was their perceived project goal attainment.

Fischetti *et al.* (1989) deployed undergraduates to tutor language minority high school pupils, one-to-one and in small groups for two to three hours per week, with the objective of improving their academic performance and college readiness. Tutors received modest payment and helped also with study skills, writing and thinking skills. The evaluation used an open-ended qualitative approach, unfortunately difficult to summarise. There was some evidence that some student tutors had expanded their personal boundaries, developed a deeper understanding of the nature of tutoring, gained understanding about other cultures, developed more interest in teaching (including as a career) and acquired greater insight into processes of teaching and learning.

Stewart & Palcic (1992) examined the role of audience in pre-service mathematics education students' writing experiences. The students completed writing assignments explaining the principles of mathematics to elementary school pupils. In one group, the students wrote to actual named students, serving as pen-pals and maths mentors, while students in the other class were required to imagine they were carrying out the exercise for unnamed students. Interview and questionnaire data indicated that the writing competence of students in both groups improved, but that the group communicating with real students improved more than the other and showed more involvement in the task, as well as preferring it to other coursework writing tasks.

Raupp & Cohen (1992) incorporated student tutoring in elementary schools within a course in child psychology, making a credit available for individual placements. The 'community service' was linked closely to the psychology curriculum. The intention was to demonstrate psychology's commitment to promoting human welfare and enable the application of principles learnt in the classroom to enhance learning in real-life settings. Subjective feedback from the participant student tutors was very positive, with increased empathy, commitment, empowerment and self-esteem reported.

Flippo *et al.* (1993) reported on the 'Student literacy course' of a state college in Massachusetts. The STC experience was an elective course for which credit was available. The intention was to improve cross-cultural communication. Tutors' understanding of themselves, the community and other cultures was increased. Tutees also made gains (see section below).

2.3 Outcomes For Tutees

Research in the UK

The 'Pimlico Connection' subjective feedback (Goodlad, 1985) involved questionnaire returns from 2,919 tutees in schools (response rate 78%), and 56% reported lessons were more interesting with student tutors, 64% found the lessons easier to follow, 55% found lessons more enjoyable and 54% felt they learned more. The percentage feeling that the presence of student tutors made things worse was negligible.

Stewart (1990) reported similar feedback from a small project elsewhere in the UK. Seventy-two per cent of pupils reported lessons were more interesting, 52% that they were easier to follow and 74% that they were more enjoyable, but no response rate was given. Fifty-nine per cent of tutees reported that they learned more in the presence of student tutors.

In the Cambridge STIMULUS project (Beardon, 1990), 30% of tutees reported lessons were more interesting, 38% that they were easier to follow, 29% that they were more enjoyable and 24% that more learning occurred than usual.

In the Birmingham architects' project (Gadsby, 1993), the tutees reported lessons were more enjoyable (67%), afforded more learning experiences (58%), were more interesting (61%) and were easier to follow (60%).

The North London Connection (CSV, 1994a) also reported positive tutee feedback (83% response rate). Sixty-seven per cent of pupils reported that learning was more enjoyable with student tutors, 61% found the lessons easier to follow and 80% found them more interesting.

Hughes (1993b) reported a study of the effectiveness of student tutoring on the aspirations of 14–15-year-old pupils. This study involved 10 secondary school classes in three schools, half of them experimental with two student tutors per class, half non-tutored control classes. They were equally divided between science and mathematics content, and matched by teacher judgement and logistic necessity. Subjects completed questionnaires about their aspirations a month before tutoring commenced and a month after it ended, an inter-test period of approximately six months. Response rates were not given, but appeared to be at least 66% at pre-test (although post-test response rate was lower than pre-test).

At post-test tutored children were more likely to report higher aspirations for college entrance, but this reached statistical significance only in maths classes, and the nature of the 'college' intended was not specified (experimental n = 202). Strangely, at post-test the science class subjects reported reduced feelings of success, more so in the tutored children. However, there was very little change in the maths classes. Conversely, at post-test the science class subjects reported making more effort, and although they showed a larger increase than controls, this difference did not reach statistical significance and the maths classes again showed very little change. No change in liking of maths or science was reported by any group and gender made little difference. There were doubts about the comparability of the groups at pre-test.

Research in Israel

The Perach Project in Israel was initiated in 1974 and has deployed thousands of students as tutors to disadvantaged children. Tutoring is usually conducted on a one-to-one basis with twice-weekly two hour meetings over the course of a school year. Tutoring content can be academic, remedial, cultural or leisure oriented. Contact is usually out of school hours, and may occur on school or college campus or in the participants' homes or community and leisure centres. The focus of tutoring varies greatly from pair to pair and is intended to be individualised to the tutee's needs.

Evaluation has tended to concentrate on the effects on the tutees. Eisenberg *et al.* (1980 a and b, 1981) compared the gains on standardised tests of tutored and non-tutored children in mathematics, reading and English. No significant differences were found, although parents, teachers and tutors all rated the project very highly and reported marked academic-related behaviour change in the children. No effect sizes were given. Affective changes were evident on pre- and post-questionnaires. Tutored children appeared to have significantly improved in attitudes towards school, self-reported participation in class and time allocated to leisure reading. They did not differ from non-tutored children on measures of self-concept and aspirations (Eisenberg *et al.*, 1982).

A follow-up study of the same children was carried out two years later (Eisenberg *et al.*, 1983a, 1983b). Tutored children dropped out of school less often than the non-tutored group. After tutoring they seemed to possess higher aspirations and some reported doing homework more regularly. However, the two groups did not differ with respect to self-concept, satisfaction in school, type and level of curriculum and eligibility to take examinations. Mathematics and reading skills were measured over a two-year period for children who had been tutored for two years, one year and not at all (Fresko & Eisenberg, 1985). Findings indicated that one year of tutoring yielded some cognitive gains, particularly in mathematics, but a second year of tutoring did nothing to augment this. Activities during the second year of tutoring may have tended to drift from an academic focus.

Thus, while studies have shown Perach tutoring to have only a small impact in cognitive and affective domains, the project goals are of course very numerous, varied and not sharply defined. It is perhaps unsurprising that blunt measurement instruments have failed to show major effect when applied to such various inputs and outputs.

Subsequently, in a study of the effects of wider recruitment of tutors (Fresko, 1988), there were indications that those joining the project only for the extrinsic reward of rebate of tuition fees tended to report less change in their tutees and were more critical of the project. Similarly (Fresko & Chen, 1989), tutor satisfaction appeared higher among tutors who felt their tutee had improved, who had established a good relationship with tutee, were from the same ethnic group and were preparing to enter a helping profession.

Research in Australia and New Zealand

Butler (1991) deployed university students as remedial reading tutors for fourth grade school children in Australia. Using structured and programmatic remedial reading materials, 40 subjects were randomly assigned to experimental and control groups and tutored for three 20-minute periods per week. The experimental group scored significantly higher than the control group on the comprehension sub-test of the Neale Analysis of Reading Ability and two sub-tests of the Standard Diagnostic Reading Test. However, other differences were not significant. Effect sizes were not given. A smaller scale replication yielded similar results.

In New Zealand, student tutoring on the UK model but with four or five tutors per class has been developed by Jones (1989, 1990, 1993a; Jones & Bates, 1987). Participant and approximately matched comparison classes were subjected to pre-test and post-test on instruments including an indication of favourite school subjects, post-school vocational intentions, a semantic differential and open-ended questionnaires. However, there were few differences between the pre-tutoring and post-tutoring responses.

Pupil subjective feedback about the tutors varied considerably from school to school and from class to class. Tutoring had affected the vocational aspirations of the tutors in both directions: some tutors who had intended to become teachers changed their minds during tutoring, while others who had not intended to become teachers formulated that aspiration. Jones & Bates (1987) commented on doubts about reliability and validity, but included a great deal of useful qualitative data in their report.

Follow-up evaluation was reported by Jones (1989). This study used a purely qualitative and illuminative methodology, concluding that there was some support for many of the claims made for student tutoring, but only in some situations. Three primary and two secondary schools were involved. Tutors received brief training and payment. Four tutors were deployed in each classroom over a ten-week period. The school pupils were asked if the presence of tutors made lessons more interesting and enjoyable, more understandable or more practical. Again, on some items responses varied greatly between schools. The school pupils' educational and vocational aspirations did not change.

Research in North America

In the survey of Cahalan & Farris (1990), tutoring programme managers perceived high levels of success in meeting programme goals concerning outcomes for tutees. Ninety per cent of programmes reported they were successful in providing role models, 82% reported success in providing exposure to college and university, 80% reported success in improving tutees' self-esteem, 74% success in improving basic skills, 57% success in providing recreational or cultural opportunities, 55% success in assisting the talented and gifted, 47% success in preventing drop-outs and 42% success in improving vocational skills. However, no clarification of actual meaning or supportive evidence was given for these claims.

Klosterman (1970) deployed students of education as tutors with 9-year-old schoolchildren. The pupils were withdrawn from class and tutored either individually or in a small group. Tutoring sessions of half an hour took place four days per week. On pre- and post-tests of reading, pupils receiving either individual or group tutoring gained more than pupils receiving an equivalent amount of classroom instruction. The tutors subjectively reported a variety of advantages of the tutoring experience for themselves, mostly related to their vocational intentions. Similar results from deploying trainee teachers as tutors were reported by Bausell *et al.* (1972).

Schwartz (1977) deployed college students as contingency managers for adolescents in a programme to develop reading skills in Vancouver. Behaviour modification procedures in an individualised tutorial programme were used to remediate reading skill deficits in seventh-graders. Structured reading materials were used and learning contracts agreed between tutors and tutees. Results of the ten-week intervention indicated significantly greater increases in the reading scores of experimental tutee groups on test compared to control groups. Six-month follow-up indicated that there was no wash-out of experimental effects. Subjective feedback from teachers and parents was also positive. Attempts were made to control for the possible effects of differential expectations of improvement. Tutoring was for one hour per week and was a course requirement for the tutors, who received course credit.

Sandler *et al.* (1979) reported a programme using college students as tutors with low achieving inner-city junior high school pupils. Tutors were recruited largely from the ethnic minorities. Participant versus control group outcomes were reported. Teacher ratings of classwork effort, quality and attitude favoured the participant pupils, who self-reported improved attitudes towards education and higher aspirations and self-expectations.

Valenzuela-Smith (1983) evaluated a project serving 22 Hispanic students in a junior high school in California involving 22 Spanish-proficient students from a community college. Tutors and class teachers completed a behaviour assessment schedule in relation to tutees. This gave some indication that tutees' school behaviour had improved. The tutees themselves reported that the tutoring programme helped reduce their anxiety about going on to high school. Evaluation indicated gains in the oral English capability and report card grades of all participants. Moreover, all 22 tutees enrolled in high school rather than dropping-out. There were however no gains in reading test scores, scores on a self-concept measure or school attendance rates. No effect sizes were given.

University and college students as tutors for schoolchildren

Turkel & Abramson (1986) reported a project in which university students acted as tutor/mentors for high school pupils, directed primarily at potential drop-outs in the ninth grade. Contact took place out of class time, and often out of school. Pre- and post-measures of the subjective self-perceptions of the pupils indicated a significant improvement in attitudes towards school, but response rates were not given. The tutees showed an improvement in attendance (not statistically significant – no effect sizes given). This was also true of the grade point average and standardised reading test scores of the tutees. The authors concluded that given the short duration of the treatment and the hitherto intractable nature of the target group, the results were encouraging.

The City University of New York and the New York City Board of Education developed a collaborative tutoring programme commencing in 1985, linking at-risk high school students with university student tutors. Substantial tutor training was involved. However, evaluation reports (Tyler *et al.*, 1987; Gregory & Berley-Mellits, 1988) found no evidence of effects on the academic performance of tutees, although subjective feedback was positive.

A programme targeted on foster children aged 12 to 15 at risk of dropping-out of high school was reported by Lee *et al.* (1987). Tutors spent at least five hours a week with their tutees, covering basic academic skills and homework assistance and also wider activities. Although both tutors and tutees improved their self-esteem during the programme, there was no evidence of improved academic skills in the tutees, despite the high level of input.

In the study of Fischetti *et al.* (1989) with language minority high school pupils, 98% of tutored minority students in one school continued to post-secondary education, 25% above the school-wide average.

Trainee teachers at Memphis State University communicated with their school-based tutees via electronic mail in a programme described by Ross *et al.* (1989). The tutors left assignments and sent messages and feedback via an electronic bulletin board system. Each tutee was paired individually with a personal tutor. The findings indicated that the performance of participant tutees was superior to that of a control group on standardised achievement tests in reading and maths, as well as in some aspects of writing. Girls used the system more than boys. The tutors regarded their activities as beneficial to themselves personally as well as to the tutees.

Fasko & Flint (1990) targeted high school pupils at risk of drop-out as tutees. Undergraduate students tutored ninth-graders from four high schools. Tutors received ten hours of pre-service training and weekly training and debriefing sessions thereafter. Bi-weekly tutoring sessions were conducted for seven weeks, each tutor serving four tutees. Tutees' self-concept and interpersonal integration appeared improved compared to control groups.

Rhodes & Garibaldi (1990) incorporated campus-based tutoring in a programme for African-American high school students. The intention was to promote minority careers in education. Some evidence of increased aspirations for some tutees was gathered.

Juel (1991) deployed male university student athletes as reading tutors for disadvantaged at-risk elementary school pupils. The intention was to improve the reading skills of the tutors as well as the tutees, since students majoring in athletics were not necessarily highly competent information-processors. Training was given in seven different kinds of tutoring activity and three or four of these were activated during each 45-minute tutoring session. In the first cohort of tutees, 18 out of 20 children were subsequently moved to a higher reading group.

For a second cohort of 27 tutees, mean pre-test score on a reading readiness test was at the 26th percentile, whereas a comparison non-participant group scored at the 46th percentile. After tutoring, the reading comprehension test scores of the tutored children were on average at the 41st percentile, while the scores of the comparison group were at the 16th percentile. Subjective feedback was also positive.

Glazer & Wughalter (1991) reported on a programme designed to attract minority students to teaching careers. The effects on participating tutees' educational aspirations and career choices are reviewed.

Huisman *et al.* (1992) deployed students from four private universities as tutors for eighth grade students in middle schools who were at-risk. Programme impact in terms of school attendance, school grades and subjective feedback is outlined. However, the reliability and validity of the instruments used is questioned.

Bacon (1992) deployed trainee teachers as tutors, focusing on increasing their experience of disadvantaged and at-risk students. Nine undergraduates in an urban university worked one-to-one in a middle school with children who were two or more years behind their peers in reading and/or maths. The tutors found the experience to be worthwhile and rewarding and tutees showed improved academic skills.

The Student Literacy Course study (Flippo *et al.*, 1993) referred to in the previous section, which deployed psychology undergraduates as tutors, reported the development in the elementary school tutees of more positive attitudes towards reading and writing and improved grades for the high school tutees.

Powell *et al.* (1987) evaluated the academic effectiveness of an inter-generational tutoring programme serving disadvantaged children. Forty-two per cent of the tutors were college students and the rest were other adult volunteers. Although the tutees had greater average gains in reading and maths achievement and better attendance records than their non-participating counterparts, the differences did not reach statistical significance (no effect sizes given).

2.4 Outcomes for Teachers

Goodlad (1985) reported subjective feedback over four years from the 'Pimlico Connection', involving questionnaire returns from 128 class-teachers. The response rate was 66%, 58% of the teachers reporting that lessons were easier to handle when student tutors were involved, 66% that teaching was more enjoyable and 63% that they felt the pupils learned more.

Hughes (1993a) reported subsequent teacher subjective feedback (response rate 79%). Ninety-six per cent felt their pupils learnt more, 70% that lessons were more enjoyable, 60% that lessons were easier to handle and 58% that teaching was more enjoyable.

In the Cambridge STIMULUS project, Beardon (1990) found teacher feedback less positive. Seventeen per cent of teachers reported that lessons were easier to handle with tutors, but a similar number reported they were harder to handle. Thirty-three per cent of teachers found lessons more enjoyable with student tutors and 42% thought pupils learned more than usual.

In Birmingham, Gadsby (1993) reported that 55% of teachers found the lessons easier to handle, 54% found the lessons more enjoyable and 57% felt the pupils learnt more than usual.

In the North London Connection (CSV, 1994a), with a response rate of 65% for teacher feedback, 52% of teachers reported lessons were more interesting with student tutors, 64% easier to handle, 73% more enjoyable, 80% felt the children learnt more and 54% felt tutee behaviour improved.

2.5 Summary

In the UK, 'student tutoring' usually means university or college students tutoring schoolchildren in classrooms supervised by the class-teacher. Outside the UK, tutoring programmes involving university students and schoolchildren vary according to tutor and tutee character-istics, the curriculum tutored, contact arrangements and goals, and outcomes and rewards for tutors and tutees.

Gains for tutors

In the UK, a great deal of subjective questionnaire feedback has been gathered from tutors. Response rates have varied from less than 50% to 83%, with some not known. Many studies document a high rate of tutor reporting of improved communication skills (92–100%) and self-confidence (76–95%), but cognitive gains for tutors in the curriculum area of tutoring are much more variable (19–60%). Usually approx-imately 25% of tutors report that tutoring interferes with their main-stream studies. There is limited and conflicting subjective evidence on the extent to which tutors manage to be role models.

In North America, most tutors are white, female, socio-economically advantaged and receive payment or course credit, tutoring equally in elementary (primary) and high schools. Tutees are mostly ethnic minor-ity and socio-economically disadvantaged. Tutoring is more likely to occur on the university campus than in school (the tutor transporting the tutee) and on a one-to-one rather than group basis. Tutoring is often focused on basic skill acquisition. The objective of raising tutee aspira-tions is rarely mentioned in tutoring programmes, although often mentioned in mentoring programmes. Large-scale surveys indicate that most tutoring programme managers believe most of their programme goals are being met, but supportive evidence is rarely accessible.

Other North American studies suggest articulating clear and achiev-able goals for tutors raises their satisfaction levels. Tutors involved in writing programmes can show gains in their own writing skills and motivation. A good deal of positive subjective feedback is also reported.

Gains for tutees

In the UK, subjective questionnaire feedback from tutees is based on response rates from 78–83%, not known in many cases. Usually a little more than half of tutees feel that with tutors in the classroom they learn more and lessons are easier to follow. There is considerable variation in tutee perceptions of whether lessons are more interesting or enjoyable (30–80%).

In Israel, the Perach programme deploys student tutors on a one-to-one basis with disadvantaged schoolchildren, meeting twice a week for one year out of school hours, on campus or in school or elsewhere for academic, cultural or leisure activities. Subjective affective feedback is very positive, but significant academic, self-concept or aspiration gains for tutees have not been found in comparison to control groups. However, at two-year follow-up, there was some evidence of lower tutee drop-out and improved aspirations, together with some cognitive gain in mathematics.

In Australia, students acting as remedial reading tutors using structured materials generated some significant gains for tutees on some reading tests. In New Zealand, student tutoring operates in a similar way to the UK model but with four or five tutors in each class. Little difference has been found between pre- and post-tutoring self-report measures, with much variation between classes. Although some effect on the vocational intentions of tutors was evident, there was no apparent impact on the aspirations of tutees.

In North America, a number of studies have evaluated tutee gains. Five of these have unequivocally demonstrated a significant positive effect on academic achievement, usually with a structured programme of relatively frequent tutoring designed to impact reading and/or maths skills with outcomes measured by norm-referenced tests. Significant self-concept gains, improved grades and reduced drop-out rates have also been recorded, and two studies showed improvements in teacher ratings of classroom behaviour. However, a similar number of studies have failed to show significant gains on reading tests or other academic performance indicators and some have not shown significant gains on measures of self-concept. There is little evidence of improved tutee aspirations.

Gains for teachers

Only research in the UK has attempted to quantify gains for the classteacher, by gathering subjective questionnaire feedback. Response rates range from 65–79%, with some not reported. Just over half of teachers typically report lessons are easier to handle with student tutors, about 50–75% find lessons more enjoyable and well over half (42–80%) feel the pupils learn more.

2.6 Conclusion

Programmes deploying university and college students as tutors for schoolchildren around the world have generated a substantial body of evaluation research of varying quality.

It should be remembered that the types and models of student tutoring encompassed by these studies are many. Two studies utilising the same gain factor may have investigated very different models of operation with very different populations for very different purposes. Thus, like is rarely adjacent to or compared with like. The overall pattern of outcomes certainly cannot be assumed to apply in its entirety to the UK model of student tutoring or any other single specific model. Future research could usefully focus on aptitude X treatment interactions – which models of student tutoring are most effective for which types of populations in which contexts.

Positive outcomes demonstrated for tutors are mostly within the social/affective domain. Relatively few studies have explored cognitive and/or transferable skill gains for tutors. Subjective post-only feedback suggests tutors often perceive gains in their communication skills and self-confidence, but there is no corroborative evidence for the former and measures of self-concept change in tutors have yielded mixed results. Self-reported tutor cognitive gains are much less frequent and there can be an adverse effect on the tutor's studies in a minority of cases.

Cognitive and attainment gains are more frequently reported for tutees, especially in basic literacy and numeracy skills. However, this is not a finding for the UK model of student tutoring, which does not tend to focus on basic skill remediation. Subjective post-only feedback from tutees in the UK suggested about half perceived immediate benefits in the classroom, with no adverse effects. However, pre-post subjective tutee feedback in New Zealand showed no difference resulting from tutoring. There is a need to establish whether cognitive and attainment gains for tutees accrue from the UK model.

In the Perach programme in Israel, subjective feedback was very positive, but more rigorous scrutiny of academic or self-concept gains for tutees suggested these were delayed and small. In Australia and North America, good quality studies have demonstrated academic and other gains for tutees, usually where the tutoring was frequent, focused on basic skills and used structured methods. However, other similar studies failed to find significant effects. Generally, evidence for increased tutee aspirations is slight.

Post hoc subjective feedback from classteachers in the UK suggests a little more than half usually perceive benefits in the classroom.

What gains might reasonably be expected from what is essentially a relatively slight intervention has not always been thought through in the fervour of innovation and dissemination. Student tutoring programmes, in whatever format, should specify clear, realistic and achievable goals. If

30

these are measurable, enabling improved quality of evaluation research, so much the better.

It may be that many of the tutoring programmes reviewed above had effects which could not be convincingly proved given the evaluation design and instrumentation used or available. However, without satisfactory evidence, this cannot be assumed. Further thought about evaluation methodologies is necessary. Meanwhile, tutoring programmes should not be marketed in a context of unrealistically raised expectations, since subsequent disappointment will damage dissemination, replication and embedding of the initiative.

Different formats of student tutoring should be actively designed, structured, contracted and operated to maximise the likelihood that the stated objectives will be achieved. This, together with adequate monitoring and quality control of the process of tutoring, should help to avoid what sometimes appears to occur at the moment – serendipitous gains for some coupled with considerable inequality of opportunity. Certainly, if raising tutee aspirations is to be an objective, the structuring and quality control of the tutoring experience would appear to need further thought by all concerned.

Further research is currently being undertaken in the UK to investigate cognitive and transferable skill gains for tutors in the UK model of student tutoring. As indicated, research on such gains for tutees from the UK model also appears to be needed as a matter of priority.

Address for correspondence: Keith Topping, Centre for Paired Learning, Psychology Department, University of Dundee, Dundee DD1 4HN. Tel. 01382 223181 ext 4628, secretary 4622/3/4. Fax 01382 229993. email k.j.topping@dundee.ac.uk

Chapter 3

PEER TUTORING IN ECONOMICS AT THE UNIVERSITY OF MELBOURNE

Carol Johnston

This chapter examines a peer tutoring model which integrates trainee teachers in an undergraduate group learning programme. It was found that small groups operate more effectively in terms of group cohesion, longevity and perception of improved performance when supported by a trainee teacher. Trainee teachers developed an enhanced range of skills in relation to small group management, cooperative learning and communication. Evaluation of the model from both the tutors' and the students' perspective is reported. The applicability of the model to cross-institutional contexts is examined.

The pressure on resources available to the tertiary education sector has increased in Australia over the past decade. An expansion in demand for places at tertiary institutions has stretched existing facilities while at the same time governments have sought to reduce expenditure in the face of unsustainable budget deficits. These two sources of pressure have provoked a search for new ways to improve the efficiency of tertiary institutions. At the same time, employers have reiterated their need for graduates who are able to analyse and synthesise information in order to solve real-world problems and for these graduates to demonstrate a capacity for effective communication. As universities are becoming more reliant on non-government funding it is clearly in their interest to be seen to respond more actively to these calls than they may have done in the past. Research in the tertiary education area suggests that the skills required by employers are likely to be best developed through a more participatory learning environment than the traditional lecture/tutorial format. In addition, resources may be used more efficiently where small groups establish learning patterns which are independent of the lecturer and tutor.

The Business Studies Department of the University of Melbourne responded to these challenges in 1993 through a project designed to foster cooperative learning strategies in undergraduate economics students while at the same time providing the opportunity for trainee economics teachers to develop teaching skills in a small group context. The project evaluated student achievement, both at the graduate and undergraduate level.

This chapter is divided into four sections. The first provides some background to the project and examines the proposition that small group learning with peer support can foster deeper approaches to learning and thereby develop the skills valued by employers. The second section outlines the project and the context in which it took place. The third examines the results from the project. The last section discusses the results and explores their implications.

3.1 Background to the Project

Graduates who are adept at analysing and synthesising knowledge to solve practical problems are likely to adopt an approach to learning during their undergraduate work which involves them intimately in the learning process. Their approach to learning is 'deeper' than that of a student who has learnt to jump through hurdles but has not retained and cannot use much of what has been 'learnt'. In their seminal work, Marton & Saljo (1976 a and b) distinguished between deep and surface approaches to learning. Students who use a deep approach seek to obtain some underlying meaning; they aim to understand relationships between the immediate task and other tasks or contexts; they are likely to read extensively, engage in discussion with others and ultimately to achieve higher grades on assessment tasks (where the assessment instrument is designed to assess more than a simple recall of facts); and are likely to be more self-confident in communicating ideas to others than students who use a surface approach.

If a deeper approach to learning improves student ability to analyse and synthesise material, then clearly there are advantages in employing strategies in undergraduate courses which would foster this approach. Cooperative learning in small group situations may be one way in which a deeper approach to learning is encouraged. Much North American research establishes the relationship between cooperative learning and improved student achievement. Studies by Slavin (1990) and by Palinscar & Brown (1984) show that an individual student's achievement is consistently positively related to the level of help that the student gives to others. The opportunity to interact in a structured way in a peer group setting compels students to externalise their thoughts and make their ideas explicit. It provides the opportunity to transmit knowledge and discover inadequacies, to correct misunderstandings and reconcile conflicting views. Enhanced understanding results because students must think about the material, develop examples and structure explanations. Small group learning improves communication skills, increases individual self-confidence and encourages openness to new ideas. There are a number of approaches to the establishment and maintenance of small groups; studies by Goodlad & Hirst (1989, 1990) indicate the efficacy of small group learning with peer tutoring support.

The project examined in this chapter aimed to encourage a deeper approach to learning and the development of valuable communication skills through the establishment of a cooperative learning context in the form of small groups supported by a proctor. Saunders (1992) argues that the term 'peer tutoring' implies an equality of status which is not present in most peer tutoring structures where more advanced students tutor those in earlier years in the course. For this reason the term 'proctor' has been used in some cases in Britain. The term encompasses a situation where students assist each other to learn. One partner in the relationship, the proctor, may be more knowledgeable in a specific discipline but will benefit from the relationship by building skills and knowledge in other areas. The other partners to the relationship, the undergraduates, will benefit from the knowledge and expertise of the proctor in the discipline area.

The term proctor rather than peer tutor was adopted for the Melbourne University project because it clearly distinguishes the role of the proctor from that of the tutor. A tutor's more formal traditional role is to expand and explain key ideas and concepts covered in lectures. It is a leadership role rather than a peer support role. Tutorials at the University of Melbourne are typically composed of 20–25 students. Commonly the approach to teaching in the tutorial is didactic. Tutors go through a series of exercises set by the lecturer. There is an expectation that students will complete the exercises prior to the tutorial. Tutorials are often conducted by postgraduate students with no teacher training who frequently comment on the difficulty in generating meaningful discussion.

The proctor's role is to guide small groups (termed 'microgroups' to distinguish them from tutorials) and to assist them in conducting meaningful discussions to solve problems. A coordinating and mentoring function is part of the proctor's role. The microgroups to which proctors were assigned were composed of around four students and the teaching approach which was encouraged was Socratic in so far as the proctor was expected to guide discussion, not direct it. Problems were set by the lecturer and were designed to foster deeper thinking and, through the system of assessment, to reward evidence of analysis and synthesis rather than recall or description.

3.2 The Project and its Context

The undergraduate students

The Business Studies Department has responsibility for undergraduate students in two degrees: Bachelor of Education and Bachelor of Social Science (Information Management). Students taking these degrees have graduated from secondary school with results which are in the lower end of the spectrum for university entrance. There are more females than males and they are drawn from a wide variety of ethnic and socio-economic backgrounds. The Business Studies Department also had responsibility for postgraduate students taking a Diploma of Education degree with teacher training in economics. These students have graduated from high school with above average results and all have passed an undergraduate degree. They tend to be more homogeneous in terms of their ethnicity, socio-economic background and motivation than the undergraduates.

In the past, undergraduate students have not been enthusiastic about forming microgroups and where they have been formed, early enthusiasm has faded rapidly, resulting in a high drop-off rate. There are several possible reasons for this: the difficulty of recognising the individual contributions of group members; a widely-held view that small group work provided a vehicle for sharing ignorance and allowed undue domination of the group by particular individuals; the demands of the course or subject which increase as the year progresses resulting in less voluntary small group discussion as students see their time as more productively spent in alternative ways. The higher drop-off rate as the year progresses is exacerbated when the group work is not assessed.

The postgraduate students

Postgraduate Diploma of Education students who have experience of a lecture/tutorial teaching structure have difficulty in adjusting to the idea that students learn more effectively when they actively participate in their own learning. There is a prevailing attitude that as the relatively passive learning approach engendered by a didactic rather than Socratic style of teaching worked for them, insofar as they graduated: this should be sufficient for everyone. This is disturbing in trainee teachers as it perpetuates an approach to teaching which may not be the most effective in stimulating deeper learning. A highly-structured learning environment is safe and comfortable for students and teachers but the learning approach which it generates tends to be surface level. A more interactive, and thereby challenging, environment stimulates deeper approaches to learning but is not as comfortable and tends to be avoided. Increasingly it is likely that employers will seek employees who have proven skills of cooperation, team learning and effective communication. These skills are best nurtured in a small group learning environment and teachers will be expected to know how to develop such an environment. There is a need, therefore, for trainee teachers to be exposed to such a learning context in their training.

Past experience suggests that it is not enough simply to expose trainee teachers to the idea of small group work through lecture and reading material: they need to have considerable practical experience of group work in order to feel comfortable with this approach. Observation of trainee teachers on school practice in Australia over a number of years suggests that they are unwilling to 'let go' of the class and will not use small group strategies in their teaching. They tend to ask 'closed' questions in their classrooms which do not allow the development of extended discussion and which often do not guide the discussion in a meaningful direction.

The observed characteristics of undergraduate students in economics subjects and the postgraduate Diploma students indicated that more needed to be done to change student approaches to teaching and learning. However, it was evident in light of the pressure on resources that any innovation would have to be accomplished within existing budgetary constraints. As a result, the new structure was designed to improve student approaches to learning and teaching without incurring extensive additional cost.

Aims of the project

In general terms the project was designed to improve teaching and learning in economics. More specifically the project aimed to:

- provide a structure to support small undergraduate learning groups in order to improve the depth of economic understanding
- to improve communication skills of both undergraduate and postgraduate students
- to provide a cost-efficient structure to link trainee teacher programmes to undergraduate courses in order to (a) enhance small group teaching familiarity and skills of new teachers and (b) provide student teachers with a mechanism for future professional development through a developed competence in working cooperatively as part of a team.

An evaluation was undertaken to judge the effectiveness of the structure in (a) enhancing undergraduate learning and (b) improving teachers' skills in small group work in order to inform prospective users in other contexts

The structure

The university year is divided into two semesters and most subjects are one semester in length. All undergraduate students in the second-year subjects, macroeconomic theory and macroeconomic policy, attended two lectures and one tutorial a week. In addition, the participating undergraduate students attended one microgroup meeting each week. Postgraduate economics trainee teachers attended one lecture per week in the Diploma of Education subject, economics teaching method, which explored strategies for teaching school economics.

There were 90 students enrolled in macroeconomic theory in the first semester. Of these, 55 (61%) volunteered to take part in the microgroup project. These volunteers were divided into 14 groups. The groups were formed by the lecturer on the basis of student enrolment numbers. As students did not know each other it was hoped that the focus of the group would be clearly work-related from the outset. During the year friendships were formed through the microgroups but by this time a group norm of behaviour focused on productive work had been clearly established. Each group consisted of approximately four students who worked together throughout the year on a series of problem-solving exercises.

A volunteer postgraduate Diploma of Education student was assigned to each group to act as the microgroup's proctor for the year. The proctor's role was to foster constructive debate and to guide in the analysis of the set problems. It was anticipated that the proctor would also play a significant role in keeping the group motivated and in ensuring continued constructive participation.

The proctors were provided with an introductory training session on small group teaching strategies, conducted by the researcher in association with the University's Center for the Study of Higher Education. This session focused on the proctor's role within the group and on strategies for dealing with common problems such as domination by a group member or unfocused discussion. In addition, two lectures in the economics teaching method subject were devoted to small group teaching. Ongoing support was provided throughout the year by a number of review sessions intended to monitor the proctor's progress and experiences.

There were three sets of problems to be completed by the microgroups in each semester, six in all. The exercises reflected a focus on problem-solving in a real-world contemporary context. In some cases they reinforced lecture and tutorial work and in others extended this work. Students were expected to be able to explain and defend their solutions to other group members.

Assessment of student work

Where assignment tasks or examination questions elicit factual or descriptive responses, students will tend to adopt a surface level approach as deeper learning will be perceived to be relatively unrewarded (White, 1992). This has implications for curriculum design in that assessment instruments must clearly reflect this aim and reward deeper, higher-order thinking. Microgroup problem sets were designed specifically to elicit and reward deeper approaches to learning.

The role which problem-solving exercises can play in stimulating deeper thinking is well established (Newble & Clark, 1986; Boud & Felleti, 1991). Problem-solving exercises encourage higher-order thinking skills and are thereby more challenging than questions which require a simple regurgitation of facts. When a problem is challenging, students must approach it from a deeper learning perspective.

The microgroup problem-solving tasks replaced an essay which the non-microgroups were required to complete. The tasks contributed to 20% of the semester's assessment; the remaining 80% was through an end-of-semester examination. The problem-solving tasks were assessed in the first instance by the proctor and subsequently checked by the lecturer to ensure that the criteria for award of marks were applied consistently across all groups. The non-microgroup essays were marked by the lecturer.

In order to more accurately value individual contributions to the microgroup problem-solving exercises, group members were given the option of deciding how marks were to be distributed between the members of the group. For example, a group of four were awarded 75 marks from a total of 100 for a given task. If it was decided by the group that one member had made a more (or less) significant contribution to the group's understanding than others, the group could reward this by allotting more of the marks to this member up to the total value of the marks awarded by the proctor, ie, $75 \times 4 = 300$. From the 300 marks available, one member may be given 90 and the remaining three members 70. This method of assessing individual contributions to group work was based on the view that students themselves are in the best position to know the contribution of each member and also that students in the group will be encouraged to contribute if they are aware of the consequences of an inadequate performance.

The proctors were assessed on the basis of a journal which they kept throughout the year which reflected on the process and their role within it. The journal replaced a more conventional assignment which non-participating Diploma of Education students completed. The journal was not assessed beyond a satisfactory/unsatisfactory grade.

Evaluation design

It was hypothesised that microgroup participants would both perform better and improve more on the assessment instruments (exams and problems) than those students who did not participate. The undergraduate's skills in communication and team work was also expected to improve, as was the cohesion and longevity of the group itself. Postgraduate trainee teachers were expected to improve in terms of their communication skills and their use of small group teaching. Qualitative and quantitative methods of evaluation were employed to test these aspects of the project:

■ A Test of Understanding of College Economics developed in the United States by the National Council on Economic Education (and modified slightly to suit Australian terminology) was administered to all undergraduate students at the start of semester one in order to establish base-line data.

■ Questionnaires were administered which sought responses in relation to the reasons why students chose to participate in the microgroups and proctoring. They sought to establish whether the groups had fulfilled the students' original expectations and to understand the process microgroups adopted to complete the problems set. Four groups of participants completed questionnaires: the microgroup undergraduate participants; the non-microgroup undergraduates; the proctors and the non-proctors. Questionnaires were administered in July and again in September at the end of semester two.

■ Interviews were conducted with a small randomly selected sample of undergraduate students and proctors in order to obtain a qualitative perspective on the operation of the microgroups. Eight undergraduates (14.5% of total microgroup participants) and six (42% of total) proctors were interviewed at the end of the course. The number of undergraduates selected for interview was relatively small due to work pressures at the end of the year and to funding constraints.

■ The end-of-semester undergraduate examination provided some further indication of any differences in performance between the microgroups and the non-microgroups.

■ The journals kept by the proctors as part of their assessment in economics teaching method provided additional qualitative data.

3.3 Results of the Evaluation

The undergraduate microgroups

Tests and exams

Students who take second-year macroeconomic theory and macroeconomic policy must pass first-year foundations of economics. Similarly, students who take the second semester subject, macroeconomic policy, must pass macroeconomic theory. This prerequisite results in fewer students taking economics in the second semester. Sixty per cent of students volunteered to participate in the microgroups in the first semester and 59% in the second semester. Of these students, 38 took

Peer tutoring in economics at the University of Melbourne

Table 3.1 Student population

Total population semester 1	91
Total population semester 2	78
Microgroup participants semester 1	55
Microgroup participants semester 2	46
Microgroup participants common to both semesters	38
Non-microgroup students common to both semesters	19

economics in both semesters. This cohort provided the basis of evaluation of the microgroups as they participated in the groups for the whole year (see Table 3.1).

The US National Council Test of Understanding College Economics was administered to establish whether there were differences in economic understanding between the participating microgroup students and those who chose not to participate. The standard deviations and mean scores for each of the groups are set out in Table 3.2. The standard deviations for each group show considerable deviation from the mean, indicating a wide variety in terms of understanding of economics within each group. It will be seen that the mean for the non-microgroup students was slightly higher than for the microgroup students. A difference in means test shows that the difference in scores between the two groups is not statistically significant. We may therefore conclude that, on average, the two groups were not significantly different from each other at the start of the year in terms of their knowledge of economics. All participating and non-participating student university entrance scores and first-year foundations of economics scores were tested and indicated that on these basis too there was no significant difference between the two groups of students.

As the TUCE test indicated that there appeared to be no significant differences on average between the two groups at the start of the year, it was possible to examine changes in student performance over the course of the year in relation to their experiences within that year.

Results in both the first semester and second semester exams indicate that microgroup students scored better than non-microgroup students. However, these results should be viewed cautiously as the standard

Table 3.2 Test of Understanding College Economics (TUCE)

	Mean	Standard deviation	Number of students in the sample
Microgroup students	17.34	4.55	38
Non-microgroup students	17.79	5.21	19

Table 3.3 Exam results

	Mean	Standard deviation	Number of students in the sample
Semester 1 exam			
Microgroup students	61.5	8.4	38
Non-microgroup students	60.9	8.6	19
Semester 2 exam			
Microgroup students	67.2	9.9	38
Non-microgroup students	64.8	9.4	19

deviations indicate a great deal of variability within each group and the differences in scores is not statistically significant. The results for both groups are set out in Table 3.3. While it is very difficult to assign causality, particularly in view of the small sample size, one factor which may have contributed to the microgroup's better relative performance on the exams may have been their participation in the microgroups. Another may have been that 20% of the assessment for microgroups was continuous, which may have contributed to the establishment of better work/study patterns in the microgroups than in the non-microgroup students.

While the microgroup's mean was higher overall on exams than the non-microgroup students, both groups improved their performance by around 9% during the year. Several factors may have been at work in the improvement in mean scores, the most obvious being that all students had simply improved their understanding of economics over the year. Other contributing factors may relate to the different subject material covered in the second semester, more appropriate exam questions, and work pressures in other subjects may have changed. Both the improvement and higher score in the microgroup students' (mean) results appear to support the idea that small group work enhances student understanding.

Questionnaires

Microgroup students were asked a number of questions which sought to understand why they had participated in the project, how the groups had worked and whether they saw the groups as worthwhile in terms of the skills and understanding they developed during the year. The first questionnaire was administered at the end of semester one after there had been sufficient time for early enthusiasm to wear thin and for problems to emerge. From a total cohort of 55 microgroup members, 45 (82% of the group) responded to the questionnaire.

The reasons students had chosen to participate in the project were examined as these would influence their view of the project in terms of its usefulness. Table 3.4 summarises responses to this on the first questionnaire. Three main reasons emerged: a recognition of the value of small groups in improving learning; insecurity about their ability in economics; a preference for the continuous form of assessment in the microgroups. Recognition of the value of small groups is a surprising result in that if students already held this view, it is puzzling that they had not formed groups of their own in first year or in other subjects. Intuitively, it seems likely that insecurity about ability in economics and a preference for continuous assessment may be more cogent reasons for participation.

Additional reasons for participation revolved around the idea that the groups provided a less threatening environment in which to voice difficulties and concerns. The proctor was seen as potentially more approachable than the lecturer and students noted that they were more willing to take risks in voicing opinions than they would have been in the larger tutorial groups.

In response to a question which asked students whether they saw the microgroup exercises as a good reflection of the focus being given in tutorials and lectures, 89% said the exercises were appropriate. The exercises which were designed to foster a deeper approach to learning were focused on a problem-solving approach to economics and required higher-order skills to solve than many of the tutorial exercises. It is likely that when students are asked to approach a learning task in a manner

Table 3.4 Reasons for participation in microgroups

	Extremely important	Very important	Important	Not very important	Not at all important
Insecurity about ability in economics	14	27	40	14	5
Participation of friends	–	2	11	41	46
Recognition of value of small groups	18	53	27	2	–
Preference for continuous assessment	14	30	30	25	2
Interest in working in pilot project	5	7	36	34	18
Time to participate	2	14	39	30	16

which is different from that with which they are familiar, they may, in the initial stages at least, fail to see the relevance or usefulness of the task and develop negative feelings towards it. If students had found the tasks to be unrelated they may have rated the microgroups as less useful.

Students were also asked to identify key strengths and weaknesses in the microgroup structure. They saw the principal strengths as the opportunity to discuss problems with peers in a language that all could understand. Effective communication is one of the skills frequently identified as desirable by employers. In light of this the perception that students were able to communicate more fluently in microgroups is interesting. The support of group members and the encouragement to work harder were also mentioned by many. The prime perceived weakness of the programme was that some members did not contribute fully to the group through infrequent attendance or failure to produce a section of work. The difficulty of setting a meeting time to suit all students and proctors was also seen as a problem. Nevertheless, over 90% of microgroup students said they enjoyed being part of the microgroup, indicating that perceived strengths outweighed perceived weaknesses.

In relation to the microgroup's relationship with the proctor, three-quarters of the students believed that their proctor was effective in providing worthwhile general support for the group and in contributing to meaningful discussion. Over three-quarters thought the proctor demonstrated a good knowledge of the subject and was well prepared for the group.

A second questionnaire was administered to the microgroups at the end of semester two. At this stage students were aware of their first semester results, had completed a multiple-choice test and a number of microgroup exercises and therefore had a clear idea of their progress in the subject. There were 38 respondents from a total cohort of 46 microgroup participants (an 83% response rate). Students were asked to rate the effectiveness of the microgroups in improving their understanding of economics: 86% rated the groups as either effective or very effective.

This questionnaire examined the way in which the groups operated. Students were asked if members attended regularly (87% positive), whether all members of the group contributed to discussion (84% positive) and came with work prepared (22% positive) and whether there was cooperation of the group in completion of set tasks (60% positive). Importantly, students saw the microgroups as worthwhile, as 89% said they would recommend participation in the groups to students taking the subject in the following year.

Interviews

The eight undergraduate students who were interviewed were asked whether the microgroup work should be assessed. It was suggested that the groups should meet for discussion purposes only. Students reacted strongly, asserting that most students would not attend a pure discussion group and that the assessment link contributed to students taking participation seriously.

Interviewees were asked to describe the way in which the group worked. Most groups appeared to have adopted similar approaches to the following:

> We met and discussed the questions so we could pick up ideas and then we'd go home and do it. Then we'd meet again to finalise what we'd got and discuss it and read out what we had and make up a final paper. . . . I realised the different views, the different angles that you could take.

Some noted their frustration when a proctor came poorly prepared and was perceived to be unhelpful. However, six students out of the eight interviewed described the proctors' participation in similar terms to the following:

> Our proctor, rather than telling us what to do . . . acted as someone to guide us. To be there for us to fall back on rather than directing us as a teacher would.

Students were asked if the group could have operated as well without a proctor. Most felt that the proctor was necessary to give the group a sense of cohesion and also to help in clarifying problems:

> . . .she was there to clarify everything. Because if the other people in my group had a different answer to me, we could discuss it but we wouldn't really know who was right, whereas the proctor could clarify it. She had more knowledge in economics.

In general terms the interviews supported the notion that groups operate more effectively when an individual whose role is to guide and support is made available to the group. It was also apparent that the proctors' usefulness was quickly identified and that considerable frustration was experienced when the proctor was not seen as helpful.

45

The experience of the postgraduate proctors

Questionnaires

The 14 proctors completed similar questionnaires to the microgroup students, seeking the reasons they chose to become proctors and to evaluate their experiences of the microgroups. In general terms, the proctors were more motivated by professional factors than the under-graduates, who were focused on jumping through the next academic hurdle.

The data summarised in Table 3.5 indicate that trainee teachers are keen to gain more exposure to direct teaching experiences in their courses and to improve their employment prospects. None of the proctors rated the form of assessment as important in their decision to participate, which is in contrast to the undergraduates who viewed this as very important.

All except one of the proctors said that they would choose to take part in the project again, although many noted that it was a great deal of work. Proctors were required to spend an hour a week with their microgroups, they had to prepare for the group and assess the work which was submitted. This represented a time commitment of around two and a half hours a week.

In a questionnaire completed at the end of the second semester, proctors were asked which of a list of skills they thought they had improved as a result of their proctoring experience. Results from this question are summarised in Table 3.6. Most proctors believed that their skill in leading small groups, assessing student work and in questioning techniques had all improved significantly. All proctors also noted an improvement in their knowledge of economics.

Table 3.5 Reasons for proctor participation

	Extremely important	Very important	Important	Not very important	Not at all important
Need for more teaching experience	25	17	35	25	0
Interested in small group work	–	33	58	8	–
Enhancement of employment prospects	8	8	42	25	17
Preference for journal form of assessment	–	–	25	33	42
Interest in participation in a pilot project	–	17	42	42	–
Lecturers' enthusiasm	8	33	50	8	–

46

Table 3.6 Skills improved as a result of the proctoring experience

	Extremely important	Very important	Important	Not very important	Not at all important
General teaching skills	8	17	42	33	–
Leading small groups	17	50	33	–	–
Assessing student work	8	75	8	8	–
Relating to students	8	50	17	25	–
Appropriate questioning techniques	33	42	8	17	–
Improvement in knowledge of economics	25	33	42	–	–

Interviews

Interviews were conducted to confirm and extend the questionnaire responses with six of the proctors chosen at random towards the end of semester two. Those interviewed thought that they had improved their questioning techniques, their assessment skills and their knowledge of economics as a result of participation in the project.

In terms of the most positive aspects of the project for the proctors, several also noted a finer understanding of the need for organisation and planning in teaching effectively. On the negative side, many expressed concern at the amount of time the groups took in terms of organisation and preparation. They also expressed some frustration in organising appropriate meeting times and disappointment when a group member did not turn up to a meeting.

In relation to assessment, one proctor noted that,

> Certain members of the group have taken this option as an easy way out of part of the assessment. This caused some resentment amongst the hard workers but the adjustment of mark allocations seems to have fixed this.

However, the pressure to give all students in the group the same mark remained strong even when the alternative option was available. Only four of the groups gave different marks to individual members of the group.

Proctors felt that the microgroups helped to overcome the detached, impersonal university culture and that this led to better learning outcomes. The more fluent expression of ideas in a risk-free context was also seen as desirable:

> The students seem to have benefited from a regular group that's really small enough for all to be well attended to and have their say without fear. It's made the usual detached Uni culture more accessible to them.

In response to an interview question which sought to establish how the microgroup experience differed from that of the more formal school practice, proctors noted the greater opportunity to guide rather than direct student learning:

> The difference was that the students teach other students in the group and you are there more in an advisory position. . . . In teaching you are. . . the center of attention.

Journals

The journals which all proctors kept throughout the year provided an insight into the dynamics of the microgroups. Proctors were required to reflect on each of the microgroup meetings. They reported on the manner in which the groups solved the set problems. This varied considerably. Some groups divided the questions between members, went away to solve them individually and then came back to the group to explain to other members how they had reached the solution. This approach depended on the degree to which group members were prepared to critically appraise solutions and their ability to defend their answers:

> My approach was to ask each member to explain to the others the section they were responsible for and if they didn't fully get something, to get it out of someone else, or build the answer by asking the right question so they would come to the conclusion. . . . There was a lot of room for what if kind of prompts, which expanded the scope of each problem, forcing them to think beyond what they had prepared.

Another approach was to 'brainstorm' what the group already knew about the questions and to then decide which elements they needed to research further in order to finalise solutions. This approach tended to be employed by the more-able groups.

The proctors noted a growing confidence about 'letting go' of the class:

> As our meetings developed I have found myself more prepared to simply sit back and guide the group in discussions. As I have become more comfortable with the group I have improved my discussion techniques.

The journals also highlighted several problems with the group structure. There was some difficulty experienced in terms of the flow of information from the lecturer to the proctor and then to the student. Proctors did not know the context in which the microgroup problem-solving exercises were set as they did not attend lectures. This meant that they had difficulty in establishing the relationship of the problems to the tutorial work and to the lectures themselves.

3.4 Discussion and Implications for Further Research

In terms of the aims of the project it appears that the structure did provide support for small groups to continue to operate over the course of the year. While the composition of groups altered slightly over the year, the same number of groups were operating at the end of the year as at the start, indicating that the assignment of a proctor to the groups was helpful in maintaining group cohesion and momentum. Thus problems often experienced in maintaining enthusiasm for small group work were to some extent avoided.

Somewhat less clear however is the achievement of an improvement in the depth of understanding of economics in undergraduate students. Microgroup participants seemed to improve more on all forms of assessment than did the non-microgroup students; however, the differences recorded were not statistically significant. But the conclusion that microgroups are not worthwhile on the basis of this test should be avoided at this stage. The evidence from this small sample is inconclusive and indicates that similar studies must be carried out on a much larger scale and/or with a student body who are more homogeneous.

Microgroup students demonstrated a keen awareness of the important role assessment had in the groups. Many chose to participate because of the continuous form of assessment and most participants recognised that the fact that the group work was assessed encouraged greater participation and quality work. The pressure to reward all group members equally remained strong and some modification of the assessment procedures would seem to be in order so that individual contributions are more clearly rewarded.

The degree of satisfaction with the microgroup exercises indicated that they were not beyond the students' capability to solve and at the same time appear to be viewed as relevant to the mainstream subject.

Undergraduate students' responses indicate a high overall degree of satisfaction with the project. Despite the ambiguous nature of the assessment results, it appears that students do enjoy working in groups when some structure is provided through the use of proctors. A more collaborative and interactive learning environment for all students was created in both tutorials and lectures in the year in which the microgroups operated, as the learning patterns which were established in the groups contributed to a change in the culture of the entire cohort of students. However, several elements of the project need to be considered further: the selection and training of proctors needs to be improved so that all proctors are comfortable with their groups and seen as useful; the method of assessment at the undergraduate level should be reconsidered so that individual contributions to group work can be more adequately rewarded; and strategies to make systems of information interchange between the lecturer and the proctors more fluent should be explored.

The proctors appear to improve significantly in terms of developing their confidence and small group teaching skills over the semester. From the journal, questionnaire and interview evidence it appears that the aim of improving trainee teachers' familiarity with small group teaching strategies and in improving communication skills was achieved. However, it is difficult to determine whether the proctoring experience was the only or even the main cause of this improvement. Nevertheless, proctors clearly felt that participation in the project was a significant factor.

Many proctors alluded to the time commitment involved in the proctoring project, but most asserted that the time was well spent and worth the effort. The time commitment is undoubtedly as substantial as it is unavoidable. In light of the extra commitment that proctoring requires, it would be unwise to make participation compulsory. As a voluntary component of a teacher training course it has the advantage of being relatively cost-neutral but profitable for both trainee teachers and undergraduates.

The use of postgraduate trainee teachers in leading microgroups in economics would seem to be a structure which could usefully be employed in other disciplines. The first-year experience is a vital one for undergraduates as it is in this year that approaches to study and work become established. Small group work strategies established in this year are likely to be carried forward into later years and on into the workplace. As an adjunct to traditional trainee teacher school experience, the microgroups appeared to have been a highly successful component of training. Postgraduate students who envisage an academic career should be encouraged to undertake a proctoring role as the skills which this role appears to develop are essential to 'quality teaching', the focus of so much current attention in Australian universities. Similarly, employers may value graduates who have been exposed to this type of experience as they would be familiar with skills appropriate to cooperative team learning in the work place.

In an increasingly competitive world economic environment it is imperative that higher education institutions prepare well-equipped graduates. Problem solving and an ability to work effectively in a collaborative context are skills which are expected of graduates in the 1990s. The proctoring project contributes to the development of these attributes in economics students and teachers and it may be appropriate to extend the proctoring structure to other discipline areas.

Note: A more detailed paper is available on request.

Address for correspondence: Carol Johnston, Department of Economics, The University of Melbourne, Parkville, Victoria 3052, Australia. Tel. +61 3 344 5289. Fax + 61 3 344 6899. email: c.johnston@ecomfac.unimelb.edu.au

Chapter 4

STUDENTS AS MUSEUM INTERPRETERS

Stephanie McIvor

In 1991 the British student tutoring scheme, The Pimlico Connection, was extended to involve educational trips to the Science Museum, London – The Pimlico Connection Science Museum Project. The objective was to link the student tutors' classroom-based tutoring to a field trip to the Science Museum. The project aims to develop good management procedures in the deployment of student tutors as volunteer museum interpreters, and to evaluate the benefits and pitfalls of such a project to students, teachers and pupils.

4.1 Introduction

The Science Museum London, at the heart of the National Museum of Science and Industry, is a unique institution. It celebrates an extraordinary story of innovation and achievement. Its collections, without parallel in the fields of science, technology and medicine, record not only the origins of modern scientific and industrial man, but chart human progress from the waterwheel to fibre optics.

Fast-changing temporary exhibitions complement the historical galleries by focusing on contemporary science, technology and medicine. An extensive programme of events for adults and children, including gallery drama, activity workshops, science shows, curator tours and Science Nights (the chance for 8–11-year-olds to experience all that the Museum has to offer and to sleep among the exhibits overnight) is on offer to all our visitors throughout the year and enhanced over holiday periods.

A selection of resource materials provide support and enrichment for group visits with children of all ages, and a range of teachers' courses provide professional development opportunities, particularly for teachers of science, technology and history.

Every year, 1.3 million visitors benefit from the museum experience, a quarter of a million of them coming in educational groups organised by school clubs and societies.

Following 17 years of running The Pimlico Connection – a student tutoring scheme linking volunteer student tutors from Imperial College London to local schools – the Pimlico Connection Science Museum Project was created. This new project aims to link student tutoring with a class visit to the Science Museum, the 'principle being that student tutors in the classroom and in the Museum, could offer the potential to bridge the gap between the visit to the Museum, and the more normal experiences back at school' (Hughes, 1993c).

4.2 Background: Pilot Project 1992/93

In October 1992, student tutors who volunteered for the well-established and popular Pimlico Connection classroom-based tutoring scheme were given the opportunity to volunteer for the pilot project. Students are attracted to the project through the student-run Pimlico Connection society, mainly through posters around campus. Student tutors were to be affiliated to certain galleries. The galleries chosen were considered less accessible than most to casual visitors, and student tutors were assigned to one particular gallery through personal choice and availability. Student tutors were then matched to a school that had already booked a visit to that gallery on a Wednesday afternoon.

Five students became museum student tutors, although the interest was far greater. The museum student tutors attended the two and half hour mandatory training session on tutoring, along with all the other student tutors. The museum student tutors were then invited to the Science Museum to visit in their own time the gallery to which they had been assigned.

The project was coordinated by John Hughes, the then Pimlico Connection Coordinator, the initiator of the project together with a member of the Education Unit and a Student Tutor–The Museum Link Tutor. The Science Museum was the principal contact for the schools and the member of staff was available to answer questions and support tutors when called upon.

Tutors visited the museum on Wednesday afternoons, the time traditionally left free for sport. Tutors contacted the museum coordinator sporadically to ask questions about the gallery, and on how to interpret it for school children.

The tutors then went into three different schools to assist the teachers with preparing the class for the visit and to assist them to integrate the visit into the normal programme of study. The plan was for the student tutors to spend at least two weeks in the classroom before visiting the museum. In reality, some student tutors had only one week with the class before the visit.

Feedback from the teachers, the student tutors and the museum was positive. There was a consensus that the pilot scheme should be expanded upon. It was apparent that there was a need to focus objectives so that it would become clear why the different parties were participating. Specifically, there appeared to be a need for:

- one recognised person to do all external liaison with schools
- an additional training session at the Science Museum
- a more detailed evaluation programme.

It is clear that more detailed support and guidance has to be given to student tutors to reassure them about what they are meant to be supporting in schools; without this they are given a task that they feel is impossible: of trying to become experts on an entire gallery in three Wednesday afternoons (Hughes, 1993).

4.3 First Year of Operation: 1993 to 1994

For the academic year 1993/94, 17 schools and 30 student tutors participated. The recruitment and mandatory tutoring training session was run, as before, by the Pimlico Connection Coordinator. Thirty students were assigned to the Science Museum, as opposed to a particular school, after attending the training session. Science Museum tutors are affiliated to different schools each term.

On top of the introductory tutoring session, the Science Museum Coordinator gave one afternoon briefing session on the practicalities of tutoring in the Science Museum and explained how school teachers booked their class into the museum galleries and what written resources and gallery programmes were available to support the visit.

The student tutors were then assigned to schools in twos and threes. One student tutor who participated in the pilot project the previous year took on the role of coordinator for the museum tutors–The Museum Link Tutor.

Schools were attracted to the project in three ways: all schools already working with student tutors were offered museum tutors; schools already booked into the museum on an appropriate Wednesday afternoon were contacted and offered museum tutors, and the Museum's *Stop Press* publication made mention of the project (sent out to teachers and local authorities each term, publicising the term's educational events and resources and providing a general museum update on new galleries and future developments).

Instead of being affiliated to a specific gallery, student tutors were first matched up to a school. The tutors then helped the teacher visit whatever gallery he or she had chosen, frequently outside the student tutor's subject area. As there was more lead time than in the previous year, tutors visited the school one or two Wednesday afternoons before the museum visit, met the school children in the museum on the afternoon of the visit, and went back into the classroom for one or two afternoons after the visit to follow up on what the children saw and did.

Evaluation questionnaires were circulated to all 30 museum tutors at the end of the academic year and feedback meetings were held with the Museum Link Tutor for the academic year 1993 to 1994 and the new Museum Link Tutor, for 1994 to 1995.

Evaluation from the academic year 1993/94 was inconclusive, with only nine of the 30 student tutors responding to the questionnaires; no firm conclusions could be made. But some problems and issues were identified:

- there was a need for better preparation and training of the student tutors
- there was a need for better briefing of the teachers receiving student tutors
- there appeared to be some misunderstanding by the tutors as to their role as student tutors

4.4 Development of the Pimlico Connection Science Museum Project

Second year of operation: 1994/95

This year's Pimlico Connection Science Museum Project has been developed to incorporate all the recommendations and feedback collected to date. The appointment of a Research Assistant/Science Museum Coordinator for the Project, in early 1994, financed by a Nuffield Foundation grant, has allowed a three-fold increase in time commitment from the Science Museum Coordinator to approximately two days a week.

The two paid coordinators of the Pimlico Connection Project based at the neighbouring institutions, (the Science Museum and Imperial College), now have more time to ensure that both projects are run in parallel with a clear line of responsibility for each project. The Museum Link Tutor – a museum tutor from the previous year – and the Science Museum coordinator introduced to students the idea of becoming a museum tutor at the mandatory training session for all tutors.

This year, the project accepted the first 17 volunteers who opted for the Pimlico Connection Science Museum Project in preference to the 15-week classroom-based student tutoring project. Students who opt for the Pimlico Connection Science Museum Project commit themselves to eight or 13 Wednesday afternoon sessions – eight in the winter term and five in the spring. After the mandatory introductory training session on tutoring, Science Museum tutors must attend two additional afternoon training sessions in the museum, learning how to enjoy the museum from two perspectives – as a teacher and as a pupil.

Once the training programme was completed, the student tutors were asked to fill out a questionnaire asking about their motivations and expectations of tutoring for the Science Museum. When asked why they chose to participate in the project, students gave varied answers. Tutors repeatedly mentioned that they enjoyed the company of children and explaining science to a younger audience, and that they wanted to spend time in the museum. There were also mentions of student tutoring being directly relevant to course work, specifically for the communication of science (undergraduate and postgraduate) courses. Students considered almost unanimously that they would gain 'communication skills' by tutoring: explaining things to school children would allow them to develop their communication skills while doing something productive. From the students' perspective, student tutoring appears to provide comparable opportunities to more formal adult education activities (Stedman, 1990).

Students seemed to clearly understand their role as an extra support and unusual resource for the teacher. They believed that tutors may provide or provoke new ideas for teaching, and an opportunity for teachers to try out new classroom projects and to reflect on current ones. They appeared quite modest about what they thought the teacher would gain: 'an extra pair of eyes, ears and hands', 'enthusiasm'. Only one tutor considered that the teachers may gain 'expert knowledge' from having tutors in the class. Students did appear more idealistic when it came to considering what the school pupils would gain from museum tutors. Most tutors commented on increased one-to-one attention, and there were a number of more ambitious comments such as 'a more thorough understanding of how science is present in the world around us', and 'an insight into science and engineering and university'.

Schools were attracted to the scheme by the same three methods as in the previous year. Only four schools requested museum student tutors for the autumn term. Three other schools did put in a request but only after the student tutors had already been assigned to a school. The 17 student tutors were assigned in groups of four and five to the four different schools. This year all student tutors visited the class for the two weeks preceding the visit and for two weeks following, which had not always been possible in the two previous years.

The small number of schools participating in the project for the autumn term, and the subsequent high student tutor-to-pupil ratio, facilitated easier evaluation of the project by allowing most of the participants to take a more objective view of their work. There was, however, the danger that student tutors thought that their time and energy was not being used effectively or that the teachers felt over-whelmed with tutors in the class.

Feedback lunches were arranged at the end of each term. In both terms, six or seven tutors attended out of a possible 17 and discussed their experience as a tutor while they looked at photos and slides of themselves tutoring on the galleries. The same questionnaire as last year was circulated to all student tutors. The core of the programme of evaluation was self-study involving individual student tutors, co-ordinators and museum staff, following procedures outlined by Kuyper (1993) and Tremper & Kostin (1993).

In comparison to the previous year's feedback, tutors responded more positively on a scale to questions such as, 'Do you believe that the school understood that you were accompanying their class to the Museum', and 'Were you clear about what was expected from you as a student tutor?' This may have been a result of the two additional tutor briefing sessions and the increased contact between the schools and the museum through visits and telephone calls by the museum coordinator.

As in previous feedback, the tutors were most enthused by the school children's reaction to science, the museum and the tutors' presence. Tutors were continuously motivated with the knowledge that their presence allowed a whole class to do something different from normal. Answers to the question, 'What do you believe the children gained from their visit?' were more positive than in the previous year. In 1993/94

57

responses tended to be short and vague and not stated with much confidence:

> I think they enjoyed the visit as an activity, and learnt about things that interested them.

> They were able to see examples of what we had talked about in class. I hope they found the museum an exciting place to be.

By contrast, 1994/95 tutors were more enthusiastic:

> Hopefully a sense that science isn't all about men in white coats. They certainly enjoyed it.

> They were so enthusiastic in the day and in the class it was brilliant. They thought it was great to meet real scientists and they all enjoyed the museum and most wanted to come back with their parents.

The warmer response was probably a result of increased training and briefing of the tutors and school teachers and in consequence more accurate expectations, ones that could be met.

There were still some doubts from the tutors as to how they could link the museum visit with the classroom experience and whether the teachers wanted to integrate the visit into the course of study or not. Students were definitely more positive in response to the second question, 'Explain why you believe that you did or did not fulfil what you believe to be the role of a student tutor'. In 1993/94, responses were more matter-of-fact and lacking enthusiasm:

> No connection between visit and class activities.

> I felt more was being asked than I gave. I think the teachers had different expectations of me.

By comparison, responses from 1994/95 included such statements as:

> We created worksheets for use in the museum, helped with experiments and due to our knowledge of what was in the museum were able to focus the activities in the classroom.

> I do not know if I really have been able to explain science to the children but I know that it was very helpful to have me in the classroom and during the visit to explain and help the children in general.

Feedback from student tutors indicates that:

■ tutors were enthused and motivated by the children's reaction to the museum and the tutors, both on the day of the visit and in class

- students considered that four tutors was too many for one class of around 25; two or three would be most appropriate
- students seemed to respond to the increased time commitment from the museum with regard to training and ongoing support, and commended the organisation of the project.

Teachers were asked to provide written feedback on the project; verbal feedback was also given on visits to the schools and by telephone. Teachers were extremely positive on the whole. Two or three of the seven schools would never have visited the museum without museum student tutors. This is due to the high adult-to-pupil ratio that is stipulated for many teachers by local government bodies for insurance purposes and practical logistical reasons when on a field trip.

Development of written support materials for museum tutors

In the Nuffield-funded project, specific attention is being devoted to creating written materials that can be used by volunteers who take on the role of museum student tutor.

The Education Unit of the Science Museum produces a host of written resources for teachers; these currently form the core of the student tutors' training. Publications and papers on what affects visitors' memories of their museum visit and of how science is taught to primary children were used at the training session. The only additional written information issued as yet is simple, practical administration details: times, dates, and details of the school visits – together with notes on how to act as a tutor (see Goodlad & Hirst, 1989, Appendix A).

A student tutors' handbook to supplement the training sessions is being developed which will include such information as: how the Education Unit supports teachers; how objects can develop skills and extend knowledge; an orientation guide; good and bad volunteer experiences; and research on how our visitors perceive the Science Museum, similar to that used by the Oakland Museum, California (The Oakland Museum, 1976). In 1994/95, the only written resources that the student tutors were given to take away were a schedule of the tutoring times and the details of their school, a *Teachers' Guide for Group Visits*, including a good plan of the museum, a list of written resources available from the museum, and an *Explorers Book* a publication which links museum objects and exhibits to practical activities that children can try at home or in class.

The development of student tutor training techniques

The development of enhanced training for the student tutors is still in its early stages. The existing introductory tutoring session, led by the Pimlico Connection Coordinator, presents an insight into classroom tutoring by means of identifying student tutors' motivations and worries about tutoring. The issues raised are then discussed openly. The discussions are led and facilitated by the Pimlico Connection Coordinator, Mrs Betty Caplan.

This year, for the first time in this introductory session, the theory and the practicalities of becoming a Science Museum tutor were presented to the students by the Science Museum Coordinator, (the author), and the Museum Link Tutor respectively. The aim was to introduce the idea of a museum experience being a positive and complex learning experience.

At the mandatory introductory training session, the Science Museum Coordinator presented the more theoretical aspects of the programme: how children can learn and what influences their memories, by focusing on Falk & Dierking's (1992) Interactive Experience Model. This was integrated into discussion by asking the group to share their earliest memory of a museum or field trip with a group, and when it was. Discussion of these experiences (what was remembered and how long ago it was), emphasised to the group the complexities of a museum visit and encouraged the group to consider the impact of a field trip in terms of cognitive and affective learning.

The second session began in Imperial College with a 45-minute talk on the benefits of student tutoring and an insight into the breadth of its operation around the world by John Hughes, Project Manager of the BP International Mentoring and Tutoring Project. The Science Museum tutors were then guided over to the museum for their first hour's induction into the Science Museum.

The emphasis of this first museum training session was observation of museum visitors and reflection on personal feelings as a visitor. The first 20 minutes were taken up with practical administration details on the location and descriptions of the schools to which the student tutors had been assigned. The following 15 minutes were spent recapping the previous week's ideas on the factors influencing learning in a museum environment and how, as student tutors, they may be able to influence children's agendas and expectations to maximise the benefit of a class visit to the museum. Ideas for this session were drawn from work undertaken by the Association of Science and Technology Centres (ASTC, 1990). The student tutors were then led into the museum to observe visitors and professional museum interpreters: explainers, actors and guides at work around the museum.

The final afternoon session looked at methods of presenting science to children by means of questioning children on what they see and observe through comparison, description and recording of their findings. Student tutors were asked to go out into the galleries and look at objects that appealed to them from two perspectives – as both school children and teachers. They were asked to pick out an object that they believed they would enjoy most as a child, and then another that they believed they would find most beneficial as a teaching resource. (Observation from Harlen, 1985; Carre & Ovens, 1994 and Hayson, 1994, were used by the presenter for purposes of comparison.) The student tutors then came back to discuss their discoveries with the group and explain what had attracted them to the objects they chose and why they chose them.

Policies and management procedures in the deployment of students as museum tutors

Recruitment and initial training sessions are run jointly by the committee of the Pimlico Society and the Pimlico Connection Coordinator. The Science Museum Coordinator participated this year in more of a support role as she was new to the project. The current scheme of management involves the two respective coordinators for the Project: the Pimlico Connection Coordinator and the Science Museum Coordinator working part-time at their respective institutions. The coordinators are the principal contacts for the schools and the tutors participating in the projects.

Tutors who sign up for the Science Museum tutoring project, after the initial training session, work separately from the other tutors. The tutors are sent details of training dates, times and places and the school that they have been assigned by internal post. The week following the completion of the training programme, the student tutors visit their respective schools, in order that the teachers may meet them and show them around the school – 'orientation day'. The tutors can then make sure that they feel comfortable with the prospect of spending every Wednesday afternoon in the coming term in their assigned school.

Evaluating the project in terms of costs and benefits to each party participating

An evaluation programme is studying what the student tutors, the museum, school teachers and school pupils gain from participation in the project. The feedback from tutors and teachers from the last two academic years has been helpful in identifying key issues and pre-empting problems. The information will be used to develop a more detailed and focused questionnaire which will be used starting in the academic year 1995/6.

In addition to providing research data on specific practices and procedures, the object of the Nuffield-funded project is to develop ways of assessing the financial efficiency of the Pimlico Connection Science Museum Project. As well as transferrable documents on training proce-dures, the project will establish the costs of running this type of operation – namely one involving three-way collaboration between a college, schools and a science centre, museum, or other such facility.

Addresses for correspondence: Regarding the Nuffield-funded project described in this chapter: Ms Stephanie McIvor, Volunteer Organiser, The Science Museum, London SW7 2DD. Tel. 0171 938 8000. Fax 0171 938 8118. Regarding the Pimlico Connection tutoring scheme more generally: Mrs Betty Caplan, Pimlico Connec-tion Coordinator, c/o Humanities Programme, Imperial College of Science, Technology & Medicine, Exhibition Road, London SW7 2BX. Tel. 0171 594 8755. Fax 0171 594 8759.

Chapter 5

GENEPI – STUDENTS TEACH IN PRISON

Heidi Schwarzwalder

GENEPI is an acronym for Groupement Etudiant National pour l'Enseignement aux Personnes Incarcerees, or National Student Group Teaching in Prison. It concerns an initiative taken by a Parisian student in 1975 which has since then become a national movement involving 800 students working in some 60 prisons all over France. A Convention has been signed between the students and the Ministry of Justice to institutionalise the activity and afford it legal status. The chapter describes the aims and procedures of GENEPI, emphasising the organisation of the Association of a national working team.

5.1 GENEPI'S Activities

The GENEPI Association has three aims: to teach in prisons; to educate the students who do the teaching; and to inform the public.

Of these, the teaching in prison is the central preoccupation. The sessions in prison take place weekly, for two hours at a time, and are very diversified. Teaching is offered to any standard and in any subject, for example in languages, history, music, and literature. The students can be creative in their approach, and usually select subjects which are asked for by the prisoners.

The aim is not just to provide 'recreation': there certainly is a recreational aspect to the scheme, because the tutors are young, dynamic and from 'outside'. Their presence does permit men and women in prison to escape from the mentality of prison for a while. However, the courses permit prisoners to acquire knowledge – often to take exams for diplomas. Also, the presence of students in the prisons is an act of solidarity with people who are usually forgotten. This requires skill and diplomacy, and open-mindedness, on the part of the students who have to enter a closed world and work in it – which is all the more difficult as they are not professionals.

GENEPI aims to educate its members as much as it can. Twenty years of experience, accompanied by regular appraisals of the activities, have generated ideas and materials with which the 'GENEPIstes' are given useful knowledge and suggestions about how to proceed. GENEPI edits several information brochures concerning the tutoring itself, the functioning of the judiciary and the penitential system, and produces two magazines – one purely informational (*La lettre de GENEPI*), one satirical and provocative (*Le GENEPItre*). Each 'GENEPIste' also has the opportunity to go to an information workshop at the National School of Penitentiary Administration in Paris.

Despite the information offered, the first visit to prison is a very personal experience which each GENEPIste has to negotiate.

The third objective is that of informing the public at large as much as possible. Media statements such as 'Prisoners live well – they are housed, fed, and sit all day in front of the television' are misleading. GENEPI is carrying out a survey throughout France to discover more accurately what the public know about life in prison. GENEPI also organises conferences in meeting halls, in schools and in universities, participates in radio programmes, writes newspaper articles, and attends workshops and conferences. The aim is not to generate pity for prisoners, but rather to work against the myths about prison. GENEPI would like people to know that the average prison cell has a surface area of 9 square metres, that there are two people living in it 22 hours a day, that prisoners are allowed only one shower per week, that the TV has to be paid for by the prisoners, etc. A significant obstacle for the social reintegration of prisoners is the uncomprehending and uninformed attitude of society towards those who have been in prison. Better public information about life in prison might contribute to an improved public perception of prisoners. GENEPI wishes to make as many people as possible to feel concerned about prison – the dark side of society that nobody wants to hear about.

A fourth aim of GENEPI, though less extended and institutionalised, is to participate in 'open' institutions and environments such as associations which deal with homeless people (informing the members about prison which many homeless people have known, and participating in socio-political activities), and offers teaching to children in marginalised sections of society. These latter activities have grown around local contacts that GENEPI has formed over the years.

5.2 GENEPI: A National Working Team

GENEPI operates through a decentralised organisation, not only because of the dispersion of prisons in the country, but also for democratic reasons. The headquarters are at the Ministry of Justice in Paris. A President, a Secretary, and a person responsible for the GENEPI publications, are elected every year by the assembly of all GENEPI members. Being an official of GENEPI can be taken as an alternative to military service. Each region of France has a coordinator who is responsible for regional meetings, collective visits to Paris, and other tasks linking the headquarters and the local groups.

The local group is the most important element of GENEPI. The responsible official is elected each year by the local group. Because of the departure of many students every year (through end of their studies, movement to study in foreign countries, etc.), the first task is to gather new people, inform them of GENEPI's aims, give them information, send them to Paris for orientation sessions, organise the intervention schedule at the local prison, stay in touch with the social assistants of the prison, and with the teachers and the head of the prison, gather and distribute the documents needed for registration for students to become GENEPI members. (Every member of GENEPI has to be checked by the French Secret Service who wish to know if he/she have already had to deal with prison, if a member of the family is imprisoned, etc.) The local responsible official is the link between the group, the prison and the headquarters of GENEPI and, if necessary, with a regional officer of GENEPI.

5.3 The Extension of GENEPI

Each year, GENEPI extends and improves its work through experience. Many workshops are organised locally or nationally for GENEPI members, and for officials responsible for local groups. In addition, every local group has to complete an appraisal form describing the activities organised in the local prison, what the prisoners and the prison staff thought about it, and how it could be improved. This constant process of appraisal and evaluation makes GENEPI an organisation which is constantly evolving.

Following 20 years of presence in France's prisons, GENEPI members are constantly thinking about extending the organisation's activities. Students who participated in GENEPI programmes in France try to get in touch with each other when they go abroad for a year or if they go back to their native countries – for example through the Erasmus programme, trying to interest students in other countries in the activity to transmit the message. A European cell has been created which is mainly working on the translation of GENEPI documents and in making contact with interested people all over Europe and beyond.

Further information about GENEPI can be obtained from: GENEPI – Bureau National, 14 Rue Ferrus, 75014 Paris, France. Tel. 33 1 45 88 37 00. Fax 33 1 45 88 94 02. Or from the author: Heidi Schwarzwalder, 17 Rue Turenne, 38000 Grenoble, France. Tel. 33 76 46 05 46.

Chapter 6

SENIOR STUDENT TUTORS: PARTNERSHIP IN TEACHING AND LEARNING
A Case Study in Social Anthropology, from South Africa

Carol Taylor

In tandem with national events, South African universities are being transformed. Students from very diverse cultural and educational backgrounds are being admitted to institutions of higher education. To help meet the needs of this heterogeneous student body, senior student tutors are being trained in tutorial methodology. Emphasis is being placed on a partnership in teaching and learning between academic staff and senior and junior students. This chapter outlines and assesses the efficacy of the student tutor programme in the Department of Social Anthropology at the University of the Witwatersrand in 1993 and 1994.

6.1 Introduction

In tandem with national events, South African universities are being transformed. At the University of the Witwatersrand (Wits), students from diverse educational, social and cultural backgrounds are being admitted in ever-increasing numbers. Such diversity in the student body represents a mosaic peculiar to the new South Africa.

67

During the apartheid era, 1948–1990, segregated education meant that South Africa's White, Indian, Coloured and Black school children were educated in separate systems each controlled by separate Departments of Education.[1] Pupils attended separate schools, wrote school-leaving examinations set by separate matriculation boards and studied for degrees in separate universities. Some private schools and four liberal universities, Wits, Cape Town (UCT), Natal and Rhodes, in defiance of government legislation, endeavoured, however, during these years, to admit pupils and students of all 'races'. But the 1959 Extension of University Education Act dictated that Indian, Coloured and Black students had to receive Ministerial permission to take up places offered to them by open universities such as Wits. During the 1950s their numbers never exceeded 5% of Wits or UCT's enrolment (Taylor, 1990:5). In 1969 only eight black doctors graduated from all of South Africa's medical schools (Tobias 1983:134). A new range of courses offered exclusively by the open universities in the mid-1970s enabled black students to obtain the necessary ministerial permission to register for them and black enrolment rose by 2% per year – the maximum allowable under state restrictions.[2] During the 1980s the government's pragmatic recognition of the need to create a black middle-class brought about the deregulation of student admissions through the University Amendment Act (Taylor, 1990:7). In 1995, black students at Wits constitute 39.8% of student enrolment.[3]

Many of these students, however, carry with them the legacy of an apartheid education in their pursuit of a degree at Wits – one of the top universities in the country. Apartheid education was not simply segregationist; it was discriminatory, intended only to produce school leavers destined for semi-skilled jobs. For example in 1987–8, the government subsidy per African pupil was one-fifth that for whites; the official teacher:pupil ratio in African schools was 1:41, for white schools 1:16.[4] Throughout the decade black education was severely disrupted and as recently as 1992, 14% of teachers in African schools did not have a teaching qualification and 57% were underqualified.[5]

As a result, a situation has arisen which is reflected in an advertisement which appeared in a local newspaper, *The Weekly Mail*, on 15 February 1991. It depicts a young African woman sitting on the steps of UCT's central building. The caption reads, 'She got A's in matric for maths and physics, but she is going to fail her first year at University.' In South Africa, in 1992 only 10% of African pupils who took the school leavers' examination received a matric exemption for admission to university.[6] Many African matriculants dream of going to university but most, due to educational neglect suffered during the years of apartheid, can never hope to be accepted, and those who are have to make a prodigious effort against all odds to complete their degree. Wits in a liberal tradition of wishing to provide equal opportunity to all, has implemented a two-tiered system of meritocratic admissions. On the one hand students who obtain a matriculation exemption and whose results match a set number of points determined by individual Wits faculties are automatically admitted. Others seeking admission may, in the Faculties of Arts, Science or Engineering, write a selection test and be admitted on the basis of 'potential to succeed', given the right educational support. In the Department of Social Anthropology at Wits, student tutors are working with selection-test students, through a tutoring scheme designed to help accelerate their intellectual development.

6.2 Student Tutors in the Department of Social Anthropology

The formal training of senior students as tutors in the Department of Social Anthropology began in 1993. The programme was conceived of as one of a number of responses to academic needs at Wits in a context of declining financial resources and an ever-increasing heterogeneity among the student body, many of whom are under-prepared for university. It was informed by an ideology of partnership in teaching and learning between staff and students, a recognition of the need for formal training and evaluation, and as having one complementary role to play among several educative approaches designed to enhance student academic development.

Student tutors are perceived as being centrally placed as mediators of innovations such as enriched teaching and learning, academic support, skills training, curriculum development, and action research which are part of a programme promoting a culture of learning within the department. The student tutor's current role as central to this process of teaching and learning within the department is conceptualised in Figure 6.1. Here the student tutor can be seen to be located at the centre of a network of strategic mechanisms designed to enhance and accelerate the intellectual development of educationally under-prepared students.

Training

Four student tutors received training in 1993, six in 1994 and currently six senior students are participating as tutorial assistants. This training is launched by initial faculty-wide workshops on academic reading and writing, and small group teaching given by the staff of the Academic Development Unit and the Department of Applied English Language Studies. Training thereafter takes the form of weekly one-hour meetings, throughout the year in the Department of Social Anthropology. The Academic Development (AD) Coordinator, a lecturer and the student tutors work together during these planning sessions. As each tutorial topic extends over a two-week cycle, the first session is preparatory and the second reflective in nature. In session one, the lecturer discusses aspects of the tutorial content, while the AD Coordinator suggests methodological approaches to presenting the material. In session two, the tutorial assistants report on their tutoring experiences and the discussion focuses on resolving difficulties and refining methodology.

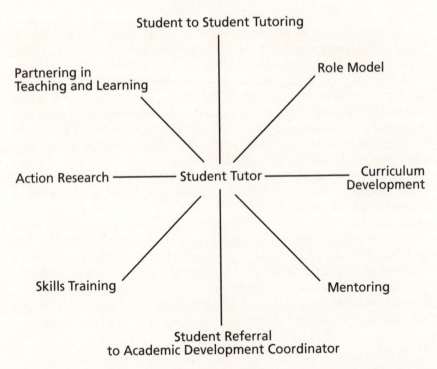

Figure 6.1 The central role of the student tutor in the Department of Social Anthropology

Session two is also important in providing the lecturer and the AD Coordinator with an opportunity to receive comments and suggestions from the student tutors. These focus on ways in which complementarity between lectures, tutorials and assignments might be enhanced, choice of reading made more germane and strategies for teaching and learning refined. Prior to session one, student tutors hand in written tutorial preparation to the AD Coordinator for comment, and a critique of their tutorials at the end of the tutorial cycle. In this way ongoing action research into the student tutor programme is made possible.

At the end of 1993 and 1994 the student tutors were asked to evaluate their training programme and the first-year students their tutorials.[7] In the 1993 and 1994 questionnaire evaluations, the student tutors unanimously agreed that training in tutorial methodology was essential for successful tutoring. They expressed an appreciation of the supportive nature of the planning sessions and on their efficacy as a discussive forum in helping overcome pedagogical and psychological difficulties encountered in tutoring academically diverse groups of first-year students. Confidence building was cited as one of the most important aspects of weekly planning sessions. The following comments reflect these sentiments:

> Regular departmental meetings have helped to make me feel more competent in giving tutorials. Meetings to discuss the lecturer's requirements and to offer solutions to problems experienced in tutorials have been invaluable.

> Feedback from other tutors and brainstorming and sharing ideas as to how to overcome problems have helped a great deal.

> I think the departmental meetings are useful to boost confidence of new student tutors.

The student tutor evaluations showed them to be very pragmatic in evaluating their tutorials. All of them mentioned compensating for under-prepared students in their tutorial groups and involving students of very diverse ability levels as being particularly challenging. Interestingly, the first-year student evaluations assessed the student tutors as having some very sophisticated skills, most notably their ability to adjust the pace of the tutorial to accommodate all participants. Student tutors were deemed to be well prepared, have a thorough knowledge of tutorial topics, to be competent in explaining difficult concepts and to have established a good rapport with their tutorial groups.

Table 6.1 1993 results for selection test students in the Department of Social Anthropology by tutorial group

Tutor	Tutorial	Total Number of Students	Selection Test Results	Pass Rate for Selection Test Results
Lecturer 1	A	10(100)	7(70)	5(71)
Lecturer 1	S	14(100)	6(43)	4(67)
Lecturer 2	D	13(100)	8(62)	5(63)
Lecturer 2	V	15(100)	8(53)	6(75)
Lecturer 3	F	14(100)	8(57)	6(75)
Lecturer 3	X	12(100)	4(33)	2(50)
Marcus	H	12(100)	7(58)	5(71)
Marcus	Z	12(100)	9(75)	7(78)
Paul	C	13(100)	6(46)	6(100)
Paul	U	12(100)	11(92)	7(64)
Megan	B	16(100)	10(63)	6(60)
Megan	T	13(100)	11(85)	10(91)

In addition to evaluation in the form of questionnaires, the 1993 end-of-year results for under-prepared students with student tutors as tutorial leaders are instructive. Table 6.1 shows the final results for 1993 for students in tutorials taken by student tutors compared to results for students in tutorials taken by lecturers.

The table shows significant pass rates for selection-test students, typically those who are under-prepared, tutored by lecturers, and by student tutors. The pass rates for under-prepared students tutored by student tutors compare very favourably with those for under-prepared students tutored by lecturers. There is in fact no statistical difference between the respective pass rates. Also, the mean pass mark for under-prepared students tutored by both lecturers and student tutors was almost identical. That for under-prepared students tutored by lecturers is 54.8% and that for under-prepared students tutored by student tutors is 54.3%.

The idea of partnership in teaching and learning has evolved over the last four years at Wits. In 1991 the university appointed full-time academic support tutors in departments with large numbers of under-prepared students. These tutors, of whom I am one, have both teaching and discipline-specific qualifications. Since 1991 our role has shifted from one of academic support to academic development, with tutors and lecturers working together on integrating academic skills with academic content and refining the curriculum to accommodate the needs of educationally disadvantaged students. As Mountney and Nicholls note, 'Many of these innovations have widened the acceptable range of pedagogies and learning techniques' (in Potter & Porter, 1992:5). A partnership is now envisaged within the Department of Social Anthropology which encompasses not only student tutors, but the undergraduates they tutor, in a joint venture enhancing a culture of learning within the department.

A number of unanticipated developments suggest such a culture is emerging. Senior students, through their role as tutors, have become more integrated into departmental structures and mature in their working relationships with staff, which facilitates their own postgraduate studies. Additionally they develop a personal interest in the undergraduate students in their respective tutorial groups, monitoring their progress in assignments, adopting in some instances a mentoring relationship with disadvantaged students, and responding to requests from students needing help with essays or lecture material on an impromptu basis. This is in addition to one hour of formal consultation time offered each week as part of their role as a student tutor. In this way students, especially those who are under-prepared, are offered a network of support by lecturers, the AD Coordinator and the student tutors. Of importance here is the range of choice available to the student. Equally significant is the student tutor's place as one resource among others, in a partnership of teaching and learning.

In extending this notion of partnership to undergraduates, one student tutor's response to an item in the 1993 evaluative questionnaire, 'What areas of your departmental function as a student tutor do you feel you have fulfilled well?' is informative. She reports, 'getting the students to interact well as a class, rather than as a group of disinterested individuals is one of my particular strengths'. Another student tutor responded, 'I think I inspired confidence in first-years in my tutorial group and have encouraged the quieter students [typically those who are under-prepared] to voice their opinions and to think about their answers'. A third student tutor's response refocuses the mechanism of partnership on curriculum development as a strategy for improving under-prepared students' chances of success. He says, 'I felt I made a contribution to the report back on the tutorials, allowing the lecturer to better understand why some of the tutorials do not work'.

In the semi-informal discussion forum of a tutorial, students are provided with an opportunity of articulating their own ideas. Allwright (1982:4–5) argues that,

> better understanding is likely to result if learners discuss their learning and
> share their various understandings. . . . They may learn directly from each

73

other, or more likely they will learn from the very act of attempting to articulate their own understanding.

Successful learning in tutorials is then necessarily dependent upon optimum levels of active participation by students, and essential to this process is the careful design of tutorial topics and the skilful facilitation of discussion by student tutors.

On the basis of action research, student tutors in the Department of Social Anthropology have helped focus attention on three important areas of successfully tutoring the diverse student groupings in anthropology tutorials. These are: the selection of topics most likely to promote lively discussion; the necessity for teaching academic skills as much as academic content to under-prepared students in tutorials; and the role the sensitivities of one student tutoring another play in facilitating the learning process.

Student tutors report that,

> topics most likely to ensure animated discussion are based on readings which deal with concepts already applied in lectures and which, being conceptual in nature, allow for discussion not restricted by the readings. . . . This encourages creative thinking and so tends to be most stimulating for students.

Length of readings and language are equally aspects in need of consideration. Many student tutors shared the sentiment that,

> sometimes the tutorial readings are too long or not entirely relevant to the topic. . . . The problem is when the tutorial readings are too long, they loose their effect and relevance to the topic.

Especially with under-prepared students in mind, student tutors recommended that,

> articles written by specialists for specialists be avoided as these are written in a conceptual language which is especially difficult for second language speakers of English, in their first year of university study.
>
> (Jeannerat *et al.*, 1994:2)

Student tutors are also critical of tutorial topics which are too difficult and so counter-productive in helping under-prepared students, who best make progress through developmental learning strategies. They also criticise tutorial topics with too narrow a focus, thus inhibiting full

74

discussion and negating the opportunity for the expression and exchange of viewpoints, necessary to Allwright's (1982) view of successful learning through articulation in tutorials.

Student tutor feedback also revealed them to be adept in equipping under-prepared students with academic skills through tutoring. It became clear to student tutors that under-prepared students needed to be taught the 'how to' of reading a tutorial text closely, with a critical eye, searching for different levels of information, extrapolating a number of arguments, evaluating this knowledge and synthesising it with a view to sharing it with other students.

Communicative skills required for tutorial discussion were imparted in a number of ways as illustrated by student tutor responses to an item in the 1994 evaluative questionnaire, 'How do you cope with diversity in your tutorial group?' Strategies such as 'asking very basic questions at the beginning, building up to more complex questions to take the tutorial further', or 'setting a pace in tutorial discussion which accommodates all students, together with striving to be a very approachable as a tutor', indicated their sensitivity to the needs of under-prepared students. Diversity in itself is regarded as being advantageous in a tutorial setting, 'as diversity adds interest to a tutorial if students are encouraged to offer new perspectives'. Affective techniques of generating energy and enthusiasm, of allowing 'anything to be said in a tutorial' while encouraging respect for divergent viewpoints, and alternating between a structured approach to tutoring and facilitating spontaneous debate, all cumulatively depicted a process of sensitive tutoring aimed at generating optimum participation and so enhancing learning through articulation.

One student tutor's empathy with undergraduate students' struggle to learn in an academic context pinpointed an important advantage of student-to-student tutoring – that of a shared common experience (Jeannerat *et al.*, 1994:4). The theme of relevance of tutorial material surfaced repeatedly in student tutor discussions of, and comment upon, curriculum development in tutorials. As student tutors mediated a tutorial topic, they reported establishing its relevance to anthropologists as well as its applied significance to their own lives before discussing the topic with their tutorial groups. Equally, they encouraged undergraduates to draw on their own personal experience as a technique for drawing quieter students into tutorial discussion and as a medium for gaining understanding of abstract concepts or exotic societies. Explanatory examples relevant to the student's experience of contemporary South African life were also used by student tutors to generate interest and clarify understanding. Students, they argued 'must be able to relate to the subject matter of their tutorials if they were to succeed in the study of Anthropology' (Jeannerat *et al.*, 1994:2). Such insights serve to demonstrate the skilled manner in which student tutors teach skills in their tutorials and, through a process of action research, inform curriculum development which facilitates both the needs of under-prepared students and enhances the learning of all students in anthropology tutorials.

Finally, student tutors act as role models for students. Many students from disadvantaged backgrounds have asked their tutor's advice on the potential value of continuing in anthropology and in helping structure their degree with a particular career goal in mind. Often students indicate an interest in continuing a debate with their tutor beyond the tutorial and many express a specific interest in improving their academic performance. One such student told her tutor, 'I really strive for the objective perspective which I feel you take with regard to the subject matter'.

Since 1993 the student tutor's role in the Department of Social Anthropology has developed into one which is central to the department's vision of catering to the needs of a diverse student body, while simultaneously placing special emphasis on addressing the needs of the growing number of academically disadvantaged students studying anthropology. As a result of student tutors inclusion in the process of teaching and learning, the diverse mosaic present in the student body is mirrored among the department's teaching staff. The inevitable variation in learning styles accompanying a diverse student body is arguably addressed by the plurality of inimical approaches to teaching and learning adopted by the department's student tutors and its full-time staff.

Such an experience has its own rewards: student tutors in the Department of Social Anthropology report personal development in professional attitudes, in self-confidence, in communication and organisational skills, and in management and problem-solving skills. Perhaps also of significance in South Africa is the fact that skills acquired in student tutoring are now being put to the service of the wider community. One student tutor, now graduated with an honours degree in anthropology, is currently employed by JCI, one of South Africa's biggest mining houses, as a facilitator of transformative negotiations between its black staff and the company's historically white management. He represents a student tutor helping not just to transform Wits university, but the new South Africa.

Notes

1. The nomenclature and spelling used is in accordance with the apartheid legislated 'race' categories, which of course have no basis in scientific fact.
2. Here the term 'black' follows Black Consciousness nomenclature which is inclusive of African, Indian and coloured.
3. Wits Academic Information and Systems Unit, (1995)
4. Race Relations Survey, (1987/88:147–9,158)
5. Race Relations Survey, (1993/4:677)
6. Race Relations Survey, (1993/4:713)
7. At the end of the 1993 and 1994 academic years, two separate questionnaires, designed to evaluate the Student Tutor Programme in the Department of Social Anthropology, were distributed to undergraduate students and to student tutors. A total of 531 undergraduates received questionnaires, with 448 (84%) responding. Ten student tutors participated in the programme over the two years with 10 (100%) responding. All comments quoted are from the questionnaire responses for 1993 and 1994.

The author would like to express her appreciation to participating undergraduates and to student tutors; Marcus Darwell, Karen Horwitz, Caroline Jeannerat, Paul Kapelus, Megan Kearns, Justine Lucas, Teresa O'Connor and Graeme Rodgers, for their valuable insights into student tutoring which helped in the writing of this chapter.

Address for correspondence: Carol Taylor, University of the Witwatersrand, Department of Social Anthropology, Private Bag 3, Wits 2050, Johannesburg, South Africa. Tel. (011) 716 111. Fax (011) 716 2766.
email 031Carol@muse.arts.wits.ac.za

Chapter 7

INVESTIGATING SUPPORT SYSTEMS IN SCIENCE TEACHING – A SOUTH AFRICAN PERSPECTIVE

Levina Furstenberg

Inequality in the education system of the apartheid era contributed to the disparity that occurs in academic achievement levels of students from different cultural backgrounds in South Africa. Raising the educational level in the natural sciences is urgent in view of the demand for scientifically literate and technologically skilled citizens in a rapidly developing country. The University of Port Elizabeth has committed itself to empowerment of the people of the Eastern Cape Province. New courses were implemented in the Faculty of Education, and opportunities created for underqualified teachers from the educationally deprived communities, to improve their qualifications. Student tutoring and mentoring programmes, administered since 1993, were evaluated in connection with some of the science courses. The findings could contribute to designing more effective support systems for teaching students to enable them as future educators, to contribute to the reconstruction and development of the new South Africa.

7.1 Introduction

With the opening of universities to all races as a result of recent political changes in South Africa, academic staff have been confronted with the reality of having to teach students from a variety of cultural and socio-economic backgrounds. Inequality in the education system of the apartheid era contributed to a great extent to the imparity that occurs in the academic achievement levels of students from different cultural backgrounds. Of all black South African matriculants, between 60% and 70% failed annually (1987–91). One of the contributing factors is the level of teacher qualification – 25,000 out of a total of 200,000 teachers in black schools have no professional qualification (Strauss *et al.*, 1991).

The situation in the natural sciences is particularly critical as illustrated by the statistics of the Department of Education of the former independent state, Transkei, which in the new dispensation forms part of the Eastern Cape Province – only 25% of all matriculants in the Transkei enrolled for physical science; of these only 20% passed with matriculation exemption (examiner's report). These statistics are based on the results of the last year of independence, thus prior to the transitional stage, when the Government of National Unity came into power in South Africa.

As one of the key roleplayers in education in the Eastern Cape Province, the University of Port Elizabeth (UPE) has committed itself to contributing dynamically to the development of this region and the empowerment of all its people (Kirsten, 1994). As part of its contribution towards reconstruction and development, the university has embarked on several programmes fulfilling not only the functions of research and teaching but also serving the community by making available scientific expertise and resources.

7.2 Formulation of the Problem

The proclamation of UPE's policy of commitment to real and visible change had the desired outcome of greater utilisation of the university's resources as a first step towards empowerment of the historically disadvantaged section of the community. Student numbers in the Faculty of Education for example increased from 570 in 1993 to 830 in 1994. Of the 5,617 students who enrolled in 1994, 40% of the first years were other than white students.

The predominantly white academic staff was confronted with situations that required not only adapted teaching strategies, but also a change in attitude and a different kind of commitment. Furthermore, from the students' viewpoint, the question could be asked: how could educationally disadvantaged students be assisted to acquire the necessary skills to meet their academic needs, especially in the field of the natural sciences, where high level deprivation occurs?

By means of action research the roles of mentors and of tutors were investigated in association with specific teaching strategies.

7.3 Purpose of this Investigation

During the 1980s educators in the United States of America began to regard mentoring/tutoring as a key component of reform in teaching (Wildman *et al.*, 1992:210).

The objectives of this study, to improve educational levels in the natural sciences, were:

- to investigate student tutoring and mentoring as support systems in association with some teaching strategies, with reference to cognitive gains for students in the natural sciences
- to determine which factors need to be considered when designing a support system for deprived communities in the South African situation.

7.4 The Survey

Although the situation in physical science teaching in secondary schools was emphasised when stating the problem, it should be kept in mind that poor conditions in secondary teaching evolved from equally poor and even worse conditions in primary science teaching. Therefore, there was no other option but to focus on improvement in primary science teaching first. For this purpose a new general science course was designed in 1993 and introduced into the primary science teaching curriculum at UPE. Mastering of the general science subject content and of specific teaching strategies would enable future primary science teachers to teach with confidence, since all the topics to be dealt with in the school curriculum were covered.

In 1993 UPE introduced a part-time Baccalaureus Primae Educationis degree in addition to the full-time degree, with the purpose of providing opportunities for underqualified teachers, mainly from the erstwhile Department of Education and Training (DET), to better their qualifications. It should be noted that the education of blacks outside the former self-governing and independent states was administered by the DET, and that teacher training in that department was generally regarded as inferior.

Investigating support systems in science teaching

A unique situation suitable for action research developed when student enrolment at UPE in 1993 and 1994 manifested in student combinations in the four primary science classes ideal for comparative study. Table 7.1 portrays particulars regarding the four classes, referred to as groups of students since variables differed in two of the classes.

The educational activities in the classes referred to in Table 7.1 served as a field of experiment for the researcher who happened to be the same person teaching either the whole method of general science, or at least the major module of the general science course to all the classes. The effect of mentor/tutor involvement in association with the different teaching strategies adopted in each class, was investigated qualitatively by means of observations and interviews and quantitatively by analysing the final examination results of the students.

Procedures in the method of general science classes

In the method of general science classes, a small group cooperative learning approach was followed in accordance with the nature of the subject. Emphasis was placed on the development of communication and other personal skills. Traditional lecturing to the whole class was minimised. A special mentor-mentee relationship developed in the part-

Table 7.1 Particulars of the different groups of UPE students investigated in 1994

Group Number	Subject for which enrolled	Full-time (FT)/Part-time (PT)	Number of students in group	First-year/ senior students	(Privileged) white (Deprived) black
1	Method of General Science	PT	32	Senior	Black
2a	Method of General Science	FT	22	Senior	White
2b	Method of General Science	PT	3	Senior	Black
3a	General Science	FT	26	Senior	White
3b	General Science	FT	25	First-year	Black
4	General Science	PT	56	Senior	Black

Note: Three part-time students (Group 2b) had to attend the early morning lecture with the full-time students (Group 2a) due to timetable clashes.
Students may enrol for general science in their first or third year of study.

time class (Group 1), between the lecturer and most of the students. Since these students were all adults from deprived communities, who were teaching in black primary schools, it did not seem appropriate to involve full-time university students of much younger age as tutors or mentors. Instead, the lecturer personally became engaged in a higher level of commitment, supporting these students outside the classroom emotionally, but not academically. This involvement which was very practical in nature, aimed basically at bridging cultural gaps, changing attitudes and developing self-esteem.

In addition, an adapted form of student tutoring was introduced, where the lecturer trained the students in class to work in small groups. A tutoring function was assigned to some students empowering them to act as tutors to their peers in class. A long-term relationship developed since the student allocation to specific groups remained unchanged throughout the year. Students met twice a week for a period of 80 minutes. The personal involvement of the students consisted of collaborative lesson planning and lesson presentation, cooperative learning, group demonstrations and other practical activities. Mother-tongue conversation prevailed in small group activities. Students in Group 1 were all Xhosa-speaking.

Similar teaching strategies were followed in the full-time class (Group 2a, 2b). It is important to note that only three part-time students in this class (Group 2b) were Xhosa-speaking and from educationally deprived communities. These students were alloted each to a different small group in the classroom. Cross-cultural tutoring therefore evolved since group members were from different cultural backgrounds. The language medium in group activities was English. Mentoring support from the lecturer was not required by the majority of the students since they were all senior students from privileged backgrounds.

Procedures in the general science classes

In this course the subject content was the focal point. Lectures and laboratory practicals were repeated by the same academic staff members for full-time and part-time students.

The full-time class comprised 26 white students in their third year of study (Group 3a), and 25 other than white first-year students all from DET schools in deprived communities (Group 3b). The 56 part-time students were teachers from former DET schools upgrading their qualifications.

UPE has embarked on a number of programmes to meet the needs of the historically disadvantaged section of the community. The Supplemental Instruction (SI) programme, administered by the Department of University Education, is just one of many academic assistance programmes aiming at increasing student performance and retention. A senior student from the faculty of the natural sciences, presented as a model student of the subject, attended the full-time general science lectures with Groups 3a and 3b. A tutoring session was conducted by the SI leader once per week for the first-year students (Group 3b), creating the opportunity for the students to become actively involved in the course material. The lecturer was in no way involved in these activities. No support system was introduced for part-time students enrolled for the same course (Group 4).

All the lectures as well as SI sessions were given in English. Black students from historically deprived communities were all Xhosa-speaking (with English as their second language) and although some of them were not in their first-year of study, they could all be regarded as high-risk students. A small number of white students in Groups 2a and 3a were Afrikaans-speaking but experienced no difficulty with English as a second language.

7.5 Results

Examination results were analysed as indicative of academic achievement in relation to support systems and teaching strategies administered in the different classes. Statistics based on the final examination results of each group of students are given in Table 7.2, along with the teaching strategies and supporting systems chosen.

7.6 Conclusions

Based on the pass rate of the different groups the following conclusions may be drawn. It would seem that:

- tutoring/mentoring programmes are only successful when administered along with effective teaching strategies (Groups 1 and 2)
- cooperative learning is ideal for peer tutoring even in educationally deprived situations (Groups 1 and 2)
- a long-term trust relationship must develop for mentoring/tutoring to be successful. SI sessions were too few and far between for trust relationships to develop (Group 3b), bearing in mind that the tutor had no other contact with the group on campus

Table 7.2 Teaching strategies, supporting systems and examination results

Group Number	Teaching strategy	Language medium	Supporting system	*Number cancelled	Pass percentage
1	Mainly cooperative (small group)	English and Xhosa	Mentoring (lecturer) plus peer tutoring	1	90.6
2a	Mainly cooperative (small groups)	English	Peer tutoring	0	100
2b	Mainly cooperative (small groups)	English	Peer tutoring	0	33
3a	Lecturing	English	None	0	100
3b	Lecturing	English	Supplemental Instruction SI leader as tutor	2	44
4	Lecturing	English	None	16	26.8

* Students who did not complete the course

- students who had opportunities to develop a learning culture (white students) were successful in their studies regardless of the teaching strategy administered (Groups 2a and 3a)
- language barriers had a greater effect on students in the all-English lecturing situations (Groups 3b and 4). In Group 1, concepts could be clarified during mother-tongue discussions in the small group. It is important to note that the only two students who failed in Group 2 where small group discussions and tutoring occurred in English, were the Xhosa-speaking students in the groups
- people from deprived communities need some form of tutoring/mentoring when they return to tertiary institutions to upgrade their qualifications although they are not first-year students
- cultural differences must be acknowledged when setting up mentor-mentee/tutor-tutee combinations
- a long-term relationship is a prerequisite for a change in attitude to occur. This only develops when a higher level of commitment and more personal input from the mentor is possible (Group 1). Only one student cancelled the course in Group 1, as opposed to 18 students in the general science classes.

Although SI programmes are internationally accepted as effective ways of dealing with students in need of support, it became clear in this study that in the South African situation a much different approach should be followed. A variety of factors are evidently influencing the success of supporting systems. These must first be investigated.

7.7 Suggestions

In order to contribute to the improvement of the education level in South Africa in general and in the natural sciences in particular, effective mentoring programmes must be designed and implemented in teacher training institutions. Target groups must not only be pre-service teaching students, but also teachers inadequately equipped for science teaching. Simultaneously projects to reach children from educationally deprived communities must be implemented only after all efforts have been made by means of an holistic approach, to unveil the needs of these children. In view of the unique situation in a number of tertiary institutions in South Africa, where academics from the minority culture group have to teach in a constantly changing situation where the the majority of the students could well be representing a number of different African cultures, research must be undertaken with special reference to the following aspects:

- communication medium and communication skills
- cultural differences and interpersonal relations
- political influences and personal attitudes
- socio-economic backgrounds and learning culture
- teaching strategies and educational needs.

It is important to focus not only on the students in need of support. The academics too need assistance, emotionally and otherwise, to contribute to the mammoth task that lies ahead in the new South Africa.

Address for correspondence: Dr Levina Furstenberg, University of Port Elizabeth, PO Box 1600, Port Elizabeth, South Africa. Tel (041) 5042111. Fax (041) 5042317.

Chapter 8

A STUDY OF ADULT STUDENTS' PERCEPTIONS OF MENTORING AS A SUPPORT SYSTEM

Val Clulow

Student support services have been identified in the educational literature as being a key factor in student perseverance and academic achievement. The study reported in this chapter focuses on a group of tertiary adult distance education students' perceptions of mentoring as a support system in their course. In-depth interviews of 12 students from an Australian retail organisation were conducted to explore and illuminate mentoring relationships and their impact as a student support system. The analysis of the data showed that students interact with a number of people in their network who can provide a mentoring function in varying degrees. The extent to which developmental relationships affect technical/ managerial skills development, psychosocial development and/ or role modelling was explored. Significant findings were that more than one type of relationship was found to be providing a mentoring function in support of the students' efforts. There were important questions uncovered relating to terms and definitions in this complex field. In relation to this particular distance education course, the impact of such relationships appeared to strengthen commitment to persevere with study. The wide range of relationships uncovered led to the view that the relationship network is a valuable concept for all students

*to understand and employ as a support system. This chapter
provides a discussion of the study and then a viewpoint which
reflects on the transferability of the findings to younger
students in schools.*

8.1 Introduction

The value of interactive discourse in relation to distance education has
been discussed by many writers. This term has been used to demonstrate
that communication beyond that provided by the learning materials,
teachers and students, can be a catalyst for understanding. Roberts
(1984:14) argues that increasing the proportion of interactive activities
improves student performance.

The need for student support services and the opportunities they
create for interaction is evident in the literature in the field. Paul
(1990:93) claims that, 'An institution's commitment to strong student
support services is critical to the fundamental value of opening up access
to a university education'. Sewart (1978) describes the student support
services offered by the Open University in the United Kingdom as a
'. . . continuity of concern for the student studying at a distance'. In
considering the phenomenon of early drop-out, Roberts (1984) cites
Holmberg (1980) and Sewart (1981) as keen advocates of more effective
student support services.

The purpose of the study was to attempt to gain a better understanding of the interaction associated with a mentor and the mentor's
protégé. In particular, the study investigates the adult students' perceptions of mentoring as a support system while they are undertaking the
Bachelor of Business (Retail Management) by distance education. This
chapter presents an overview of the study and a discussion of the
transferability of the findings to students in schools.

8.2 Mentoring

Terms used in mentoring

The definition of a mentor according to Kram (1985), writing of
mentoring in industry, is a manager who also relates well to a less-
experienced employee and, by virtue of their experience, can facilitate
the protégé's development in a manner which benefits both the
individual and the organisation. The mentor is generally regarded as

older than the protégé who is typically a young career aspirant (Hunt & Michael, 1983).

Informal mentoring is distinguished from formal mentoring (Noe, 1988; Zey, 1988; Klaus 1981). Informal mentoring is a natural pairing which results in a nurturing relationship and occurs in a wide range of settings such as the work environment, in educational institutions and in personal settings such as leisure activity groups, community groups or clubs. The term 'primary mentor' has been applied to the mentor in the informal process. Kram (1985) describes these people as unselfish, caring and altruistic, who act as mentors to protégés they have identified for themselves.

'Secondary mentors' are described as people who offer the exchange of ideas and ideals on a more businesslike basis (Kram, 1985), more in keeping with a coaching process which is a feature of formal mentoring. In this regard secondary mentors often act as a confidante, fulfilling a counselling role in addition to exchanges about work and other experiences (Noe, 1988).

It has been noted (Kram, 1985) that the benefits resulting from informal mentoring by 'primary mentors' are not easily duplicated in formal mentoring programmes. Several studies discussed by Noe (1988) indicate that successful formal mentoring programmes in organisations are characterised by a supportive organisational culture including management support, careful pairing of mentors and protégés, training and orientation of pairs on responsibilities of each person and expectations concerning the relationship, and the establishment of a minimum contact requirement (Lean, 1983; Phillips-Jones, 1983; Zey, 1985).

A model known as 'The Patron System' developed by Shapiro *et al.* (1978) provides another interesting perspective within this topic. They proposed that there were a range of professional patronage and sponsorship relationships whose role included that of protector, benefactor, sponsor, champion, advocate, supporter and adviser. They presented the system as a continuum, with 'mentors' and 'peer pals' as end points and 'sponsors' and 'guides' as internal points. Mentors were the intense patrons, 'sponsors' were strong patrons but less powerful than mentors in promoting and shaping the careers of their protégés. 'Guides' were seen as less able than mentors and sponsors to fulfil the roles of benefactor, protector or champion, but invaluable in explaining 'the system'. 'Peer pals' was the term used to describe the relationship between peers helping each other to succeed and progress. This concept belies the idea of patrons as more senior and more powerful than their protégés.

This model is useful in providing a framework for discussing different perceptions of students of all ages in relation to the personal meaning they attribute to the mentoring concept. The definitional issue raised in the literature reflects the notion that aspects of a mentoring relationship can be detected in a wide range of personal interactions. Kram (1986:171) shows how,

> The relationship constellation is the range of relationships with superiors, peers, subordinates, and (outside work) family and friends that support an individual's development at any particular time. . . . It reflects the fact that. . .

mentoring functions are embodied in several relationships rather than just one.

The concept of 'relationship phases' discussed by Kram (1985) is important in considering the mentoring literature. She describes four predictable phases which are not always distinct. These are the initiation phase, a cultivation phase, a separation phase and a redefinition phase. This is a useful framework for understanding the evolution of a wide range of different developmental relationships over time, but is not explored to any extent in this study.

Mentoring in education

Mentoring of students as a strategy for improved academic success and higher quality educational outcomes has been active for many years. Informal mentoring, of course, has been recognised as a feature of educational institutions for centuries but the extent and nature of this phenomenon has not been measured. For example, Professor Isaac Barrow, a mathematics professor from Cambridge University, acted as mentor to Isaac Newton. Professor Barrow provided Newton with tutelage and, recognising his genius, provided personal encouragement and support as Newton developed his skills and ideas.

Theoretical models of mentoring in higher education – mentoring as a student support service

Astin (1977, 1984) contends that the extent to which a student is involved in the educational process is a good predictor of graduation and academic achievement. Jacobi (1991) views mentoring as a vehicle for promoting involvement in learning and suggests that empirical studies should assess the impact of mentoring on student investment in their own learning and subsequent achievement, satisfaction and persistence with educational experiences.

Tinto (1975) has proposed a model in which retention or attrition are viewed as outcomes of commitment to and integration with the educational process and the particular institution; this has been validated in a number of studies (Pascarella & Terenzini, 1977; Terenzini & Wright, 1987). The role of mentoring in this model could be viewed as one which embraces student commitment to and integration with the educational process and the institution.

Contact with faculty linked to academic success has been studied (Astin, 1977; Pascarella & Terenzini, 1977; Tracey & Sedlacek, 1985). Jacobi (1991) discusses these studies and implies from the results that mentor relations may positively influence retention and achievement, but is critical of the lack of study of the processes involved in a successful mentoring relationship and the issue of matching diads.

Mentoring linking education and business

Up to 600 youth mentoring programmes have been found to be operating by The National Media Outreach Center based in Pittsburgh (*Across the Board* magazine, April, 1991). The objectives of these groups vary and include activities such as the improvement of literacy amongst underprivileged youth, courses to 'stretch' high school juniors beyond their limited career expectations and companionship partners for troubled children from single-parent homes.

Little research has been found on formal mentoring as a link between higher education and industry. Rowntree (1992) discusses the concept of line managers being trained as coaches to staff who are undertaking open learning courses relevant to their jobs. He cites British Airways and the Royal Bank of Scotland where this relationship is encouraged. He reports that some open learning packages include guidance notes for line managers and that the extension of such line management involvement into a more formal mentoring scheme is already part of the broader training and development function with Jaguar Cars Ltd and employees undertaking open learning courses, but that this idea is still new to many organisations.

In a programme at the University of South Australia, 40 students in their second and third year of the Bachelor of Business in Property course were paired with a 'mentor' who is a member of the Australian Institute of Valuers and Land Economists, for a 12-month period. From discussion with the Head of School of Real Estate, this arrangement is fairly casual. Students are introduced to a person employed in the industry who is experienced in their area of special interest. This provides students with access to a person for general course assistance and advice on matters of practice.

Rennie (1989) suggests that education–business partnership programmes can have a positive impact on educational outcomes of schools through business offering 'mini grants', equipment, company facilities, work experience and industry skills, and importantly the provision of mentors.

8.3 Methodological Orientation of the Study

Given that very little research was found on formal mentoring as a link between higher education and industry, an exploratory research method was appropriate for this study, which would illuminate the complex phenomenon of organisational interrelationships. The in-depth personal interview was selected as the most appropriate method.

The study constitutes a 'case study' (Stenhouse, 1988; Taft, 1988; Simons, 1977; MacDonald & Walker, 1977). Walker (1986:189–90) offers a general definition of the 'case study' in an educational setting as the study of particular incidents and events and the selection of relevant evidence which meaningfully interprets such evidence.

8.4 Research Strategies

Personal, in-depth interviews

To collect personal data from the participants about complex relationships involved within an organisational setting, the 14 in-depth, unstructured interviews were held between July and August 1993. Material was sought about the interrelationship between student and mentor(s) within the organisational context of the company. Most interviews were conducted in business locations in and around Melbourne, and all associated notes were confidential.

Location and sample

The study was centred in a retail business in Victoria, as there were several students from the one company involved in the degree course.

During the period of the study, some students were transferred out of the company. A group of 12 students formed the final sample; the mentors of two students were also interviewed.

8.5 Analysis of Data and Discussion of Findings

Mentoring in education

Discussions with the participants offered broad support for Jacobi's (1991) view that mentoring offers a vehicle for promoting involvement in learning generally. The links are associated with self-image within one's learning (working) environment offering opportunities for self-development. This benefit can be viewed in relation to the findings of Pascarella & Terenzini (1977) and Terenzini & Wright (1987) where retention or attrition in an educational context was linked to the extent of commitment to and integration with the learning process and the particular institution.

Mentoring and the distance education course

Of the 14 participants interviewed in the sample, only two felt they had a particular organisational mentor whose role was clearly identified around their progress in the degree. However, all other participants discussed relationships with other people from which they gained positive input concerning their involvement in the degree.

In the following section of the analysis, findings concerning the nature of these various relationships will be discussed and illustrated with relevant individual accounts.

A. 'Nominated' organisational mentors – specific to the distance education course

The following section is the analysis of a case where the student discusses their nominated 'mentor', and the mentor was interviewed about their protégé.

Although the pair knew of each other previously, there was no regular contact or supporting relationship. On the commencement of the degree, when the idea of establishing a mentor/protégé relationship was suggested by the course director, the student approached the mentor seeking his involvement. There was a 'loose' agreement made, but no particular commitment to timing of contact, nature of discussions, etc. The pair make contact usually by phone about once a month. They normally discuss progress in the course generally and sometimes particular successes (failures) in assessment work:

> We just talk about how I'm going generally; I sometimes discuss my successes (or failures) and I also use him as a sounding board. Mostly I get

most value from having a confidante who I can be sure will give me an unbiased response. He enjoys my friendship and honesty.

PF (student)

This seems to indicate that the relationship is providing a mixture of 'coaching' and 'counselling' which bridges both mentoring functions identified earlier, that is technical/managerial and psychosocial. This description suggests that the student has a primary mentor (Kram, 1985; Noe, 1988) who performs both a career and psychosocial function.

The difficulties discussed by Kram (1985) in trying to duplicate the benefits of informal mentoring appear to be minimal in this case. The steps in setting up formal mentoring pairs, suggested by Lean (1983), Phillips-Jones (1983) and Zey (1985) were not formally taken. However, in my discussion with the mentor in this case, I noted that he had instinctively done this to some extent:

It is important to set up the ground rules because it (mentoring) involves a mutual sense of confidentiality and trust. I think it is also important to establish a 'use-by' date. We need to understand where we are going and agree on how it will work. Of course the protege contributes to this setting-up of the ground rules and we discuss issues such as where we should draw the line on personal matters, etc.

GW (mentor)

The strength of this relationship with regard to the distance education course is that it appears to act as a focusing mechanism. That is, the student gains course focus from the contact because the mentor regularly encourages discussion about issues on course progress, provides encouragement and input on assessment work and expects that the student is 'continuing'. In support of this concept, Astin (1977, 1984) maintains that the extent to which the student is 'involved' in the educational process is a good predictor of graduation and academic achievement. The contact with the mentor described by PF appears to be contributing to his 'involvement' with the educational process in this sense. This also seems to describe a focus on the student's commitment to persevere in the course. Tinto's (1975) model, validated by several studies (Pascarella & Terenzini, 1977; Terenzini & Wright, 1987) indicates that retention or attrition can be viewed as outcomes of commitment to and integration with the educational process and the particular institution. The mentors' role in this case appears to contribute to the commitment to the educational process. The distinction between primary and secondary mentoring combined with the two dimensions of career and psychosocial development can be usefully considered in tandem with a study by Clawson (1979). He delineates:

1. comprehensiveness of influence – how many aspects of an individual's life a relationship affects, and
2. mutuality of individual commitment to the relationship.

His description characterises the primary mentor relationship as being that where the influence is comprehensive and where the commitment of both people is high.

B. Mentoring relationships outside the organisational environment (with impact on the distance education course)

Kram (1985) found that 'spouses' were generally viewed as key supporters, providing critical psychosocial functions. Seven of the 12 students interviewed (and one of the two mentors), clearly indicated their 'partner' as contributing to their development in a mentoring context in relation to the course. Such support, which is highly desirable, makes any attempt to find strict cause-and-effect relationships in mentoring impossible.

The following account has been selected to illustrate the function of partners in this role. This account not only indicates the influence of the partner on the psychosocial development of the student, but illuminates the issue of managing the tension between personal and work commitments (Kram, 1985) and adult study:

> My husband is the most significant support I have. He understands both the course content and the commitment needed to study. There is mutual support. He admires my focus and accepts that I need to spend time on this achievement. I think I would still do the course without his help, but it is really beneficial knowing he support my efforts. I feel more comfortable knowing that the other person is there when I need him.
>
> FL (student)

This student has identified both psychosocial and technical/managerial support from her partner, although she had elected not to seek out an organisational mentor. A senior executive was mentioned as showing general, informal interest in her work role. She commented on the need to be self-motivated as you were 'on your own' in the organisational context.

This case is indicative of the role a partner can play in providing input to aspects of technical/managerial development and/or psychosocial development.

C. Mentoring and peer relationships – in the context of student support systems

Is there potential for peer relationships to offer similar or unique opportunities for learning and personal development?

Each individual develops a unique interaction network during their lifetime. A wide range of relationships have been shown to be important to development throughout successive life and career stages (Levinson *et al.*, 1978; Neugarten 1975; Storr 1963). Kram & Isabella (1985) suggest that peers may be able to function well as mentors. This is an important issue, particularly for women in situations where like-gender mentors may not be available.

Peer relationships appear to have the potential to provide strong interactive communication in relation to some of the mentoring functions. Kram & Isabella (1985) found that three types of peer relationships emerged from their study. The primary functions of these relationships are shown in Table 8.1.

Naturally each mentor or peer relationship will be unique in terms of the nature of the interaction and the learning and development outcomes. Within the broad definitions assumed there are some significant differences between the two types of relationships.

Formal mentoring relationships are generally formed between people with both a considerable age difference and a difference in status in terms of the setting, whereas the attributes of both age and status could be the same in the peer dyad.

Table 8.1 Types of peer relationship

INFORMATION PEER	COLLEGIAL PEER	SPECIAL PEER
– information sharing	– career strategising – job-related feedback – friendship	– confirmation – emotional support – personal feedback – friendship

Adapted from Kram, KE and Isabella, LA (1985) 'Mentoring alternatives: the role of peer relationships in career development', *Academy of Management Journal*, 28, 1, 119.

Table 8.2 Developmental functions – comparison of mentoring and peer relationships

Mentoring relationships	Peer relationships
Career enhancing	*Career enhancing*
sponsorship	information sharing
coaching	career strategising
exposure and visibility	job-related feedback
protection	
challenging work assignment	
Psychological functions	*Psychological functions*
acceptance and confirmation	confirmation
counselling	emotional support
role modelling	personal feedback
friendship	friendship
Special attribute	*Special attribute*
complementary	mutuality

Source: Kram, KE and Isabella, LA (1985) 'Mentoring alternatives: the role of peer relationships in career development', *Academy of Management Journal*, 28, 1, 117.

Kram & Isabella (1985:129), in comparing the two relationships, also point out that while there is some overlap in the developmental functions of the two types of relationships, peer relationships involve a two-way exchange, whereas mentoring relationships involve a one-way helping dynamic. Their comparison is summarised in Table 8.2.

Peer relationships offer a degree of mutuality that enables both people to give and receive. This contrasts with a mentoring relationship where one individual is acknowledged as the sponsor in the interaction. Peer relationships often operate spontaneously. That is, they may not work to any formal agenda, nor attempt to achieve specific objectives. Work-related advice and support may be exchanged periodically, touched on, returned to at another time. 'Negative' feelings and attitudes towards the environment may also be shared and even promoted. This feature of peer relationships contrasts sharply with the positive goals of mentoring relationships.

Structured programmes with peer dyads, designed for school-age students, are reported in the literature (Fuchs *et al.*, 1994; Duin *et al.*, 1994), providing examples of the formal application of a process which was found to occur informally with adults in the workplace.

Several students discussed relationships with peers that were directly connected to their support system in relation to the course. The following account is illustrative of the role peers are playing in this regard and supports the findings of Kram & Isabella (1985) that peers can function effectively as mentors:

> In relation to the degree specifically RL is supportive (another student). It's mutual. He helps me and I've helped him with the maths. We meet together to go through study material.
>
> NT (student)

It was difficult to tell from this interview the extent to which the personal friendship between NT and RL has developed. However, from this account there is 'information sharing', described by Kram & Isabella (1985) as a function of the information peer relationship, and elements of the special peer relationship (Kram & Isabella, 1985) evidenced by personal feedback and friendship.

The strongest case of an important peer relationship in this study is one where two students began the course together. They have been temporarily in different businesses for part of this year, and are now working in the same organisation again, outside the company.

From discussions with PF, all primary functions of peer relationships noted by Kram & Isabella (1985) were in evidence in this peer dyad. That is, each person was able to function for the other as an information peer, a collegial peer and/or a special peer:

> We are in contact at least once a week, usually by phone now, on either work or study issues. We use each other as a sounding board and find it useful because we look at things from a different perspective. In relation to the course, although we've been working in different states for part of this year, we still send or fax notes all around Australia! Like we send each other copies of summaries. We look after one another. If he's behind one week I fax him my notes. I'm sure I wouldn't be doing it if it wasn't for him!
>
> PF (student)

From these case reports it is clear that peer relationships are able to fulfil a number of functions similar to those provided by a mentor. As students are more likely to have access to a larger number of peers than prospective mentors, the benefits of developing a peer relationship as a student support system should be encouraged. In addition, as a peer relationship involves greater reciprocity and mutuality than a mentor relationship, where the dyad is two students, gains in relation to progressing with study are doubled.

The term 'peer pal' is used by Shapiro *et al.* (1978) to describe a reciprocal supporting relationship: 'Through sharing information and strategies and providing sounding boards and advice for one another, peer pals help each other while helping themselves' (p. 56). They suggest that a peer pal relationship by comparison with a mentor relationship tends to be more egalitarian and peer related, less intense and exclusionary and potentially more democratic. In relation to such a relationship being established by two students, the common concern of progress in study in particular and matters relating to study more indirectly, could create a strong bond. In this case, both people could gain incrementally in their study, from the relationship.

Developing a greater awareness amongst younger students of the potential of peer interaction for improved learning therefore has merit, in relation to both formal and informal peer dyads.

D. The 'patron system'

During the analysis of data, the relevance of another model, the 'patron system' (Shapiro *et al.*, 1978) became clear. Students described the study support they receive from a range of workplace relationships.

Shapiro *et al.* (1978) presented the system as a continuum, with 'mentors' and 'peer pals' as end points and 'sponsors' and 'guides' as internal points. Mentors were the most intense patrons, 'sponsors' were strong patrons but less powerful than mentors in promoting and shaping the careers of their protégés. Guides were seen as less able than mentors and sponsors to fulfil the roles of benefactor, protector, or champion but invaluable in explaining the 'system'. 'Peer pals' was the term used to describe the relationship between peers helping each other to succeed and progress. This concept belies the idea of patrons as more senior and more powerful than their protégés. This model is more specific to workplace support and offers a less complex, but none the less useful framework for adult students to consider, in encouraging the establishment of a support network in the workplace.

Table 8.3 The 'patron system' – devised from the continuum described by Shapiro, Haseltine and Rowe, 1978

Mentors	*Sponsors*	*Guides*	*Peer pals*
Intense	Strong patrons	Explain the system	Reciprocity
'Paternalistic'	Promote and shape careers	Shortcuts	Share information/ strategies
'Godfathers'		Pitfalls	Sounding boards
'Rabbis'		Provide 'intelligence'	Advice

The following quotations from students in the study have been selected as examples of some of the workplace relationships described in this model:

...they show me the ropes. Like one of the guys might sit next to me at a meeting and sort of coach on who's likely to say what – and, what I should do.

KP (guide)

...There is TS who is a great friend. He is a good sounding board; he's studying another course.

DC (peer pal)

My exposure through K has got to have helped. I am sure he has referred me to people who make the moves.

MD (sponsor)

E. Relationship 'constellations' – in the context of student support systems

The analysis of data to this point has indicated that there are a range of relationships which vary in influence and comprehensiveness and impact on psychosocial and/or career enhancement dimensions and role modelling.

The concept of the 'relationship constellation' was introduced by Kram (1985) to account for this phenomenon. It takes into account a range of relationships with people both within an organisational environment and outside the workplace that supports an individual's development during their lifetime. Figure 8.1 illustrates this concept and reflects the idea that students gain different mentoring functions from several relationships.

The relationship constellation of individuals varies and changes as needs and circumstances change. While an individual is an adult student and an employee, their relationship constellation may resemble that shown in Figure 8.1. However, in later life the same individual may be involved in teaching others, through mentoring. Subordinates then would become a more prominent element in their relationship constellation.

In this study there was evidence that students had a range of relationships which were contributing some aspect of a mentoring function. The following accounts demonstrate this point. They illustrate the value in having adult students consider patterns of relationship constellations so that they might more consciously identify and build supportive relationships to provide for particular developmental and learning functions:

I don't have a mentor in Kmart to support me with the degree specifically. I am friends with LM (student outside Kmart) I have an area manager studying and I'm supporting him and encouraging him. I get something back from that. There is TS who is a great friend. He is a good sounding board. . . . My father and grandfather before him are retailers so I get strong encouragement from the family to carry the family torch as a retail professional.

SE (student)

There's no particular person in Kmart who discusses the degree with me. The three managers I mentioned earlier all show sort of general interest. They're all helpful and we have professional friendships, they show me the ropes. Like one of the guys might sit next to me at a meeting and sort of coach on who's likely to say what – and, what I should do. . . . Like when I was appointed, SO rang and said, 'I'm so proud of you!' That meant a lot.

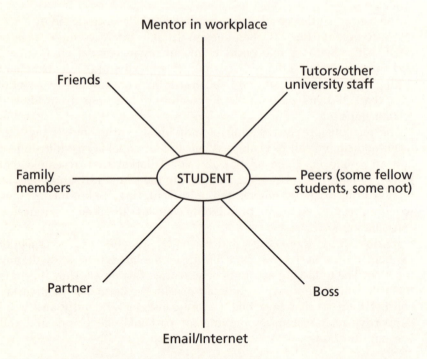

Figure 8.1 The relationship network as a student support system: adapted from Kram and Isabella (1985)

Also my father has always supported my achievements. He's always there
if I need him.

MO (student)

8.6 Significance of Findings and Implications

Summary

The following elements were considered significant.

■ Two students discussed their relationship with workplace mentors
which are having a positive impact on their progress in the course.
From the analysis it was clear that each relationship offers different
supportive functions depending on the individuals concerned.
However, in both cases the role of the mentor is significant in their
continuation and achievement in the course.

■ Partners of students were clearly significant. Partners were discussed as playing a crucial role particularly in relation to support
and encouragement to persevere with study. Discussion of their
relationships also indicated the need for adult students to manage
the tension created between personal, work-related and study
commitments.

■ Peers were evident as a valuable student support system offering a
range of mentoring functions depending on the individuals in the
dyad. The reciprocity of this particular relationship was clearly a
strength in relation to the possible benefits for adult distance
education students. The applicability of this finding to younger
students is apparent from formal peer-tutoring programmes reported in the literature. The value of promoting informal peer
interaction for enhanced learning with younger students should be
explored further.

■ Other workplace relationships not strictly fitting the 'mentor'
definition were shown to be providing different but positive
functions for several students, both with regard to study and with
technical/managerial development and role modelling.

■ In review of the overall analysis, it was clear that a wide range of
relationships varying in both influence and comprehensiveness
were contributing to the students' support networks. These relationships were from either the workplace, outside the workplace or
a combination of both. Different mentoring functions were found
to be provided by more than one individual and peers were found
to be an influential support source.

■ Although the issue of gender and mentoring was not actively canvassed in this study, some participants' perceptions about this issue were noted. Cross-gender relationships were not highlighted as a particular issue. However, there was evidence of perceived paternalism in the organisational culture. Opportunities for women to be mentored by same-sex mentors would be limited by the number of senior female managers available. The cultural climate of the organisation, although changing slowly, could also act as a barrier to any extension of cross-gender mentoring for the younger female mangers at the company. Preparation for such an initiative would need to be thorough.

Terms and definitions

In this study a range of operational definitions have been canvassed through the discussion of different models. In the analysis, the linking of participants' descriptive data as examples of aspects of different models demonstrates that each model has merit. This is helpful in providing a deeper understanding of the intricacies of developmental relationships and the opportunities that effective networking can provide.

Further, to attempt to isolate some 'basics' about mentoring in order to facilitate the opportunity for comparative research seems to me to devalue the concept. The complexity of individuals and their developmental relationships cannot be meaningfully simplified to this extent.

Student support in education

The analysis of data has demonstrated that whatever the nature of the developmental relationship, the students were gaining a range of benefits. Clarity of focus on the objectives and intrinsic value of the course was one broad gain in evidence. Having meaningful others involved in support and encouragement appears to strengthen the commitment to persevere.

Support for study was more clearly identified by participants in relation to people outside the workplace. This support was available from partners, friends and family. However, the 'support' described by some participants from inside the organisation was less obvious in nature. In relation to the course specifically, occasional general queries about 'How's the course going?' were more typical.

Although the data indicated that students gained from a wider source of developmental relationships than one particular mentor, whatever the nature of that relationship it acted as a focusing mechanism. That is, discussion with the support person about a wide range of issues relating to the course appears to build the student's involvement in the educational process – a factor identified by Astin (1977, 1984) as one which increases the likelihood of academic achievement and graduation. This feature is likely to apply to students of all ages. Similarly, studies by Pascarella & Terenzini (1977) and Terenzini & Wright (1987) support Tinto's (1975) model which claims that retention and attrition can be viewed as outcomes of commitment to and integration with the educational process.

In this regard, a wider range of benefits may be gained for school-age students involved in peer-tutoring or mentoring programmes than those relating to the learning curriculum only. Such relationships may influence psychosocial development and attitudes and values relating to learning and the educational process.

Implications for further research

The diversity of developmental relationships which can be explored by people in the establishment of networks for study support, technical/ managerial skills development or psychosocial development is the feature of this field of study. The complexity of the concept should not be devalued in future research by imposing arbitrary definitional boundaries around some of the aspects of the mentoring function.

In particular, the opportunity to better communicate to students of all ages the opportunities for personal development through the establishment of effective relationship constellations is a great challenge for all 'educators'.

Address for correspondence: Ms Val Clulow, Department of Marketing, Faculty of Business and Economics, MONASH UNIVERSITY, PO Box 197, Caulfield East, VICTORIA, AUSTRALIA 3145. Tel. (03) 903 2727. Fax (61) (3) 903 2929. e-mail val.clulow@symbus.monash.edu.au

Chapter 9

PEER ASSISTED LEARNING AND RAISING STANDARDS

Toni Beardon

This chapter gives an analysis of various types of peer assisted learning programmes and of the contrasting paradigms which underlie different models. It is argued that the effectiveness of peer assisted learning, as an educational strategy, is robust and stable in so far as it is shown to be effective in many different contexts, in different countries, within different educational systems and with learners of all ages. It is sufficiently robust to succeed as a strategy despite local difficulties, and it is stable enough to withstand changes in organisation and personnel. Some of the pedagogical issues surrounding the teaching and learning relationships are discussed with reference to the author's research which focuses on the classroom management and teaching skills required by teachers to work effectively with teaching assistants. The research is based on the Cambridge University STIMULUS project which enables university students to assist regularly in schools. The aims of the project are to raise standards of learning in the sciences and mathematics, to encourage an interest in these disciplines, to raise the aspirations of pupils (especially girls), and to give the university students an educative experience.

9.1 Introduction

The term 'peer assisted learning' (PAL) refers to learners assisting other learners with their studies. The examples compared in this chapter include same-age and cross-age PAL programmes, set up to meet well-defined educational objectives, and where data have been collected on their effectiveness in relation to the intended outcomes. When PAL is used as a deliberate pedagogical strategy, research shows that there are positive academic and social benefits for the participants compared to other groups of learners (Bloom, 1984; Palinscar & Brown, 1984; Hedin, 1987; Benard, 1990; Slavin, 1990). This chapter gives examples of some contrasting PAL programmes, including an in-depth case study of the Cambridge STIMULUS project and a report on the author's research. Many of the case studies discussed in this chapter provide models which could usefully be copied and adapted in other situations.

In this chapter the term 'peer assisted learning' (PAL) is used as a blanket term to cover a variety of different forms, known variously as peer tutoring, student tutoring, mentoring, etc. The learning may be academic or vocational, and the location may not be in an educational establishment, but the peer exchange must be directed by a professional teacher. The term 'teaching assistant' is used in this chapter for the peer teachers involved in PAL schemes who are neither qualified teachers nor trainee teachers. The equality of age and status, implied by the term 'peer', does not always apply. For this reason terms are used such as 'proctor' or 'mentor'. Cambridge STIMULUS is described as a peer assisted learning project, using the more general term, in order to avoid some of the connotations associated with the term 'tutor' and to reflect a particular philosophy of teaching and learning. Topping (1995) gives helpful definitions of some of the terms, and this chapter gives a more detailed analysis based on Cornwall's (1979) definitions. There is a need for the adoption of standard conventions for the terminology.

The use of the term mentor in the context of peer assisted learning is confusing. Topping (1995) defines 'mentoring' as an encouraging and supportive one-to-one relationship with a more experienced worker. Some mentoring schemes fall under the PAL umbrella but those in which the mentor has a professional responsibility for assessing the trainee do not. For example, in initial teacher training in the UK, the mentor is an experienced teacher who makes the assessment of teaching competence of the trainees on which their qualification to teach depends.

PAL is characterised by having three significant parties or groups, namely the class teacher (or teacher in charge), the teaching assistant and the learners. In the STIMULUS project, and in many of the examples given in this chapter, the three parties work together in the classroom. This terminology is used for the sake of consistency although it does not suit all institutions. For example, the term 'lecturer' or 'professor' may be more appropriate than 'class teacher'. There may be, as in the STIM-ULUS example, an external agent or coordinator who has a role in making introductions, giving advice and conducting research.

Every student who assists another student with his or her studies provides an instance of PAL and many teachers actively encourage this, though not in any formalised way. Significantly it is found to be the case across a range of subject areas, ages and different educational systems that the teaching assistant gains as much cognitively as the learner. Research in this area suggests that peer teaching leads to 'deep' rather than 'surface' approaches to learning on the part of the teaching assistants (Jones & Bates, 1987; Entwistle, 1987) and there is ample scope for further research. There has recently been a resurgence of interest in peer assisted learning as a cost-effective way of raising standards (Levin *et al.*, 1987) and of increasing learner motivation (Gartner & Reissman, 1993).

9.2 Peer Assisted Learning Developments in the United Kingdom

In the UK there has been a big expansion in peer assisted learning in the last few years. The Pimlico Connection, founded by Sinclair Goodlad at Imperial College, London in 1975 (Goodlad & Hirst, 1989) provided a model for the five projects which, like Cambridge STIMULUS, were set up in 1987 with grants from the University Grants Committee (UGC), as it then was, the government committee which controlled the funding to universities. These were the pioneers for over 180 projects which have since sprung up in the UK.

The grant from the UGC was part of an initiative to improve the supply of mathematics, physics and technology teachers. Different agendas can be served by the same PAL scheme, as the range of aims of the STIMULUS programme and the evaluation evidence demonstrates. Since 1990 STIMULUS, like many of the other projects, has depended on sponsorship funding.

The City of London Lord Mayor's appeal in 1991 adopted peer assisted learning as one of its charities. Through Community Service Volunteers (CSV), and with sponsorship from industry, many new projects were set up. In order to promote PAL as part of a 'Raising Aspirations of Young People' initiative, BP funded a fellowship in peer tutoring, a training video and a tutoring resource pack to provide the guidance needed for all those involved in such projects (Beardon *et al.*, 1991).

9.3 The Cambridge STIMULUS Project

The Cambridge STIMULUS Project is one model of cross-age peer assisted learning. STIMULUS is an acronym for Science Technology Informatics and Mathematics Undergraduate Links between University and Schools. University students, with appropriate backgrounds in mathematics, engineering, natural sciences or computing, volunteer to assist in local schools on a regular basis, meeting the same classes each week, getting to know the pupils, and working alongside and under the direction of experienced teachers. The volunteers work with learners of all ages from 4–19, and of all abilities, from those with learning difficulties to the most gifted.

STIMULUS offers a free resource to schools through which learners receive more individual help and encouragement than teachers are able to give on their own. The National Curriculum in England and Wales has placed heavy demands on teachers. For example, primary schools are now required to teach much more science and technology. Teachers who are not science specialists often gain confidence from discussing the subject with the volunteers, and from their help in setting up experiments and using computers.

The STIMULUS scheme simultaneously serves many purposes. The general aims are to provide support for the teaching of mathematics, science, computing and technology in schools; to raise the standards of learning in these subjects; to maximise the benefits in cognitive gains for both university students and pupils through research into classroom management strategies and teacher helper relationships; and to provide a link between the university and the local community. The project aims to provide pupils with positive role models of young scientists, mathematicians and technologists and to encourage them (particularly girls) to develop and maintain an interest in science and technology. The aims for the university students are to give them the opportunity to develop their social, organisational, problem-solving and communication skills in a practical context; and to give them first-hand experience of the classroom, and a better understanding of the education service, which may help them in their choice of career.

Over eight years, through STIMULUS, 485 Cambridge University students from 25 colleges have assisted in 20 schools, many for two or more terms. The scheme now operates with approximately 65 volunteers per year. The schools are all within five miles of the university and the volunteers walk or cycle to their school. They do not get any academic credit or payment. The project depends entirely on sponsorship funding, raised through triennial appeals, from local and national industry, from Cambridge colleges (which are independent of the university), and from research funding. Representatives from all the university faculties concerned sit on the steering committee, together with an elected student representative, and the university Faculty of Education provides office and secretarial facilities and rooms for meetings.

The introductory training session lasts two and a half hours and further training sessions take place every half term. Strong emphasis is placed on the importance of being a good listener and of encouraging the learners to talk about their work before offering any explanations. In the current research, which is not yet complete, 81% of teachers say that volunteers realise that encouraging learners to talk about their work helps them to learn and that the volunteer's questioning was effective. In the post-experience questionnaires (return rate 88% so far) 83% of primary volunteers and 100% of secondary volunteers agreed with this, and 74% of the sample of pupils agreed with the statement, 'I think that talking to someone about my work helps me to understand better and helps me to put my ideas into words'. The training session gives the volunteers some idea of what to expect in the classroom through viewing a locally made video, and through discussion, meeting local teachers and meeting some of the previous year's volunteers. The National Curriculum and the programmes of study for the learners they are to help are explained and discussed. There are exercises designed to develop their communication skills and to raise awareness and understanding of the teaching and learning processes, some of which appear in the tutoring resource pack (Beardon *et al.*, 1991). The volunteers discuss their expectations and those of the school, and there are exercises to help the volunteers to know how to adapt to their role. For example, the volunteers discuss in pairs how they would react to some carefully chosen classroom incidents and then the whole group discusses what to do in such circumstances.

Recognising what each has to offer, the school placements are arranged by matching requests from volunteers and schools. The head teacher, or head of department, in the school allocates the volunteers to work with particular class teachers. The class teacher has complete freedom to direct the volunteer in whatever way best suits his or her teaching style, classroom management patterns and curriculum plans. Teachers' beliefs, and their skills at working as a team with other adults, greatly affect the outcomes of this partnership. The teachers who believe that volunteers help them to achieve their objectives for lessons, take account of their role when planning lessons, plan to use the volunteer's subject knowledge where possible and, on the first visit, discuss their plans and tell the volunteers how they want them to assist in lessons. These teachers introduce the new teaching assistant by first name, telling the pupils in a way that is meaningful to them that this is a student from the university who has volunteered to come every week to help them with their work.

In the annual evaluations, the returns on the questionnaires over eight years are remarkably consistent. Teachers want more volunteers and typical comments are: 'Vital! I have 27 12-year-olds and only four computers. The volunteer helps the learners who are using the computers while I work with the rest of the class. Same again please!' 'Keep them coming'. 'A life saver at times!'

The following comments are typical of those made by learners: 'They were young, interesting and knew what they were doing, and yet were not deadly serious'. 'He cheered our lessons up and we did learn lots about the computer'.

About two-thirds of the volunteers had previously considered a career in teaching, and over 80% are as keen or keener to teach afterwards. Of those who had not previously considered a teaching career, 45% say it has encouraged them to consider teaching as a possibility. A small but significant proportion go straight into teacher training once they finish their degrees. On the basis of subjective evidence it appears that the interpersonal skills, which are valued by employers generally, are fostered through the STIMULUS experience; it gives university students a better understanding of the learning process and of the education service, and many say that it improves their own study skills. Over the eight years responses from volunteers have not fallen below the following percentages:

- 80% say it has helped them in thinking about their career;
- 75% say it has given them a feeling that they were doing something useful;
- 70% say it has given them an insight into how others perceive their subject;
- 60% say it has helped them to develop their communication skills;
- 60% say it has increased their self-confidence.

The evaluations indicate that the STIMULUS volunteers, both as role models and in passing on their own enthusiasm for their subjects, play a part in raising the aspirations of young people. One of the intrinsic advantages of PAL as a teaching strategy is in the affective area, as learners relate more easily to those they see as their peers than they do to their teachers, and this is suggested by learners' comments. Girls benefit from the opportunity to learn from female teaching assistants and they are sometimes more forthcoming and ready to ask questions of them than of their male class teachers. Forty per cent of the volunteers are women, which contradicts the gender stereotyping and prejudices associated with women and science. The percentage of girls taking up these subjects is low and it is of national importance to foster the talents and confidence of girls in these areas (Committee on Women in Science, Engineering and Technology, 1994). STIMULUS operates only in co-educational schools and many young girls, through meeting and being encouraged by female university students, become more confident in their own abilities, and are made more aware of the opportunities for further study in mathematics, the sciences, engineering and computing.

Some of the claims for the benefits of STIMULUS should, more appropriately, be called conjectures. The current research programme, set up two years ago, seeks to substantiate these conjectures. The author is working on research into the cognitive gains derived from PAL through the collaboration of teachers with teaching assistants, the classroom management skills and strategies employed in this teaching teamwork, the teacher-helper relationships involved and the teaching strategies which prove the most effective. The research methodology involves classroom observation, structured interviews with teachers and with volunteers, questionnaires, discussions and audio-recorded conferences. In order to disseminate good practice the author is editing a collection of articles written by classroom teachers about how they work with teaching assistants. This is part of a programme of research, sponsored by British Telecom and coordinated by Community Service Volunteers.

9.4 What is PAL? A Discussion of its Different Forms

Any discussion of a PAL project and any claims made for the benefits it brings to the participants raise fundamental questions about the nature of the teaching–learning process. In many programmes measurement of the cognitive gains for the teaching assistant and learners is impossible because of the difficulty of separating out those factors which relate to the peer exchange relationship from other factors influencing the development of the participants over the same period of time. It is only in the case of large university classes, taught simultaneously by the same teacher, where a subgroup engages in PAL, that a reliable control group can be used for comparison of the effects of peer teaching. Johnston and Loh offered two case studies of this type in the proceedings of the Auckland Conference (Jones (ed.), 1993). Loh's example is particularly interesting in relation to raising standards. By early identification of 'at-risk' nursing students, and by arranging peer assisted learning for them, he has very significantly reduced the failure rate on the course.

In programmes like Cambridge STIMULUS, evaluation is qualitative rather than quantitative and it depends on the judgements of the three groups of participants. It can be argued that the professional judgements made by the class teachers are reliable and, if they themselves are users rather than providers of the PAL scheme, their judgements are objective. Moreover, the perceptions of all three parties are important, particularly in relation to emotional and social gains. It is claimed that such programmes not only have educational benefits for the teaching assistants and learners but also meet some of their social and emotional needs (Gartner & Riessman, 1993).

If the academic, emotional and social gains derived from one project can be validated, the question arises as to whether the example is generalisable to other contexts. There is considerable evidence that the benefits of PAL are recognisable, and in some cases even measurable, across many subject areas, all age groups, and for different types of organisation and in different cultural and social contexts. In probing the reasons for this we need to discuss the theoretical basis of PAL and to analyse the different types and models of organisation of PAL schemes.

The classification of four types of teaching–learning relationship in PAL is based on that given by Cornwall (1979): the teacher substitute; the teaching assistant; teacherless groups and co-teaching. Of the four types of PAL relationship, the teacherless groups and co-teaching depend on exchanges between students who are learning the same material, and will invariably involve participants who are at the same stage in their education, whereas the teacher substitute and the teaching assistant are usually at a more advanced stage than their pupils. The distinction between the teacher substitute and the teaching assistant needs clarification. The teacher substitute acts in place of the class teacher, with a small group or with the whole class according to a pre-arranged plan, under the direction of the teacher in charge, and for a limited time. The teaching assistant on the other hand works in partnership with the class teacher, very occasionally as a 'double act' in front of the class (for example in role play, or demonstration of science experiments). More usually, at any one time, the assistant works with an individual learner or with a small group.

Topping (1995) defines different organisational frameworks for PAL. He defines the student tutoring framework, of which the STIMULUS project is an example, as the practice of students from universities and colleges of further and higher education tutoring learners in primary (elementary) and secondary (high) school classrooms under the guidance of the class teacher. In such programmes the tutor acts for most of the time as a teaching assistant but on occasions may be invited by the class teacher to act as a teacher substitute. This sometimes occurs in the STIMULUS project when jointly planned by the class teacher and volunteer. It is also a feature of the Sydney University Dentistry example (Arneman in Jones (ed.), 1993) which is an example of what Topping defines to be 'peer tutoring', namely people from similar social groupings who are not professional teachers helping each other to learn and learning themselves by teaching. Within any one scheme, different teaching–learning relationships may occur at different times. The quality of the relationships provides a key factor determining the effectiveness of PAL when judged in relation to intended outcomes.

Research also shows that PAL is effective in case studies where the underlying philosophies of education are radically different. However, as has already been noted, PAL programmes can serve many different agendas, and the desired outcomes and the judgements of effectiveness dependent on these desired outcomes, may differ. We shall compare different philosophies, the consequent motives for employing a PAL strategy, the attitudes towards it and the effect on patterns of implementation. We give examples from research showing the effectiveness of the four types of PAL across the philosophical spectrum, in different phases of education and in different social and cultural contexts.

The author has consistently used the teacher substitute strategy in upper secondary school and in higher education mathematics teaching. The explicit aims are to develop not only a better understanding of the subject matter but also the learners' communication skills and their responsibility for their own learning. The principle is that each student should, in turn, present and explain a prepared section of work to the class having had the opportunity for help beforehand as needed. The philosophy is that we are all part of a learning community and that my role as teacher can sometimes be most effective, once having selected appropriate material for the peer teaching exercise, by taking a back seat in the classroom. By involving all the learners as teacher substitutes it is possible to build a climate in which relationships are mutually support-ive rather than competitive.

Two PAL programmes involving teacher substitutes have been oper-ated at the University of Sydney Faculty of Dentistry (Arneman & Prosser, in Jones (ed.), 1993). In one, selected fifth-year undergraduates assisted in the teaching of first-year students, each teaching assistant being assigned to a university staff member, thus enabling the class sizes to be increased. Teaching assistants and university staff met weekly, before and after the teaching sessions, to plan lessons and to review the lessons that had been delivered. They also met with the other teaching pairs to exchange ideas. In addition, each teaching assistant acted as a teacher substitute and gave a prepared and rehearsed lecture to the whole first-year group. In the evaluation, the university staff reported that their own teaching methods were constantly under review and that justification for the way they presented lessons was important. They also reported that, through working with teaching assistants, they had gained insights into some of the problems which the undergraduates were facing. These issues, namely cost-effectiveness in relation to class sizes, teaching loads, teachers feeling that they are under scrutiny, the bridging of the teacher–learner gap and the function of teaching assistants as mediators are all key factors in PAL programmes.

Other examples of teacher substitute PAL programmes include a Colloquium Program at the University of Massachusetts (Flanagan, 1976) in which selected undergraduates planned and gave courses. Learners submitted proposals which were rigorously validated by a faculty student committee, attended training sessions and earned academic credit. The outcomes claimed were efficient use of resources at a time of financial restraints, demonstrable effectiveness of learners as teachers, and the legitimacy of teaching as a learning experience.

The second type of PAL organisation involves teacherless groups. The professional studies component of the postgraduate teacher education programme at the University of Cambridge, in which the author is involved, provides one example of this type. Students from different subject specialisms, all training to be secondary teachers, meet twice weekly. Many teaching strategies are used but a recurrent pattern involves pre-session reading, an introduction by the staff member, a stimulus (which may for example be a case study, examples of pupil's work, classroom observation, role playing or a video) followed by discussion of key questions in small teacherless groups and the presenta-tion of group or individual reports. Through discussion of complex issues such as improving learner motivation, pastoral care in schools, catering for special educational needs, multicultural education, equal opportunities, etc. students become more aware of alternative points of view and of some of the variety of practical approaches to meeting the problems and challenges which face them as teachers. This method, involving teacherless groups, has been found to be a much more successful and motivating mode of learning than large lectures given by subject experts.

Other examples of teacherless groups include the widespread use of writing groups set up as a means of improving student skills in written communication, as well as to stimulate positive attitudes to writing, intellectual growth and rhetorical skills. Ian Hay described one such programme at Flinder's University, South Australia, in a paper given at the 1993 conference on peer tutoring in Auckland (Jones (ed.), 1993). The programme involves learners' critical appraisal of each other's work in mutually supporting groups using criterion-referenced assessment. Evaluation compared responses from Australian and American classes. One of the outcomes reported was that learners were critical of misplaced 'kindness' shown by lenient peer reviewers and appreciated honest criticism. Other research reports on peer assisted learning in teacherless groups are found in Collier (1983) and courses in American politics (Goldman *et al.*, 1975) and in accountancy (Leveson in Jones (ed.), 1993).

Co-teaching involves two learners from the same class helping each other as part of a planned teaching strategy. Paired reading is one, widely used, method of this type (Topping, 1988). Other examples involve learners being given different readings on the same subject, preparing a list of questions, then being required to discuss the topic, try to answer each other's question and produce an assignment on it (Goldschmid & Shore, 1974).

Finally the fourth type, teaching assistance, generally involves an older student teaching younger learners, as in the Cambridge STIMULUS programme. The teaching assistant and learner may come from the same educational institution and may be at different stages in the same course so that the teaching assistants have an empathy and a shared understanding with their pupils of the learning, and sometimes social, difficulties they are encountering. Four case studies of schemes in which this was a significant factor were presented at the Auckland Conference by Howse, Loh, Loo and Miles (Jones (ed.), 1993). In some projects, assistant teachers are paid for their work (Jones, 1989), and in others university students earn academic credit. One example of the latter type occurs at Nottingham Polytechnic where engineering students plan and lead a group of school students who carry out a design project as part of the school technology course (Saunders, 1992).

Before coming to the question of why PAL is found so widely to be a successful teaching strategy, we consider an adaptation of Cornwall's two contrasting paradigms from educational philosophy and the consequent effects on the aims and organisation of PAL programmes (Cornwall, 1979). In one paradigm the peer tutor is regarded as an inferior 'stand in' for the proper teacher. Under this model the teacher is seen as the source of knowledge and the educational objectives emphasise subject content and examination performance. The teaching style is didactic and there is rigorous selection of teaching assistants who are seen as superior to their peers in ability and in academic achievement. In such examples the rewards are extrinsic, with the teaching assistants either being paid or given academic credit, and the evaluation of the project depends on performance tests compared to other matching groups not involved in peer teaching. At the opposite extreme is the view that collaborative teaching has benefits which are derived from the intrinsic advantages of peer assisted learning. The teacher is seen as a facilitator of learning and the educational objectives emphasise motivation, understanding and the personal and social development of the participants. The teaching styles involve mutual help, investigational and open-ended enquiry, self-supported learning and group work. Learners regard the teaching assistant as an equal despite differences of age, academic attainment or ability, and all learners are assumed to be competent, in the right circumstances, to teach peers. The rewards are intrinsic, arising from interest in the subject, in teaching or in working with young people, or arising from a sense of personal fulfilment or satisfaction through personal development. Evaluation is likely to be from subjective reports from the three participating groups.

These descriptions caricature the two opposite viewpoints and most PAL projects have features of both types. In considering the effectiveness of any teaching method the system needs to be considered with reference to the value system underlying the project, the educational objectives it is intended to serve, the outcomes desired and the methods of evaluation employed.

9.5 Why is PAL Effective?

Explanations for the success of PAL can be found whether one looks at the behaviourist, the role theory or the gestalt theory of learning. According to the behaviourist model, a student's learning is improved when they receive more instruction, when they are given more in-dividual help and when their questions are answered quickly. Some quotations illustrate recognition of these advantages:

> I like having STIMULUS volunteers because if you don't understand what to do they are there to help you.
>
> I liked having someone to turn to if the teacher was busy.
>
> When I missed a lesson she showed me what the rest of the class had done.
>
> If you needed help you didn't have to wait for 15 minutes in a queue.
>
> The teacher was able to come around and help us individually as there were other adults in the room.

These advantages are also explained in some typical comments from teachers:

> He brought his own expertise to help with practical science, his encourage-ment to write was invaluable in helping to keep pupils on task.
>
> Some pupils were able to have far more extending work with her, and the other pupils in the class benefited from having more of my time.
>
> He was able to encourage more able pupils to extend their thinking.

In the role theory model of learning, students learn more when they can relate more easily to their teachers, they are less reluctant to appear ignorant and more ready to ask questions. However successful teachers are in relating to their pupils, they will still be perceived in a different light from teaching assistants and it can be argued that working with teaching assistants as mediators can be a very effective teaching strategy on this account. As an example, the author observed a class of 8- and 9-year-olds where a STIMULUS assistant and a trainee teacher were both teaching groups of children. They were both second-year under-graduates of exactly the same age, working under the direction of the class teacher, and they both showed similar teaching skills. The trainee teacher, a very reflective student, remarked after school was over that, in her opinion, the volunteer had a big advantage over herself as a teacher because he had been introduced to the class as a student helper and she had been introduced as a teacher. As a result the pupils seemed to regard him as a sort of older brother figure and 'opened up' to him much more readily than they did to her.

Some learners' comments from other classes also illustrate this:

He explained everything very clearly and made us feel comfy.

She is very approachable and clarifies most maths problems quickly, it is an ideal time for extra teachers because our exams are coming up.

In relation to the wider issues of social and personal development, the STIMULUS experience has provided many examples where learners clearly relate well to the teaching assistants as role models and are encouraged in their studies by them. For example:

I liked having a chance to talk to him about what he was doing and just talking to him about future maths I might be doing.

The teacher–learner relationship can be modelled as a two dimensional space, one dimension being the affective and the other the cognitive domain. In the affective dimension, the relationship between teacher and learner ranges from authority–dependence at one end of the spectrum to an equality relationship with some degree of reciprocity at the other end. Some teachers may perceive themselves, and be perceived as being, authority figures, while others may have a personal philosophy by which they strive to be facilitators of learning as authorities in relation to the subject matter only. The second dimension, in the cognitive domain, ranges from low cognitive congruence between teacher and taught to high cognitive congruence. Peer teachers and learners usually have relatively high cognitive congruence and a more nearly equal relationship. This can make it easier for the peer teacher to give assistance and for the learner to learn in this exchange, than in the class teacher–pupil exchange where there is a lower cognitive congruence and an unequal relationship. Recognising this, many experienced teachers use PAL when they have the opportunity, as a deliberate strategy, to augment their own teaching by using the help of younger teaching assistants as mediators.

The gestalt theory of learning emphasises the importance of structure and of fitting newly acquired knowledge into a pattern. We form our own conceptual structures which we have to modify to accommodate new ideas. The closer cognitive congruence of the peer teacher and learner enables the peer teacher to empathise with the learner and instinctively to appreciate, or maybe to remember, how it feels to be confused about the topic. The peer teacher understands the learner's perceptions of the subject matter and can identify the patterns of thinking and the difficulties being experienced, and find ways around the difficulties that have worked in his or her own experience. Here

117

again there is a rationale for PAL. Again this is often perceived by the learners and two typical quotes from questionnaires exemplifies this:

> It gave me insight into different ways of approaching problems.

> I like having STIMULUS volunteers because I might get something wrong and I might think it is right and she can correct me.

Some teachers enjoy the opportunity to work with teaching assistants and feel that on occasions it relieves them of some of the pressures in the classroom. Teachers often say that they value the chance to work collaboratively with other adults in the classroom, that it breaks down the sense of teacher isolation, and that they value the chance to discuss the subject matter and to hear other people's ideas on the subject. The following are typical quotes from teachers:

> I enjoyed her cheerful regular attendance, the benefit to the pupils she works with and to me.

> I liked the contact with university-level students and the chance to talk to someone involved with recent maths developments.

9.6 How Can PAL Be Most Effective?

The author's current research project seeks to identify the key issues which distinguish successful classroom collaboration. The fieldwork for the research was completed in March 1995 and the findings will be reported in detail later in the year.

The abilities and attitudes of the class teacher are the most significant variable in the equation whatever the ideals of the overall project, whatever the policies and ethos of the school, whatever the knowledge and skills of the volunteer, whatever the subject, and whatever the ages and levels of achievement of the learners.

The way in which the teaching assistant is deployed depends on the class teacher's philosophy of teaching and learning. PAL assistants are usually flexible in response to this because they see themselves as amateurs. Compared to trainee teachers, these volunteers are much more likely to adapt to the class teacher's general classroom systems and manner of teaching and to follow the class teacher's general philosophy of teaching and learning. This is because they are visitors in the classroom, they do not have to prove that they can take full responsibility, and they know they do not have the professional skills and training. Trainee teachers know that ultimately, in their chosen profession, they have to be true to their own beliefs and personalities and they know that there are different styles of successful teaching. The most successful collaboration occurs when the class teachers make their aims and objectives explicit and when they engage the volunteers as partners, giving them a share in the responsibility for achieving the objectives.

The key factors contributing to successful outcomes of PAL include the following:

- the class teacher is a volunteer and not a conscript to the PAL programme;
- the class teacher knows the ideals and conditions of the scheme, knows the qualifications and expectations of the assistant, and aims to make full use of the assistant's skills;
- in planning the lessons, the class teacher sees PAL as a way of achieving his or her own educational objectives and of accomplishing ways of teaching which would be more difficult to achieve, or even impossible, without assistance;
- time is taken for the class teacher to tell the teaching assistant something about the needs of the learners, to explain aims and objectives and lesson plans, and for debriefing sessions from time to time;
- if time is not available to explain lesson plans, the assistant is given notes on what the learners are to do and what they are to be encouraged to think about;
- a list of key words can be helpful to the teaching assistant;
- the teaching assistant is introduced to the class, the learners are told a little about what he or she is studying and where, and his or her role in the classroom is explained;
- the teaching assistant is a volunteer, with specialist knowledge of the subject, who is reliable and committed to the ideals of the scheme;
- the teaching assistant has had suitable preparation and training, and in particular is aware of the importance of being a good listener;
- the teaching assistant is, on occasions, given specific responsibility for an activity with a group of learners, and is given feedback as to whether this contribution had been at the right level and whether the class teacher would have liked anything done differently;
- learners are encouraged to understand the value of developing their own communication skills;
- learners are helped to realise the advantage of being able to talk about the work they are doing to someone who has time to listen

119

and who will perhaps offer useful feedback. This encourages learners who are confident about their work (but perhaps shy or inarticulate) to benefit from contacts with the teaching assistant as well as those learners who want to ask for help because they know they are having problems;

- the roles in the classroom are defined to take account of the extra teachers available and these roles are clearly understood by all concerned;
- both class teacher and teaching assistant are keen to learn from each other, neither is anxious about the limitations of their own knowledge and both see learning as a worthwhile and interesting pursuit.

9.7 Conclusion

Seen in terms of cultural transmission or in terms of social construction, PAL schemes are educational instruments which have proven value. The aims may be to promote a set of values related to the advantages of education, to raise learner aspirations, to impart existing knowledge or to foster particular skills, or they may be to promote the public understanding and appreciation of the arts, or of science or some other discipline. Alternatively, the aims may be much more politically motivated with concomitant social objectives, such as to raise educational standards (without increased expenditure), to attract more graduates into the teaching profession, to help to produce more scientists and technologists to boost the national economy or to promote women in science or economics. All these objectives appear in some form in at least one of the case studies in this chapter, and gains in these respects are demonstrated. It is apparent that the enthusiasm shown for the benefits of peer assisted learning schemes is not unfounded, that research is needed to support the development of such schemes and that other teachers may well be able to have more success through employing PAL in their repertoire of teaching strategies.

Address for correspondence: Ms Toni Beardon, University of Cambridge, Department of Education, 17 Trumpington Street, Cambridge CB2 9QN.

Chapter 10

NEW DIRECTIONS IN STUDENT TUTORING: THE UK EXPERIENCE

John Potter

This chapter sets out the background to the recent 'explosion' of student tutoring in the UK, outlines the critical success factors that made it possible, and explores the nationwide support mechanism developed by CSV Learning Together to underpin and develop the programme. It shows how student tutoring has benefited all parties, and explores new directions of student tutoring in schools, colleges and universities and reviews the lessons for future partnership among key stake-holders in education.

I enjoyed sorting out my ideas and knowledge in order to communicate with others – student at Bath University (CSV Learning Together Bath Connection)

They are great, they are helpful and they are friendly – I liked working for them – pupil (CSV Learning Together Northern Ireland Connection)

I would recommend the tutoring scheme to other schools – link teacher, Monks Park School, Bristol (CSV Learning Together Bristol Connection).

10.1 Introduction

Following a 'controlled explosion' of student tutoring in the UK over the past five years, it is clear that tutoring is here to stay. Students from

121

universities and colleges volunteer to work alongside teachers for an afternoon a week over a period of at least ten weeks, helping pupils with their studies, raising their aspirations and encouraging them to go on to further and higher education.

Student tutoring is fast becoming an accepted and valued part of the education system in the UK. More than 180 institutions of higher and further education have now embarked on student tutoring throughout Britain. Over 15,000 students have volunteered around 600,000 hours to help children and young people with their studies under the supervision of teachers. The programme makes a major contribution to our nation's quest for raising standards, expectations and achievement in education.

The majority of tutoring schemes are free-standing, stimulated by conferences and supported by resource materials. Universities and colleges set up their own schemes with their local schools. However, student tutoring does not happen by accident: development, start-up grants, consultancy and hands-on support are needed to establish critical demonstration projects in key areas. Since 1992 Community Service Volunteers has, through CSV Learning Together, appointed a team of 11 student tutoring regional coordinators in England and Northern Ireland to stimulate, promote and support a network of new schemes across the country. BP, as part of the BP Aiming for a College Education (ACE) initiative, pioneered the early development of tutoring in the UK and now sponsors coordinators in Scotland and Wales as well as promoting student tutoring and mentoring internationally.

The value of student tutoring is well established and the rationale for promoting the initiative in the UK was put simply by Sir Brian Jenkins who, as Lord Mayor of London in 1992, was leading the CSV Learning Together Appeal for student tutoring in the UK:

I know, first, that tutoring offers a simple and proven mechanism for raising educational standards.

Second, I am confident that student tutoring offers fresh models of effective partnership between those who have an active interest in the quality of our education and training.

Thirdly, I believe that student tutoring offers a springboard for new and positive ventures in education that will equip our young people to be the kind of citizens that our society most needs if we are to survive and flourish as a nation.

In short: student tutoring benefits everyone involved. (Jenkins, 1992)

10.2 The Background to Student Tutoring in the UK

Student tutoring in its modern form was invented in the late eighteenth century by the British. It was first pioneered in 1789 by the British Army Chaplain Andrew Bell in his school in Madras. It was then taken up in England by Joseph Lancaster who was faced with 350 children to teach single-handedly at his Southwark school.

In our own century the movement was rediscovered in the 1960s in some developing countries and in inner-city North America. Work in the United States proved highly encouraging. By 1988 more than 63,000 college students, primarily volunteers, worked with nearly 200,000 school pupils. Clear benefits to tutors and students were reported.

The Pimlico connection

It was not until the mid-1970s that the initiative came back to Britain. Dr Alec Dickson, founder of CSV and VSO, had visited Portland, Oregon, in the late 1960s. He was greatly impressed. He saw young people tutoring each other, and then those who had been tutored themselves helped others. 'It worked like a cascade', he said. 'Everyone was encouraged to pass on something of what they had gained'. He then added, in his own inimitable fashion, 'And there was another thing I learnt: You don't have to be good to do good. Nor do you have to be clever. You just have to know a bit more than the person you are helping!' (Dickson, 1972:99–103).

A few years later these ideas were put into practice in Britain. The first scheme was launched in 1975 from Imperial College by Dr Sinclair Goodlad as a course project for 12 engineering students who tutored pupils in the local Pimlico school.

10.3 Critical Success Factors

An effective strategy for social or educational reform requires three things (Fullan, 1991). There has to be a clearly perceived need; there have to be people who are ready to do something about it; and there have to be the resources to take action.

A widely perceived need

The debates over education in Britain during the first two years of the decade focused on four widely perceived needs: (1) The need to ensure

123

that more young people stay in education after the age of 16. (2) The need to ensure that more support is put into all education and in particular into teaching maths, science and languages; (3) The need to ensure that we educate for capability as well as for knowledge and analytic skills; (4) the need to foster the motivation as well as the ability of students and pupils (Hughes, 1993:6ff).

People ready to do something about it

Over the past five years there have been increasing numbers of educators and other stakeholders who have not only seen the need but have been ready to do something about it. Student tutoring was seen as one practical response to a national challenge. By 1989, in response to the pioneering Pimlico Connection, there were five tutoring schemes in the UK. In the following year, BP in partnership with Imperial College appointed John Hughes as the BP Fellow in Student Tutoring and began a major piece of development work nationwide. The project aimed to run and expand the Pimlico Connection, promote the growth of similar schemes and to research student tutoring.

The resources to take action

Generating financial and other resources to promote student tutoring has been central to tutoring in the UK. In 1991 the then Lord Mayor of London, Sir Brian Jenkins, made CSV Learning Together the focus of his appeal. CSV, with the active support of BP, sought four additional principal partners from among major companies with a commitment to education. BT, National Power, NatWest Bank and Royal Mail each responded warmly and very positively to the invitation to join that small but crucial group of key players who would together set the pace for other sponsors. 'I am proud to say that by the end of October we have raised in total £1,626,203 from all sources', said Sir Brian Jenkins towards the conclusion of his appeal in 1992 (Jenkins, 1992).

The combination of these three circumstances enabled CSV Learning Together to foster the rapid growth and success of tutoring in the UK.

10.4 CSV Learning Together

CSV Learning Together established a small central team based at CSV's London headquarters. Regional coordinators were appointed in Belfast,

Birmingham, Bradford, Bristol, Manchester, Leeds, London (North, South East and South West), Sheffield and Swindon (linked to Reading and Bath). The NatWest Financial Literacy Project Manager joined the team at headquarters. The locations selected included a significant number of Britain's largest conurbations with a strong university and college presence. It was possible for each coordinator to take an active part in starting up projects, recruiting students and matching them into what often proved a complex web of local schools.

During the first two years, CSV Learning Together worked closely with the BP Tutoring Fellow in England and Ireland. Thereafter BP handed over that work to CSV Learning Together, maintained their presence in East London, Scotland and Wales, and went on to promote an international network of student tutoring.

Where appropriate, CSV Learning Together has involved its principal partners in local and regional launches of new schemes. This has given a high profile to student tutoring and the opportunity to recognise the achievements of all involved. Conferences have always played a key role in promoting tutoring, particularly among the institutions. Between them, CSV Learning Together and BP have promoted events in Bath, Cardiff, Dundee, Glasgow, London, Manchester and Sheffield. In addition, coordinators throughout the UK have made presentations to institution staff, teachers, students and other stakeholders in places where there is an active interest in starting student tutoring schemes.

Good quality materials have always been critical to disseminating good practice. At the start BP brought CSV Learning Together on board in supporting a quality resource pack along with a student tutoring brochure, flyers and poster, and together, BP and CSV with additional sponsorship from British Gas, produced a video for training student tutors. CSV Learning Together is now producing further material on financial literacy, steering groups, student induction, resource raising and other issues. CSV Learning Together also produces a full national annual report along with regional reports and a newsletter. We also produce and disseminate other materials such as stickers, posters, badges and certificates.

CSV Learning Together has distributed nearly 50 grants to institutions committed to setting up fresh projects. These have proved critical in encouraging pioneers to overcome some of the initial financial challenges posed by student tutoring. Increasingly, however, those involved in local schemes are finding their own resources locally (Potter & Daniel, 1994:1–2).

Research and evaluation

CSV Learning Together with funding from British Telecom called together a team of researchers based in the universities of Birmingham, Cambridge and Dundee to research and evaluate key aspects of student tutoring. The focus is on the extent to which tutoring improves pupils' aspirations and enriches student tutors' transferable skills and learning. The results of this research deliberately complement the ongoing evaluation programme that is part of every CSV Learning Together tutoring project. A full set of research papers on the CSV Learning Together/BT work will be published in November 1995 and papers on the preliminary findings constitute Chapters 11 and 13 of this book.

CSV Learning Together is now working towards implementing a quality assurance programme based on the European TQM framework. This will take time, but it is likely to provide stronger monitoring and evaluation of the work. It will assess the impact of the new directions that are emerging and will offer more sharply focused issues for further research.

10.5 General Lessons Learned

The benefits of student tutoring

From the start, the Pimlico Connection has recorded feedback from participants in the programme. New tutoring schemes adopted the evaluation model set out by the first project (Hughes, 1993:19ff). For 20 years, participants in the tutoring schemes have been asked to comment systematically on their experience. There can be no doubt about the benefits of the programme. Teachers found lessons more enjoyable, easier to handle and valued the additional learning opportunities open to pupils. The pupils valued the additional personal attention, found lessons more interesting and fun and gained from working with positive role models. The students' tutors also gained from the experience of tutoring. They appreciated the opportunity to do something useful, developed in confidence and communications skills and in a number of cases developed a stronger grasp of their own subjects through having to teach it to others. The schools valued the extra help and the new possibilities that this brought, and benefited from the links with higher and further education which also record benefits from their involvement in tutoring. The universities and colleges appreciated the additional links with schools and their local communitites and valued the opportunity for their students to develop transferable skills through tutoring. In an increasing number of cases, institutions began to look for ways in which to accredit students' experience of tutoring and so make it an option within mainstream course provision (Potter & Daniel, 1994).

The benefits of partnerships with industry and commerce

Industry and commerce also valued the opportunity to contribute to a high-profile initiative that makes a significant contribution to learning and student and pupil effectiveness and aspirations. Each commercial partner has, however, specific interests and needs, and it is vital that the programme's contribution reflects those interests. For example, NatWest provided a secondee to manage a special programme on financial literacy (Dinsdale, 1994); Royal Mail and National Power were interested in the career development opportunities offered by secondments; and British Telecom was interested in fostering both projects and research.

Education Business Partnerships offer ways for local employers to become involved in supporting tutoring. The Birmingham Education Business Partnership, for example, regards student tutoring as one important strategy within its portfolio of initiatives to raise standards in education through partnership with industry, schools and colleges (Gadsby, 1994:6).

10.6 New Directions in Schools

The general benefits of student tutoring are familiar to those who have participated in such a programme. There are, however, tougher lessons and it is these that point up the new directions for student tutoring. They concern both strategy and tactics at every level and they also produce fruitful lines of further inquiry about the benefits of tutoring as an educational initiative.

Raising aspirations

It is not enough to invite participants to comment on the general benefits of student tutoring. For example, it is hard to show concrete evidence that tutoring on its own makes a significant difference to pupils' aspirations. Much depends on two factors: (i) the saliency of the role model – successful and highly intelligent middle-class undergraduates do not necessarily encourage young people from an educationally deprived inner-city housing estate to aspire to higher education, and (ii) the extent to which a school offers a coherent range of opportunities for its pupils to think seriously about further and higher education. This confirms research in New Zealand by Jones (1989:34). The obvious question is, 'How many of the changes in vocational/educational attitudes which did occur, can be attributed to the presence of university tutors? In an unequivocal sense, the answer has to be "Not many"', writes Jones. He then adds that the potential for student tutoring raising aspirations is perhaps 'best seen as an element of a more comprehensive programme'. This conclusion, though salutary, is hardly surprising in the light of the fact that student tutoring is usually for only ten or twelve weeks and is only one among many experiences aimed at helping pupils think positively about their future.

The value of student tutoring has to be seen in the wider context of the work of the individual teacher and the strategic approach that a school takes to encouraging an appetite for continuing learning. This raises critical questions about how individual teachers and whole-school policy make the most of student tutors. It is a question of both strategy and teaching styles. Tutoring schemes that are simply bolted on to existing practice rarely prove an effective tool for promoting learning and personal development (Campbell, 1995).

Making the best use of tutors

The most effective schemes in schools are those that set out to make the most imaginative and systematic use of the students' skills. Architecture students at the University of Central England have been working as consultants on environment projects in 20 local schools. The emphasis was on enabling school pupils to grasp the design process and to apply it to practical projects in their school and local community.

The financial literacy project, supported by Natwest Bank, was a similarly focused initiative that capitalised on the needs of young people in school and the opportunities for students from higher education to be actively involved in developing the project. NatWest describe financial literacy as the ability to understand money and to appreciate the value of proper financial management; not just being financially numerate but being completely comfortable with the prospect of handling finances. Good financial discipline is not a skill young people inherit: it has to be learnt. The scheme was phased over three years and was developed through seven pilot projects linked with selected universities throughout the country. The results in the form of case studies and relevant support materials have been published (Dinsdale, 1994).

Some schools take very few tutors and make poor use of those they have. Induction and support materials for teachers are important, as is the opportunity for teachers to enjoy in-service training. Teachers have often found it difficult to attend out-of-school seminars and conferences. CSV Learning Together is, therefore, now paying increasing attention to ways in which in-service training can be conducted by teachers in their own schools. In Leeds, for example, a group teachers were brought together to produce in-service training materials that can be used flexibly by teachers in their own schools (Pride & Slater-Simmons, 1995).

In some places reading support has been approached systematically with the use of tutors. The Kick Start programme in Manchester is one example. The University of Newcastle is pioneering a major programme on reading support which will lend itself to the use of tutors and other adults offering learning support in schools. The BP Science across the World project can involve tutors in imaginative ways. All these initiatives are based on the premise that student tutors are most effectively used within a clearly developed framework that is designed to offer focused learning opportunities on clearly identified themes.

In Cambridge, Toni Beardon has been researching the relative impact of using one or several tutors in the classroom in comparison with lessons where the same teacher takes the same lesson but without the benefit of tutors. (This research will be published in November 1995.)

Peer tutoring: the new model

The use to which student tutors are put in schools depends on the vision of peer education. Dr Alec Dickson, CSV's founder, always saw tutoring as a cascade under the banner 'Each one, teach one'. In some places, such as Glasgow, Rotherham and Birmingham, students are cascading tutoring from university to further education and from FE into schools. Audrey Gartner and Frank Riessman (Gartner & Riessman, 1993) in New York have pointed out that there are two distinct models of what peer tutoring is about. The new vision of tutoring,

> puts the tutor at the centre; it aims for significant academic improvement; and it is cost effective because both tutors and tutees benefit. Building on research that stresses learning through teaching, the new vision seeks to universalise the tutor role, enabling all students to tutor. For example, all sixth graders in a school tutor all second graders who tutor all students in kindergarten.

Gradually, tutoring in the UK is moving towards the newer and more radical vision.

10.7 New Directions in Universities and Colleges

Universities and colleges are increasingly aware of the benefits of student tutoring and there is a growing trend among institutions to support tutoring by making it a part of their mainstream provision for students. At London University, for example, medical students and speech therapy students are involved in tutoring as their future careers will involve work with children. Scientists and engineers are often encouraged to opt for tutoring to enable them to develop good communications skills with people who are neither professional scientists nor engineers.

Tutoring in this context is increasingly accredited through reflective diaries, reports and presentations, along with brief feedback from teachers. The advantage of this approach is that tutoring becomes integrated within course options and its organisation can be financed through departmental budgets. The disadvantage can be that tutoring is felt by some students to loose its voluntary, altruistic flavour. The ideal situation is one where voluntary tutoring is managed through the Student Union and accredited options are offered through course work. In many cases university enterprise units have taken on responsibility for promoting tutoring, but in most cases the funding for enterprise developments is likely to run out in the next year or two.

There is extensive evidence that tutors find the tutoring experience both valuable and enjoyable. More recent research (Hill & Topping, 1995) on cognitive gains and transferable skills has, as in schools, sharpened the questions. There are positive cognitive gains for student tutors and these include a growing awareness of the gaps in their subject knowledge. Among transferable skills, oral communication, leading others in group situations and improvising, innovating and being creative, are all areas where student tutors show specific gains after their tutoring experience.

One further relevant factor is clear from the national survey of tutoring. The majority of students involved in tutoring are female (70%) and the great majority are white Anglo-Saxons. This raises the need for a growing emphasis on involving male students and ethnic minorities. The Black Engineers project in North London illustrates one way in which more attention can be given to black students as role models for young people in schools.

Managing tutoring in institutions

Experience has further shown that universities and colleges vary considerably in their formal support for tutoring. The aim is to encourage all institutions to accept responsibility for recruiting, inducting and supporting their student tutors. In some places there are inventive solutions to the issue of coordination. At Aston University, for example, managerial and administrative studies student Cathy Gill has taken on the daunting task of organising the university's student tutoring programme as a part of her sandwich course placement. For this she enjoys a modest honorarium. Cathy says, 'I have been given a worthwhile job which allows me to prove my ability. It is definitely a valuable experience'. Others may follow the Aston lead.

10.8 New Directions: Regional and Local Development

Until now CSV Learning Together has provided hands-on support through coordinators in a number of the major metropolitan areas, and has consistently sought to embed tutoring schemes in the local institutions. In future, the role of coordinators will become increasingly regional rather than local and may well move towards becoming part-time. The new directions will be on the dissemination of good practice through seminars, conferences, in-service training and publications. This will demand prioritising needs. In schools we shall increasingly be looking for examples of the new model, and in universities and colleges at those who embed tutoring as an ongoing part of the learning environment.

The value of a regional approach has nowhere been better demonstrated than in Northern Ireland. Initially when CSV Learning Together was launched, the intention was to work mainly in the university campus areas of Belfast, Newtown Abbey, Londonderry and Coleraine. However, due to the demand from schools in rural areas and from students wanting to go to schools in their home area, student tutoring has spread its tentacles to all areas of the province. Many student tutors offer help to pupils in their home villages and towns as well as in the main centres of academic life. A development of this kind requires central encouragement, coordination and support. Once the network is established it may prove possible to develop a more local network of honorary coordinators to assist in ensuring that this complex programme runs smoothly and effectively. The essence of the approach is that the local community must be enabled to feel that tutoring belongs to them.

10.9 New Directions: Strategic Partnerships

Embedding has to happen at a national and regional level as well as in schools and institutions. CSV Learning Together has been fortunate in enjoying the help of a highly competent team of secondees from National Power, Royal Mail, the Halifax Building Society and Natwest Bank along with the help of BP in North London. Secondees, however, are only effective if they can be in post for a reasonable time. In most cases our seconded staff have been offered placements for 18 months to two years.

One of the most effective arrangements has been with the Birmingham Education Business Partnership, whereby an experienced ex-headteacher has been forging links between schools and higher education and has had, as a key part of his brief, the development of student tutoring. This approach has a number of major advantages: it has enabled someone with wide experience of education and the local situation to promote complex relationships in the context of an ongoing relationship with local business and the City Education Authority. BT's tapered financing of the project has provided the critical resources for CSV Learning Together's involvement. The results have been rewarding and have been seen as a part of the Birmingham Education Business Partnership's contribution to the National Education and Training Targets. Such arrangements are well placed to access regional government and business funding through the Single Regeneration Budget.

CSV Learning Together is seeking similar partnerships where possible in other regions and has, for example, established good working relationships with Education Business Partnerships in Merseyside and Manchester.

Quality support for student tutoring needs to happen at the regional level within a national framework, but the long-term funding of development staff has to be built into regional commitments to education and learning.

10.10 Summary of New Directions

1. Quality and effectiveness in the classroom are critical to the success of the programme.
2. Initiatives that match imaginatively the specific needs of schools with those of student tutors are likely to be the most fruitful in the long term. This demands a continuing emphasis on quality development work.

3. Teachers need encouragement and support to make the most effective use of their student tutors. It is not enough to think of them as just another potentially useful pair of hands.
4. The new model of tutoring offers a coherent and radical vision for the future of tutoring based on a learning cascade: 'Each one, teach one'.
5. Institutions must embed tutoring schemes as part of mainstream learning and continue to offer, in parallel, voluntary opportunities for tutoring.
6. Regional coordination to disseminate best practice remains crucial to a programme that still requires stimulus, direction and support.
7. Implementing a quality assurance framework will help to assess the impact of student tutoring at all levels.
8. Regional and national partnerships need to be embedded in the context of strategic education and training initiatives such as Education Business Partnerships.

Address for correspondence: John Potter, Education Manager, Community Service Volunteers, 237 Pentonville Road, London N1 9NJ. Tel. 0171 278 6601. Fax 0171 837 9621.

Chapter 11

COGNITIVE AND TRANSFERABLE SKILL GAINS FOR STUDENT TUTORS

Shirley Hill and Keith Topping

Students involved in student tutoring schemes in England and Northern Ireland completed a questionnaire before they started tutoring and at the end of their school tutoring experience. Both the pre- and the post- questionnaires asked to what extent they believed they had developed a range of cognitive abilities and transferable skills. In addition, the post-questionnaire asked whether they believed they had enhanced each ability and skill as a result of tutoring. Information on the demographic characteristics of the student tutors and the organisational structure of their school tutoring placements was also collected. Analysis revealed several significant differences between the student tutors' pre- and post- ratings, and several abilities and skills that the majority of students believed had been enhanced. Given that professional 'transferable' skills in communication, interpersonal interaction and organisation are increasingly in demand by employers, the results of this study have implications for the role of student tutoring in enhancing such skills.

11.1 Introduction

In the UK, 'student tutoring' refers to a specific method of teaching and learning where students from further education (FE) and higher education (HE) establishments tutor pupils in primary (elementary) or secondary (high) schools under the supervision of the classroom teacher. The vast majority of student tutors in the UK are volunteers and typically tutor for one morning or afternoon a week for ten or more consecutive weeks.

Students from universities and colleges act as tutors for school children in other ways in other countries. A typology of such activities and a review of relevant evaluation literature can be found in Topping & Hill (1995).

The first student tutoring scheme in the UK, The Pimlico Connection (Goodlad *et al.*, 1979), was introduced in 1975 and involved students from Imperial College London who tutored pupils at Pimlico Comprehensive School. Since then, student tutoring has spread rapidly throughout the UK, with the majority of schemes in England and Northern Ireland coordinated by the Community Service Volunteers (CSV) agency through its Learning Together student tutoring programme.

Since its inception in 1992, the Learning Together programme has established more than 170 schemes involving over 10,000 students (CSV, 1994a). Many student tutoring schemes have also been established and supported by British Petroleum as part of its 'Aiming for a College Education' initiative.

One rationale for student tutoring is to raise school pupils' aspirations and motivation to continue their education at a higher level through the positive role model provided by the student tutors. In addition, the student tutors can make cognitive gains in relation to the tutored subject, such as developing their understanding of and confidence in the subject by applying their knowledge in practical contexts. Student tutoring also gives them the opportunity to develop many of the professional 'transferable' skills increasingly in demand by employers, such as communication, interpersonal and organisational skills.

This chapter reviews the results of a pre-tutoring and post-tutoring questionnaire study of further and higher education students involved in CSV student tutoring schemes in England and Northern Ireland. The study aimed to establish whether student tutoring enhanced cognitive abilities in relation to the tutored subject and which transferable skills, if any, could also be enhanced.

11.2 Method

Development of questionnaires

An extensive search was made of relevant literature sources (School of Computing and Information Studies, 1990; Personal Skills Unit, 1993), to produce a comprehensive list of cognitive abilities and transferable skills. This list was then refined through consultation with students from Dundee University who had recently participated in a student tutoring programme, to form a list of cognitive abilities and transferable skills most relevant to tutoring.

A draft pre-tutoring questionnaire was then developed and piloted with the Dundee students, whose suggestions for changes were incorporated. A revised version of this questionnaire was subsequently distributed for comment by CSV regional and national coordinators. A final version was agreed and distributed to the 11 CSV regions nationwide in time for completion by the student tutors at their pre-tutoring training sessions before they commenced any tutoring.

The post-tutoring questionnaire was subjected to similar consultation with CSV coordinators. Once a final version had been agreed, this was distributed to the 11 CSV regions with the aim of completion at the students' post-tutoring feedback sessions.

Content of questionnaires

The final versions of both the pre- and post-tutoring questionnaires were divided into three parts. The first part of the pre- questionnaire asked the student tutors to provide personal and demographic details. The first part of the post- questionnaire asked the students to provide organisational details of their school tutoring placements.

The second part of both questionnaires asked the students to estimate the extent to which they believed they had developed the ten cognitive or 'intellectual' abilities listed below in relation to the subject they expected to be tutoring (pre-), or the subject they had tutored (post-). They were asked to rate the extent of their development as 'not at all', 'a little', 'some', or 'a lot', for each cognitive ability separately. For the pre-questionnaire, students were asked to complete this section only if they already knew which subject they were going to tutor. The ten cognitive abilities were:

- recall of subject
- understanding of subject
- accuracy with subject

■ speed and fluency with subject
■ awareness of gaps in knowledge of subject
■ confidence in knowledge of subject
■ understanding how others learn subject
■ communication of the subject facts and principles
■ practical demonstration of subject skills
■ application of subject knowledge in new situations.

The third part of both questionnaires asked the students to estimate the extent to which they believed they had developed the 11 transferable skills listed below. Again, they were asked to rate their development as 'not at all', 'a little', 'some', or 'a lot', for each transferable skill separately. All students were asked to complete this section. The 11 transferable skills were:

■ selecting, retrieving, organising and summarising information
■ managing workload, priorities and time allocation
■ communicating information/ideas orally
■ listening, questioning and clarifying effectively
■ communicating information/ideas in writing
■ collaborating with others in a group situation
■ leading others in a group situation
■ identifying problems
■ planning actions and identifying problem solutions
■ improvising, innovating and being flexibly creative
■ evaluating and interpreting results and outcomes.

In addition, the post- questionnaire asked if tutoring had enhanced any of the cognitive abilities and transferable skills, providing an indication of a positive tutoring effect, if any, for each ability and skill.

The students were not required to provide their name for either questionnaire and were reassured that all information supplied would remain confidential. They were asked to give their date of birth only for the purposes of matching pre- and post-tutoring questionnaires from the same individuals.

Processing of questionnaires

Pre- questionnaire returns were manually coded for region and institution of origin. They were then checked for duplicate date of birth identifier codes. Questionnaires originating from each institution that had duplicate dates of birth were further identified by gender, if this was possible, and then by subjects studied/tutored, where these had been specified. In this way, all pre- questionnaires were uniquely identified to enable cross-matching with post- questionnaires from the same individuals. They were then processed by an optical mark reader.

Returns of the post- questionnaire from each institution were cross-matched by date of birth with pre- questionnaire returns originating from the same institution to identify pre- and post- questionnaires completed by the same tutor. All returns for the post- questionnaire, both matching and non-matching, were then manually coded and processed in the same way as the pre- questionnaire.

11.3 Results

Distribution and return figures

Distribution and return figures for both questionnaires are given in Table 11.1. In total, 910 students completed the pre-tutoring questionnaire, 853 students completed the post-tutoring questionnaire, and of these, 358 completed both the pre- and the post- questionnaire (26% of all students responding to either questionnaire). The difference in the return rates of the pre- and post- questionnaires reflects the fact that the pre- questionnaires were completed during the pre-tutoring training sessions which were very well attended, whereas the post- questionnaires were either completed at post-tutoring feedback sessions which were less well attended, or were sent out to student tutors for postal return.

Table 11.1 Distribution and return figures for both questionnaires by region

REGION	PRE-		POST-	
	Distributed	Returned	Distributed	Returned
Bath	107	47	104	86
Birmingham	249	245	193	131
Bradford	43	43	109	56
Bristol	110	51	0	0
Leeds	0	0	153	38
London North	0	0	100	89
London South East	82	67	108	44
London South West	148	137	140	66
Manchester	153	110	150	71
Northern Ireland	88	88	400	229
Sheffield	122	122	102	43
Total	1102	910	1559	853
RETURN RATE	83%		55%	

Table 11.2 Tutor gender (total responding = 839/853)

GENDER	N	%
Male	253	30.2
Female	586	69.8

Demographic results

Table 11.2, taken from the post-tutoring questionnaire data, confirms the tutor gender distribution obtained from the pre-tutoring questionnaire and reflects the overall trend of a predominantly female student tutor population apparent from the latest regional reports in the 1993–94 annual review of the CSV Learning Together student tutoring programme (CSV, 1994a).

Tables 11.3 and 11.4 show that the vast majority of student tutors in the sample were white and were from upper- or middle-class backgrounds.

Other demographic results for student tutors in the sample included:

- 78% within the age range 18–23 (16–17: 7%; 24–35: 12%; over 35: 3%)
- 86% studying at university (HE college: 5%; FE college: 9%)

Table 11.3 Ethnic background (total responding = 904/910)

ETHNIC BACKGROUND	N	%
White	758	83.8
Afro-Caribbean	24	2.7
South Asian	63	7.0
Oriental	24	2.7
Other	35	3.9

Table 11.4 Parental occupation (total responding = 887/910

PARENTAL OCCUPATION	N	%
Professional	431	48.6
Semi-professional	162	18.3
Skilled non-manual	81	9.1
Skilled manual	146	16.5
Partly skilled	47	5.3
Unskilled	20	2.3

■ 50% in their second year of study (first year: 20%; third year: 22%; fourth year: 6%; other: 2%).

Organisational results

Table 11. 5 shows that the vast majority of students in the sample tutored in either a primary or secondary school and were evenly distributed between these two types of school. Other organisational results for students in the sample included:

■ 75% tutored for between five and 12 weeks (less: 9%; more: 16%)
■ 95% tutored once a week (less: 1%; more: 4%)
■ 55% tutored for two to three hours each session (less: 22%; more: 23%)
■ 57% had studied/tutored the subject at university/college (secondary school only: 25%; not at all: 18%).

The post-tutoring questionnaire also asked for the nature of the students' interest in teaching as a possible future career; 72% reported that they had become more interested in teaching as a result of their tutoring experience.

Table 11.5 School type (total responding = 852/853)

SCHOOL TYPE	N	%
Primary (elementary)	394	46.2
Secondary (high)	384	45.1
Special	42	4.9
Further education college	30	3.5
Nursery (pre-school/kindergarten)	2	0.2

Cognitive and transferable skill ratings – matched pre- and post- results

A comparison was made between the ratings given pre- and post-tutoring for each cognitive ability and transferable skill for the 358 students who completed both questionnaires. The number of pairs of cognitive ability ratings which were included in these analyses was 128. This was a consequence of the fact that many students had not completed the section on cognitive ability development on the pre-tutoring questionnaire (they had been asked to complete this section only if they already knew which subject they were going to tutor).

In addition, the post- questionnaire asked students if they had eventually tutored the subject they had expected to tutor when they completed the pre- questionnaire. Of the possible 180 students in the matched cognitive ability ratings analyses, only 128 responded that they did tutor the subject they had expected to tutor. It was therefore assumed that only these 128 students completed both the pre- and the post-questionnaire section on cognitive ability development with reference to the same tutored subject.

A Wilcoxon Matched Pairs Test was conducted for each of the ten cognitive abilities and 11 transferable skills. Several significant differences emerged which are presented in Tables 11.6 and 11.7. Table 11.6 shows significant differences between the students' pre- and post-ratings of their development in six cognitive abilities. For five of these, 'Accuracy with subject', 'Speed and fluency with subject', 'Confidence in knowledge of subject', 'Understanding how others learn subject', and 'Communication of subject facts', the students rated the extent of their development higher post-tutoring (Post> results). 'Awareness of gaps in knowledge of subject' was rated lower post-tutoring by a significant number of students (Post< result), as might be expected.

Table 11.7 shows significant differences between the students' pre- and post- ratings of their development in eight transferable skills. For three of these, 'Communicating orally', 'Leading others in a group situation', and 'Improvising, innovating and being creative', the students rated the extent of their development higher post-tutoring (Post> results). 'Selecting, retrieving information', 'Managing workload, priorities and time',

Table 11.6 Cognitive ability ratings – significant differences (two-tailed probability levels; n = 128 pairs)

COGNITIVE ABILITY	RATINGS			α	direction
(in relation to subject tutored)	% POST higher	% POST lower	% TIED		
Accuracy with subject	34	14	52	$p < 0.02$	Post >
Speed and fluency with subject	24	10	66	$p < 0.05$	Post >
Confidence in knowledge of subject	33	12	55	$p < 0.01$	Post >
Understanding how others learn subject	42	9	49	$p < 0.0001$	Post >
Communication of subject facts	30	12	58	$p < 0.005$	Post >
Awareness of subject facts	16	32	52	$p < 0.002$	Post <

'Communicating in writing', 'Collaborating with others in a group situation', and 'Evaluating and interpreting results', were rated lower post-tutoring by a significant number of students (Post< results). An additional measure of the effect of tutoring is provided by the 'Tutoring effect' results.

Tutoring effect results

The post-tutoring questionnaire contained an additional question for each cognitive ability and transferable skill which asked the students to indicate if they believed they had enhanced that ability or skill as a result of tutoring. All students who completed this questionnaire (853) were included in the tutoring effect analysis.

Figures 11.1 and 11.2 show the percentage of responding students who gave a 'Yes' response to the enhanced tutoring effect question for each ability and skill. (For enhancement in cognitive abilities, 6% of students gave no response of any sort. For enhancement in transferable skills, 1% of students gave no response of any sort.)

Figures 11.1 and 11.2 clearly show that the majority of students felt that tutoring had enhanced their:

Table 11.7 Transferable skill ratings – significant differences (two-tailed probability levels; n = 349 pairs)

TRANSFERABLE SKILL	RATINGS			α	direction
	% POST higher	% POST lower	% TIED		
Communicating orally	42	12	46	p < 0.0001	Post >
Leading others in a group situation	44	18	38	p < 0.0001	Post >
Improvising, innovating and being creative	39	21	40	p < 0.0005	Post >
Selecting, retrieving information	13	49	38	p < 0.0001	Post <
Managing workload, priorities and time	14	48	38	p < 0.0001	Post <
Communicating in writing	15	47	38	p < 0.0001	Post <
Collaborating with others in a group situation	25	34	41	p < 0.01	Post <
Evaluating and interpreting results	21	41	38	p < 0.0001	Post <

143

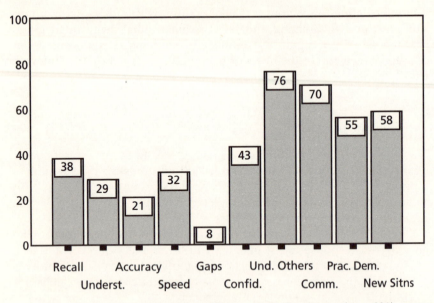

Figure 11.1 Enhanced cognitive abilities – % 'Yes' responses (n = 801)

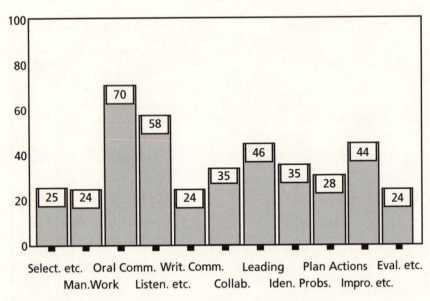

Figure 11.2 Enhanced transferable skills – % 'Yes' responses (n = 846)

- understanding of how others learn the tutored subject
- communication of the subject's facts and principles
- practical demonstration abilities
- application of their knowledge in a new situation
- oral communication skills
- listening, questioning and clarifying skills.

A minority of students reported enhancement in the other cognitive ability and transferable skill areas.

Distribution of tutoring effect responses

Figures 11.3 and 11.4 show the number of students who indicated a positive tutoring effect for different numbers of cognitive abilities and transferable skills. These distributions show that the overall tutoring enhancement results depicted in Figures 11.1 and 11.2 were not due to a small number of respondents reporting many enhancements. The average respondent reported four enhanced abilities or skills (mean number of cognitive abilities selected = 4.26, sd 2.70; mean number of transferable skills selected = 4.14, sd 3.04).

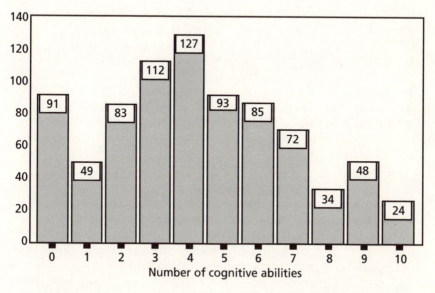

Figure 11.3 Enhanced cognitive abilities – number of students responding 'Yes'

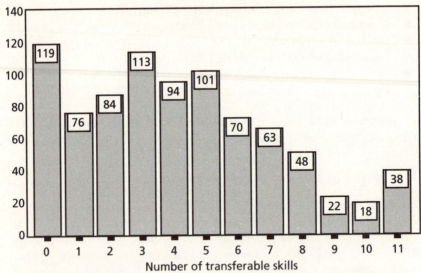

Figure 11.4 Enhanced transferable skills – number of students responding 'Yes'

Factors related to tutoring effect

Analyses were conducted on the tutoring enhancement outcome data to investigate any differences in response on the basis of the following four parameters:

- return rate   (high v. low post-questionnaire return by region)
- gender   (male v. female)
- school type   (nursery + primary v. secondary + FE)
- tutoring duration (one term or less v. more than one term).

Return rate

A comparison was made between the tutoring effect responses of students from regions with a high return rate (more than 65% of post-questionnaires returned, three regions, 306 students) and responses of students from regions with a low return rate (less than 45% of post-questionnaires returned, three regions, 125 students).

Separate chi square analyses were conducted for each cognitive ability and transferable skill. Significant differences between the 'high' and 'low' students' responses emerged for only two out of the possible 21 areas (the ten cognitive abilities and 11 transferable skills):

- application of knowledge in a new situation $(\chi^2 = 6.254$, (df = 1), $p < 0.02$; low > high)
- planning actions and identifying solutions $(\chi^2 = 4.208$, (df = 1), $p < 0.05$; low > high)

For these two, students from 'low' responding regions indicated a positive tutoring effect more often than those from 'high' responding regions.

Correlational analyses (Spearman) were also conducted to investigate the relationship between regional return rate and tutoring effect response for students from every region. Significant positive correlations were found for only three out of the possible 21 areas:

- practical demonstration of subject skills $(\chi^2 = 0.080, p < 0.05)$
- application of knowledge in a new situation $(\chi^2 = 0.095, p < 0.01)$
- planning actions and identifying solutions $(\chi^2 = 0.082, p < 0.02)$

However, the lack of significant differences or correlations for the many other abilities or skills suggests that variations in return rate were not a major factor in the tutoring enhancement outcomes depicted in Figures 11.1 and 11.2.

Gender

A comparison was made between the tutoring effect responses of male and female students (242 males, 31%; 546 females, 69%). Separate chi square analyses were conducted for each cognitive ability and transferable skill. Significant differences between the male and female students' responses emerged for only four out of the possible 21 areas:

- awareness of gaps in knowledge of subject $(\chi^2 = 6.070$, (df = 1), $p < 0.02$; males > females)
- application of knowledge in new situations $(\chi^2 = 4.602$, (df = 1), $p < 0.05$; females > males)
- managing workload, priorities and time $(\chi^2 = 5.371$, (df = 1), $p < 0.05$; females > males)
- leading others in a group situation $(\chi^2 = 10.341$, (df = 1), $p < 0.005$; females > males)

For three of these, 'Application of knowledge in new situations', 'Managing workload, priorities and time', and 'Leading others in a group situation', female students indicated a positive tutoring effect more often than males. However, for 'Awareness of gaps in knowledge of subject', male students indicated a positive tutoring effect more often than females.

School type

A comparison was made between the tutoring effect responses of students who tutored in a nursery (N) or primary school (P), and students who tutored in a secondary school (S) or further education college (FE) (396 N/P students, 46%; 414 S/FE students, 49%). Separate chi square analyses were conducted for each cognitive ability and transferable skill. Significant differences between the N/P and the S/FE students' responses emerged for five out of the possible 21 areas:

- recall of subject $(\chi^2 = 4.034, (df = 1), p < 0.05;$ S/FE > N/P)
- understanding of subject $(\chi^2 = 7.509, (df = 1), p < 0.01;$ S/FE > N/P)
- accuracy with subject $(\chi^2 = 5.688, (df = 1), p < 0.02;$ S/FE > N/P)
- managing workload, priorities and time $(\chi^2 = 4.125, (df = 1), p < 0.05;$ N/P > S/FE)
- improvising, innovating and being creative $(\chi^2 = 8.231, (df = 1), p < 0.005;$ N/P > S/FE)

For three cognitive abilities, 'Recall of subject', 'Understanding of subject', and 'Accuracy with subject', S/FE students indicated a positive tutoring effect more often than N/P students. However, for two transferable skills, 'Managing workload, priorities and time' and 'Improvising, innovating and being creative', N/P students indicated a positive tutoring effect more often than S/FE students.

Tutoring duration

A comparison was made between the tutoring effect responses of students who tutored for one term or less (up to eight weeks, '1 term'), and those who tutored for more than one term (more than eight weeks, '1+ terms') (382 '1 term' students, 45%; 460 '1+ terms' students, 55%). Separate chi square analyses were conducted for each cognitive ability and transferable skill. Significant differences between the '1 term' and the '1+ terms' students' responses emerged for three out of the possible 21 areas:

- understanding how others learn subject   (χ^2 = 4.211, (df = 1), p < 0.05; 1+ terms > 1 term)
- practical demonstration of subject skills   (χ^2 = 5.487, (df = 1), p < 0.02; 1+ terms > 1 term)
- listening, questioning and clarifying   (χ^2 = 4.025, (df = 1), p < 0.05; 1+ terms > 1 term)

For all three of these, students who tutored for more than one term indicated a positive tutoring effect more often than those who tutored for one term or less.

(Note that for all analyses of group comparisons described above, significant differences between the groups on their positive tutoring effect responses did not necessarily imply that the majority of students within the more positive group actually indicated a positive effect.)

Gender by school analysis

A chi square analysis was conducted to investigate differences in the type of school in which male and female students had tutored:

Nursery or primary school: 104 male students (41%); 284 female students (49%)

Secondary school or FE college: 143 male students (57%); 265 female students (45%).

The result of this analysis confirmed that significantly more females than males had tutored in a nursery or primary school (χ^2 = 6.317, (df = 1), p < 0.02). (Note that 5 males, 2%, and 37 females, 6%, tutored in a special school but were not included in this analysis.)

Tutoring duration by school analysis

A chi square analysis was conducted to investigate differences in the type of school in which '1 term' and '1+ terms' students had tutored:

Nursery or primary school: 173 '1 term' students (45%); 216 '1+ terms' students (47%)

Secondary school or FE college: 186 '1 term' students (49%); 224 '1+ terms' students (49%).

The result of this analysis confirmed that there was no significant difference in the type of school in which '1 term' and '1+ terms' students had tutored (χ^2 = 0.064, (df = 1), ns). (Note that 23 '1 term' students, 6%, and 19 '1+ terms' students, 4%, tutored in a special school but were not included in this analysis.)

11.4 Summary of Results

The typical student tutor in this study was a female, white, middle-class, second-year university student aged 18–23, who tutored for two to three hours, once a week, for 5–12 weeks. This tutoring was equally likely to have taken place in a primary or a secondary school, and only 57% was likely to have been in the subject the tutor was currently studying. After tutoring, a substantial majority of students (72%) became more interested in teaching as a possible future career.

On pre–post matched self-ratings of cognitive ability and transferable skill development, six out of ten cognitive abilities were rated significantly improved during tutoring (n = 128). Three out of 11 transferable skills were rated significantly improved, but five out of 11 rated significantly declined (n = 349).

On post-only self-ratings of enhancement due to tutoring (n = 801), four out of ten cognitive abilities were reported enhanced by a majority of students (understanding of others' learning, communication of facts, practical demonstration, applying knowledge in new situations), and all other cognitive abilities were reported enhanced by some students. Two out of 11 transferable skills were reported enhanced by a majority of students (oral communication, listening and questioning), and all other transferable skills were reported enhanced by some. Various numbers of enhancements were reported by different students.

Differences in return rates for the post- questionnaire appeared to affect tutoring enhancement outcomes very little. Of 21 possible differences between male and female students, only four were significant, with females responding more positively. Tutoring in primary schools was associated to a degree with greater enhancement in transferable skills, while tutoring in secondary schools was associated with greater enhancement in cognitive abilities. Females were more likely than males to tutor in primary schools. Finally, longer duration of tutoring was associated with enhanced effects in three out of the possible 21 areas.

11.5 Discussion

The demographic information obtained from the pre-tutoring questionnaire revealed that the sample of students in this study were predominantly white and from upper- or middle-class backgrounds. This may simply reflect the distribution of ethnic and socio-economic backgrounds in the student population in general or it may be indicative of the nature of the student population volunteering for student tutoring.

Given that one role of student tutors is to encourage school children to pursue their education at a higher level, whether that be at university or college (of an academic or vocational nature), then the degree to which such students provide a proximate and credible 'role model' for children of ethnic minority descent or those from less advantaged backgrounds is questionable.

An examination of the distribution of ethnic background and socio-economic status within the UK and specifically within the student population is still to be undertaken, but if the figures obtained from this survey are not reflective of these general distributions then they may have implications for the future recruitment of student tutors.

Another point to consider here is the relevance of the tutor's role in raising school children's aspirations for further and higher education when the student is tutoring in a primary school (almost 50% of the students in this study tutored in a primary or nursery school). It is unlikely that children of primary school age (5–11 years old) will have considered or be interested in thinking about 'life after school'.

Preliminary findings from an additional study of student tutoring currently ongoing at the Centre for Paired Learning suggest that, not only is it unlikely that children of this age will have considered post-school education or indeed have much understanding of the concept, but that the opportunity for tutors to discuss such a topic rarely arises in a primary school setting (the extent to which such opportunities arise in a secondary school setting also appears to be variable).

Several significant differences on the matched pre–post cognitive ability and transferable skill ratings emerged in the expected direction, ie, extent of ability or skill rated higher post-tutoring (see 'Post>' results). However, the actual significance of these results is debatable. A large percentage of paired ratings were tied, ie, the students had given the same rating for that ability or skill both pre- and post-tutoring. The Wilcoxon Matched Pairs Test does not correct for these sort of ties, excluding any tied paired values from the analysis.

In addition, it is possible that some tutors may have over- or under-rated their development in these abilities and skills pre-tutoring and that tutoring may simply have made them more aware of, and perhaps more realistic about, their actual level of development in these areas. This may account for the curious pre–post phenomenon of some transferable skills appearing to decline. The restricted nature of the response scale may also have contributed to this.

However, an additional measure of any gains from tutoring was provided by the tutoring effect results. The majority of students believed they had enhanced several abilities and skills as a result of tutoring. This positive tutoring effect was spread across and arose from the entire sample of students and was not a product of a very positive minority.

One consideration here is the extent to which the students were able to choose and were eventually placed in a school type (primary, secondary, etc) of their choice. If students were placed in the type of school for which they had expressed a preference, then they were possibly more likely to have had a positive attitude towards the school and to what they had gained from the experience.

Although this study did not ask students whether they were placed in a school of their choosing, consultation with CSV coordinators confirmed that individual institutions made every attempt to accommodate both student preferences and school needs and wishes. Thus it can be assumed that the majority of students in this sample were placed in the type of school they preferred, if indeed they had expressed such a preference.

Although the sample of students in this study was predominantly female, the tutoring effect analyses revealed very few significant differences between male and female responses. In addition, significantly more females than males tutored in a primary school, and this may account for the few significant differences which emerged between the genders. Certainly 'Managing workload, priorities and time', which females indicated was enhanced significantly more often than males, was one skill which students in nursery or primary schools felt was enhanced significantly more than students in secondary schools or FE colleges.

The 'School type' tutoring effect analysis revealed an interesting distinction between the kinds of abilities or skills which were enhanced in the different types of school. Students in secondary schools or further education colleges indicated a more positive tutoring effect for some cognitive abilities whereas students in nursery or primary schools indicated a more positive tutoring effect for some transferable skills. This may reflect the impact of the different tutoring experiences in these different types of school, or it may be that different student personality types tended to seek to tutor in particular types of school.

The cognitive demands of tutoring secondary school pupils or further education students may be expected to be higher than those of tutoring nursery or primary pupils. Such tutoring may therefore be more likely to result in greater cognitive gains for the student tutors involved. This may be one explanation for the more positive cognitive ability enhancement results indicated by students who tutored in secondary schools or FE colleges.

The two transferable skills for which students who tutored primary or nursery pupils indicated a more positive tutoring effect, 'Managing workload, priorities and time', and 'Improvising, innovating and being creative', seem particularly relevant to a primary or nursery school setting. It was perhaps to be expected that tutors in these types of school would be more positive about gains in these particular skills.

The 'Tutoring duration' analysis results were also fairly predictable. However, it is somewhat perplexing that the three abilities and skills which revealed a difference between '1 term' and '1+ terms' students ('Understanding how others learn subject', 'Practical demonstration of subject skills', and 'Listening, questioning and clarifying') should be particularly enhanced over time when there was no significant increase in the other abilities and skills.

An analysis of the type of school in which the '1 term' and '1+ terms' students tutored revealed no significant difference between the two groups, so this can not account for the enhancement effect of these particular abilities and skills over time. An analysis of the range of subjects the '1 term' and '1+ terms' students tutored is yet to be undertaken.

In conclusion, the student tutors in this study did indicate both cognitive and transferable skill gains as a result of their school tutoring experience. School type and duration of tutoring seemed to be significant factors in this and further research is currently exploring these and other factors in more detail. Additional analyses will also investigate the effect of different tutored subjects on the nature of any cognitive and transferable skill gains for tutors. Finally, given some of the demographic results of this study and the high proportion of students who tutored in primary schools, additional work is also necessary on gains for tutees, particularly in relation to their aspirations for further or higher education.

This research was supported by British Telecom and CSV 'Learning Together'.

———————

Address for correspondence: Shirley Hill, Centre for Paired Learning, Department of Psychology, University of Dundee, Dundee DD1 4HN, Scotland. Tel. 01382 223181. Fax 01382 229993. email k.j.topping@dundee.ac.uk

Chapter 12

STUDENT TUTORING AND PUPIL ASPIRATIONS

Ian Campbell

This chapter summarises the findings of a research project which was undertaken in Birmingham in the spring term of 1994. The project was designed to investigate objective evidence with regard to the impact of student tutoring on pupil aspirations, and focuses on the findings from four secondary schools in which it was possible to identify closely matched tutored and control groups. The major finding was that it was not possible to identify changes in aspirations towards further and higher education which could demonstrably be shown to result from the impact of student tutoring. However, the results with regard to the aspirations of secondary school pupils were significant in themselves and showed major gender differences. These findings can form a basis to inform research on how tutoring schemes might be planned in the future. The chapter also identifies reasons why it was not possible to show a clear link between the impact of student tutoring and changes in aspirations, and goes on to consider the rapidly changing context with regard to further and higher education in the UK.

12.1 Introduction

This research project was sponsored by Community Service Volunteers and British Telecom with a specific brief to investigate objective evidence with regard to student tutoring and pupil aspirations towards further and higher education. The research took place between January and May 1994, with pre- and post-tutoring questionnaires being administered to pupils in seven schools in Birmingham involved in the local student tutoring scheme. The scheme places students from all three universities in Birmingham (The University of Birmingham, The University of Aston and The University of Central England) in a range of schools and colleges across the city. The model followed is that tutors attend for one half day a week for a term, and in the year the study took place, tutors attended 80 institutions in all.

12.2 Methodology

A total of 845 first-stage, and 679 second-stage questionnaires were returned, giving a response rate of 80%. This chapter is based on the evaluation of a smaller sample of 286 first- and second-stage questionnaires returned by pupils in the four secondary schools involved in the study. In these schools, it was possible to identify parallel classes to those with student tutors, enabling control groups to be established.

The questionnaires were administered by class teachers at the start of the term in which tutoring was to take place, and at the start of the following term. No connection whatsoever was made between the questionnaires and the student tutoring scheme. The first- and second-stage questionnaires were in fact identical in content, although their appearance was somewhat different.

In addition, a senior member of staff in each school was interviewed in order to gain an insight into the context within which tutoring was taking place, and to identify the school's overall strategies with regard to increasing pupils' aspirations towards continuing education post-16.

The four schools involved in this research are typical of the secondary schools in Birmingham (see Table 12.1). All were in predominantly working-class areas of the city.

Four science students (two male and two female) attended School A working with Year 10 science sets. Not all sets were involved, thereby enabling a close control group to be established. Three science students and one modern languages/geography student attended School B. Two (male) worked with a Year 10 science set in the upper of two bands, one (female) worked with an upper band geography set in Year 9, and the fourth (female) worked with pupils with special needs who were not

Student tutoring and pupil aspirations

Table 12.1 Schools involved in the study

	SCHOOL A	SCHOOL B	SCHOOL C	SCHOOL D
TYPE	Mixed	Mixed	Girls	Mixed
Ethnic Origin				
White	79.5%	50.0%	38.6%	19.1%
Black	8.4%	21.2%	2.9%	0.4%
Asian	12.0%	23.1%	57.8%	77.3%
Other	0%	5.7%	0.7%	3.1%
Number on roll	631	542	1567	661
Sixth form	Yes	No	Yes	No

Source: City of Birmingham Education Department Internal Document, January 1993

included in this study. Arrangements were made for parallel Year 9 and Year 10 sets to be used as control groups.

Four arts/modern languages students (all female) attended School C. Two worked with pupils in Year 11: one working with individual pupils practising modern languages conversation, and another who was a music undergraduate working with small groups of pupils who were taking music GCSE. The other two students worked with classes in Years 7 and 9 in English and science lessons. These were the groups which were included in the study, with two closely matched control groups.

Three students attended School D. One (female) worked in the language development base for pupils who are learning English for the first time, and who need intensive tuition and support before gradual integration into the mainstream. The pupils she had contact with were not included in this study. The other two students (one male, one female) worked with a Year 8 mathematics group, and a closely matched control group was identified.

In each case the students were introduced to the groups and their roles were explained. In general, they assisted the teachers in class activities, and worked with individual pupils or small groups. Time was not set aside for specific discussion between students and pupils. The sample of pupils involved in the study is summarised in Table 12.2.

Table 12.2 The sample of pupils

GROUP	FEMALE	MALE	TOTAL
Tutored	78	65	143
Control	88	55	143
Total	166	120	286

157

Table 12.3 *Responses to question 1: 'What do you think you will be doing when you are 17?'*

RESPONSE	FIRST STAGE		SECOND STAGE	
	Respondents	Percentage	Respondents	Percentage
Job	21	7.3	19	6.6
College of FE	133	46.5	160	55.9
School sixth form	83	29.0	70	24.5
Dole	0	0.0	0	0.0
Training scheme	15	5.2	17	5.9
Staying at home	5	1.7	4	1.4
Something else	7	2.4	9	3.1
Multiple response	21	7.3	6	2.1
No response	1	0.3	1	0.3
TOTAL	286	100.0	286	100.0

12.3 Results and Analysis

Question 1: What do you think you will be doing when you are 17?

The overall responses are shown in Table 12.3. It is clear that among the sample there was a high level of aspiration towards continuing education post-16 either at a college of further education or in a school sixth form (over 75% of the respondents both pre- and post-tutoring). Few respondents expected to go straight into employment, and training schemes appeared to be very unpopular. At the end of the four-month period, continuing education was slightly more popular, though this was largely accounted for by fewer multiple responses. A movement away from school sixth form towards college of further education can also be discerned.

There was no evidence to show that the desire to continue in education at age 17 was affected in any way by the experience of being tutored, as is shown in Table 12.4. However, there was evidence that gender had a significant influence on aspirations (see Table 12.5). Male respondents were significantly more likely than females to aspire towards employment at age 17, whereas female respondents were slightly more inclined towards continuing education. Training was more popular with females.

Table 12.4 *Respondents selecting college of FE or school sixth form in question 1*

GROUP	FIRST STAGE	SECOND STAGE	% CHANGE
Tutored (% of category)	76.2%	81.1%	+4.9%
Control (% of category)	74.8%	79.7%	+4.9%

Table 12.5 *The influence of gender on aspirations*

RESPONSE	FIRST STAGE		SECOND STAGE	
	Female	Male	Female	Male
Job	4.8%	10.8%	3.0%	11.7%
College of FE	41.6%	53.3%	57.8%	53.3%
School sixth form	34.3%	21.7%	24.1%	25.0%
Training scheme	7.2%	2.5%	8.4%	2.5%

For male respondents, college of further education was consistently much more popular than school sixth form. There was, however, a significant change in female attitudes towards college of further education and school sixth form during the course of the study. College of further education became considerably more popular at the second stage, the bulk of the change being accounted for by school sixth form becoming less popular.

Question 2: What do you think your parents or guardians would like you to be doing when you are 17?

Responses to this question indicated a high degree of perceived parental support for continuing in education post-16. For those pupils who selected college of further education or school sixth form in question 1, the data were analysed to discover how many perceived their parents/guardians as supporting their aspiration (that is, indicating one of these options in question 2). The results are shown in Table 12.6. Females perceived their parents/guardians as more supportive of the desire to continue education post-16 than did males. The experience of being tutored was found to have no bearing on these results.

Questions measuring pupils' awareness of further and higher education

Several questions were included in order to obtain a measure of the awareness on the part of pupils of the further and higher education sectors. These questions were concerned with the number of colleges and universities which the respondent could identify, the number of people

Table 12.6 *Perceptions of parental support for continuing in education post-16*

GENDER	FIRST STAGE	SECOND STAGE
Female	91.7%	91.9%
Male	82.2%	80.9%

the respondent knew at college and university, and whether the respondent could name courses or qualifications which could be studied at each type of institution. The rationale was that realistic aspirations cannot be formed without an effective knowledge base.

Space does not permit a detailed analysis of these findings, but the following general statements can be made:

- Tutoring could not be shown to have a significant effect on any of these measures. In the majority of cases the mean figure obtained for the control group increased by a larger margin than did the corresponding figure for the tutored group.
- There was a consistent pattern of female respondents being better informed than males at both stages, and of showing a larger percentage increase between the first and second stages.

Question 9: What do you think you will be doing when you are 21?

The overall responses are shown in Table 12.7. The high percentage of respondents at both stages selecting university is striking, although no judgement is made with regard to whether this is a realistic aspiration for the individuals concerned. Employment is the only other substantial response at either stage. Interestingly, the figures seem surprisingly stable over the four-month period, though a certain amount of movement between options is masked.

Table 12.7 Responses to question 9: 'What do you think you will be doing when you are 21?'

RESPONSE	FIRST STAGE		SECOND STAGE	
	Respondents	Percentage	Respondents	Percentage
Job	103	36.0	101	35.3
College of FE	14	4.9	17	5.9
University	126	44.1	123	43.0
School sixth form	2	0.7	0	0.0
Dole	0	0.0	0	0.0
Training scheme	9	3.1	12	4.2
Staying at home	6	2.1	5	1.7
Something else	5	1.7	10	3.5
Multiple response	13	4.5	8	2.8
No response	8	2.8	10	3.5
TOTAL	286	100.0	286	100.0

Student tutoring and pupil aspirations

Table 12.8 Respondents selecting university in question 9

GROUP	FIRST STAGE	SECOND STAGE
Tutored (% of category)	43.4%	42.7%
Control (% of category)	44.8%	43.4%

Tutoring was not found to have an impact on the aspirations towards university, with almost identical results being recorded for the tutored and control groups (see Table 12.8).

These figures were further analysed in order to determine the number of pupils who changed their response between the first and second stage questionnaires. Tutoring was not found to have an effect, as shown in Table 12.9.

Gender was once again found to have a much clearer impact on aspirations (see Table 12.10). Female pupils were more likely to see themselves at university at age 21 while male pupils were more likely to see themselves in employment.

While it was not possible to determine whether aspirations towards university were realistic for the individuals concerned, it was possible to determine whether respondents had chosen a realistic route, by referring to question 1. Individuals who selected university for question 9 were considered to have chosen a realistic route if they also selected college of further education or school sixth form for question 1. On this basis, the level of realism was very high (over 96% for all groups at the second stage) and was found to be unaffected by tutoring or gender.

Table 12.9 The number of pupils who changed their response between the first- and second-stage questionnaires

RESPONDENTS	TUTORED	CONTROL
Changing from another response to university at second stage	13	13
Changing from university at first stage to another response	14	15
Selecting university at both stages	48	49

Table 12.10 Respondents selecting university and employment at age 21

GENDER	UNIVERSITY		EMPLOYMENT	
	First stage	Second stage	First stage	Second stage
Female	46.4%	45.2%	30.7%	33.1%
Male	40.8%	40.0%	43.3%	38.3%

161

12.4 Discussion

It is clear that in Birmingham student tutoring takes place in a context where there is already a high level of aspiration towards continuing education at age 17, and towards higher education at age 21. The reasons for this level of aspiration at age 17 are seemingly related to three distinct factors:

1. *Unemployment.* In a declining manufacturing area such as the West Midlands, very few school leavers are able to find jobs. This means that for most 16-year-olds continuing education or taking part in a training scheme are effectively the only choices. This is confirmed by the latest figures available from the Careers Service in Birmingham for school leavers in 1994, shown in Table 12.11. It can be seen that 66.43% of school leavers continued in education (an increase of 5.33% over 1993). Only 6.64% of school leavers found employment, which was very close to the percentage of respondents in this study who aspired to do so.
2. *Training.* There appears to be a widespread reluctance on the part of school pupils and parents to regard training positively, although it should be noted that the percentage of school leavers who went on to training schemes in Birmingham in 1994 was approximately twice the percentage who aspired to do so in this study.
3. *Expansion of further education.* In recent years there has been a significant expansion of FE provision in Birmingham, reflecting a national trend which can be traced back for several years in Department for Education statistics (see Table 12.12).

This expansion has coincided with the widespread introduction of General National Vocational Qualifications. In Birmingham in 1994, 24% of school leavers who continued in education enrolled on GNVQ courses. It seems that among the reasons for the popularity of GNVQ are

Table 12.11 Destinations of Birmingham school leavers 1994

DESTINATION	% SCHOOL LEAVERS
Further Education	36.28
School sixth form	30.15
Training	11.10
Employment	6.64
Unemployed	8.17
Not seeking work	1.33
Not known/Left area	6.33

Student tutoring and pupil aspirations

Table 12.12 *Percentages of 16-year-olds in full-time education 1988/89 to 1992/93*

ACADEMIC YEAR	% OF 16-YEAR-OLDS IN FULL-TIME EDUCATION
1988/89	51
1989/90	55
1990/91	59
1991/92	67
1992/93	70

Source: DfE, 1994

its clear routes for progression, the equating of the various levels with traditional academic qualifications, and the intention that GNVQ will be an accepted route towards higher education.

From interviews with senior staff in the various schools involved in this study, it is clear that student tutoring is also taking place in a context where there are a large number of other measures in place designed to raise aspirations. Included among these are:

- the Birmingham Compact Scheme
- university visits
- Girls into Computers (at Birmingham University)
- visits to colleges of FE
- bridging courses to colleges of FE
- staff mentoring of pupils
- summer schools
- supported homework facilities
- programmes in personal and social education
- careers days
- links with business
- work experience and work shadowing.

The implications for student tutoring are very great. In a situation where there are already high levels of aspiration towards continuing in education – and schools are making concerted efforts to increase these – it is unlikely that any significant changes in aspirations which can be demonstrably attributed to the effect of student tutoring could be found. This is not to say that student tutoring will not have a bearing on the aspirations of individual pupils.

With regard to the scheme as a whole, two schools independently raised the point that they would like to place the student tutors in personal and social education lessons where there would be an opportunity for structured discussion of pertinent issues involving the students directly. Both schools felt that the value would be in the students being able to explain to pupils the practicalities of continuing education after 16, the reality of the various choices at 18, and the advantages and disadvantages of living away from home.

In terms of raising aspirations towards higher education, the issue is essentially that of increasing the participation of young working-class people in education after the age of 18. In this sense, the student tutoring scheme needs to adapt to the likely pattern of increased involvement. In Birmingham, a rapidly developing route is via the colleges of further education into degree courses franchised from the University of Central England. The student may spend his/her first year of the degree course at the college of further education and the following two years at the university, living at home or in the local community throughout. In this way, the financial difficulties resulting from attendance at university may be decreased – clearly a vital issue for people from a working-class background. Student tutors themselves are not likely to have followed this route, and thus the potential for role modelling may be limited.

Financial considerations have an enormous bearing on young people in higher education. The senior teacher from School A, for instance, felt that in his school the majority of those pupils who might aspire to university would rule it out because their parents would not be able to afford to support them. In addition, he felt that there was a growing trend among more-able pupils to look for a professional job with training opportunities, as opposed to aiming for university. The issues related to finance in higher education and the declining value of the student grant are of crucial importance in the UK in the 1990s. How far can student tutoring schemes make an impact in the face of such powerful influences on the choices open to young people?

12.5 Conclusion

There is a great challenge ahead for student tutoring if it is to be instrumental in raising young people's aspirations towards further and higher education. In many parts of England, economic necessities may have a far greater bearing on the decisions which young people make than at any time for a generation. In the development of tutoring schemes in the future, the following issues which have emerged from this study should be considered.

Schools have a large number of other measures in place designed to raise aspirations. Tutoring, if it is to be fully effective, needs to be included in a broader integrated approach, and seen by all participants as a central part.

Although working alongside classroom teachers is a fundamental aspect of student tutoring, particularly in terms of its other aims, there is a clear desire on the part of some schools to set up circumstances in which student tutors can discuss with pupils issues related to further and higher education in a more structured fashion. The opportunity for student tutors to be able to give first-hand information and advice might be as important as any role modelling effect.

Important gender issues emerged from this study. In the vast majority of cases, female pupils were better informed with regard to further and higher education and more likely to aspire in these directions. Male pupils on the other hand were more likely than females to aspire towards jobs at both 17 and 21. The typical student tutor has been found by Hill & Topping (1995) to be 'female, white, (and) middle class'. The implication is that tutoring schemes need to try to involve more male and working-class students, if the young people involved are to be successful role models for pupils, particularly young males.

In view of the rapidly changing context of further and higher education in the UK there is an urgent need to attract participants into student tutoring schemes who are not following the traditional academic route through higher education. Among these participants, ethnic minority groups clearly need to be represented, especially in multi-cultural cities such as Birmingham. Two headteachers independently raised this point during interviews.

The fact that this study could not produce any evidence of quantifiable changes in pupil aspirations due to the influence of student tutoring should not be interpreted as devaluing the concept of tutoring in any sense. In all seven schools studied, the members of staff interviewed were enthusiastic about the scheme and were in no doubt that it had considerable value. This study points towards the need to prepare student tutors with regard to the reality of the options facing pupils in schools today and to the kinds of aspirations which they may have. Student tutors can then play a very important role in speaking to pupils on their own terms, bringing to the classroom the wealth of their own first-hand experiences.

Address for correspondence: Ian Campbell, 96 Sharmans Cross Road, Solihull, West Midlands B91 1PH.

Chapter 13

PERSPECTIVE TRANSFORMATION OF INTENDED TEACHERS AT DIFFERENT LIFE STAGES WHO PARTICIPATE IN A TUTORING PROGRAMME FOR AT-RISK STUDENTS

Sharon H Harwell

This chapter describes the results of an exploratory study of intended teachers' current perceptions of teaching. Qualitative data document perspective transformation of the personal construct of 'teacher self' as revealed through self-reflection journals and field observations over the duration of participation in a ten-week tutoring experience for at-risk elementary students. Programme evaluation showed a positive impact upon tutors and an overwhelming support and advocacy for programme continuation. Results lend credence to the idea that students contemplating a career in teaching should be placed in field experiences, such as tutoring, as soon as possible.

13.1 Introduction and Background

Personal insights related by students of all ages through autobiographical self-reflection papers, anecdotes shared in class, and formal observations of intended teachers in previous class projects prompted this author to observe that students experience changes in perspective about their perceived role of teacher as a direct result of hands-on teaching experiences. Significant and meaningful learning experiences incorporating social interaction, discovery, negotiation and sharing coupled with reflection seemed to make it possible for these individuals to move beyond their present level of development to attain higher levels of understanding and integration. Bruner (1994) relates that narratives allow individuals to reflect and to make sense of self and self in the world. Despite the common knowledge that 'reflection' is widely recognised as crucial to the professional growth of teachers (Dewey, 1938; Combs, 1972; Grimmett, 1988; Gipe & Richards, 1990; Knowles, 1993) the process of perspective change and transformation has rarely been documented. Calderhead (1989) and Diamond (1991), in an attempt to discover the emerging understandings of ten student teachers, concluded that researchers have discovered little understanding of the reflective processes involved in learning to become a professional teacher and that additional research should be initiated to identify specific concerns.

Diamond's (1991) exploratory work with pre-service and practising teachers offers a glimpse into the reflective views of the teacher role and the change in perception of that role over the course of an academic year. Kelly's (1955) personal construct theory and Mezirow's (1981) ideas about perspective transformation provided the theoretical framework for his research. Diamond contends that when people develop an understanding of their personal perspectives, as well as those of others, they can understand their past experiences and project themselves into a future situation, such as the classroom, because they possess prior knowledge about what those events mean to themselves and to others. Diamond notes that teacher educators should seek to empower beginning teachers with the reflective capacity to become students of their own teaching.

Critical retheorising and reflection upon experience helps an individual attain new perspectives and to transform old perspectives.

Tann (1993) believes that students should be encouraged to elicit and articulate their personal theories of life and to discover the relationship of that theory to their individual educational theory of teaching, learning and curriculum. Awareness of individual interpretative frameworks can assist intending teachers in contrasting and connecting their personal perspectives with peers and colleagues. Field experiences in teacher education such as tutoring that demand a high emotional investment must be followed by reflective analysis if students are expected to realise qualitative changes in growth and development.

Boyd & Fales (1983) provide a concept of personal reflection that demonstrates the personal orientation needed by teachers. Reflection as described by these authors focuses upon reflective learning as the creation and clarification of meaning related to past and present experiences of self in relation to self and self as it relates to the world. Reflection upon experience involves exploration and examination of a concern of central importance to the self, such as the teacher role. A shift from one perspective to another or the confirmation of a perspective represents the change brought about as a result of the reflective process. Individuals display varying levels of reflective abilities and each person employs different strategies for reflection. Different experiences may precipitate reflection in different persons. Basically, the source of reflective learning revolves around the self.

13.2 Purpose of Study

The primary aim of this study was to discover intended teachers' current perceptions of teaching and explore their personal constructs of the 'teacher self' over the course of their participation in a tutoring experience designed for an entry-level pre-service teacher education course. Additionally, it was anticipated that results would demonstrate the impact of the programme upon at-risk student participants.

13.3 Method

Constant comparative methodology, specifically analysis of reflective journals (Glaser, 1978; Bogdan & Biklen, 1992; Miles & Huberman, 1994) and multiple field observations coupled with some descriptive statistics provided the methodology for this study. Research on journal writing supports the value of journals as a medium useful in documentation and promotion of reflective thinking and self-evaluation among students (Gipe & Richards, 1990; 1992). Diamond (1991) successfully used journal writing to elicit teachers' pedagogical theories and found that writing enabled teachers to first create their worlds through text and then to recreate their worlds if those worlds proved less than satisfactory. The process of writing encourages change in a person and can modify the direction of that person's life. Documentation of these narrative worlds can be easily shared with oneself to encourage self-reflection and self-evaluation as well as documentation for others' interpretation. Observations provide insights about behaviours that are not readily obtained through other means, while descriptive statistics allow data to be quantified, promoting more meaningful interpretation (Borg & Gall, 1979). Loevinger's (1976) theory of ego development provided the 'frame of reference' for meaning in this study and describes the self in a hierarchical world view. The Tennessee Self Concept Scale (Fitts, 1965) measured self-concept in the pre- and post-test situation.

The participants were 14 students enrolled in a human development course designated as a prerequisite for admission to the education programme. Students received three semester credit hours for successful completion of the course. An integral component of the course was the requirement of tutoring an at-risk student enrolled in an elementary school committed to a school-university partnership. At-risk students were identified by classroom teachers in collaboration with the school at-risk programme coordinator. An at-risk student was identified as a child who exhibited poor academic skills, who needed help with social abilities or had difficulty with appropriate classroom behaviour to the point that intervention was necessary, had low self-esteem and inconsistent school attendance. Tutors met tutees each week, for a period of ten weeks, for two prearranged 30-minute sessions and assisted students with lessons or reinforcement activities planned by the classroom teacher. No additional costs were incurred by student, university or school. All tutoring sessions took place in the school library, cafeteria or other rooms designated by the school. The school at-risk coordinator provided a one-hour training session outlining responsibilities of tutors, school policies and appropriate tutor conduct prior to the tutoring experience. The course instructor and tutee's classroom teacher provided continuous observational feedback throughout the term.

Each tutor kept a journal of their experiences. Journal entries focused upon four open-ended statements patterned after Diamond (1991) to reveal the construct of 'teacher self': My pupil and I. . ., The teacher I am today. . ., The teacher I fear to become. . ., and The teacher I hope to become. . . . The portion of self considered to be pedagogical in this analysis was 'The teacher I am today. . .'. The meaning of the teacher role (what one believes oneself to be as a teacher) was qualitatively explored as that perception was changed or not changed over the ten-week period.

Data collection and criteria for reflection appraisal

Loevinger's (1976) Sentence Completion Test (Form 9-62) and the Tennessee Self Concept Scale (Fitts, 1965) were administered to students prior to signing up for the tutoring experience. Self-concept was measured again at the conclusion of the experience. The Sentence Completion Test was scored by this researcher who previously completed training in the use and scoring of the instrument and who has used the instrument extensively in research. Journals were analysed from beginning to end of the term to uncover recurrent themes and document insights about the construct of 'teacher self'. This procedure was patterned after Holly and McLaughlin (Tann, 1993) who advocate the charting of themes and shifts in interpretation and the tracking of those themes over time.

The at-risk programme coordinator and this researcher interviewed individual classroom teachers concerning the overall benefits of the programme. Privacy laws prohibited access to tutees' records; therefore, the at-risk programme coordinator provided evaluation related to improvements in school attendance, work habits, letter grades, self-esteem and attitude toward school. The principal was also interviewed.

Description of the sample

Fourteen students with no prior professional teaching experience or training and who were planning future careers as teachers comprised this sample of tutors (13 females and one male). Five students (36%) were considered traditional students while nine (64%) were non-traditional, re-entry female students. All tutors fell within the postconformist level of ego development. Persons at this stage of development are very self-aware and demonstrate concern with solving problems, finding meaningful reasons for understanding and adjusting to situations and roles. They are able to think in terms of alternatives and multiple possibilities. Long-term, self-evaluated goals and ideals, differentiated self-criticism and a sense of responsibility characterise this stage. A rich and differentiated inner life enhanced by reflective thinking distinguishes this group (Loevinger, 1976).

Table 13.1 presents the pre- and post-test mean scores for self-concept as well as the percentage change over time for several components of the Tennessee Self Concept Scale. As a group, these tutors reflect an overall level of self-esteem slightly higher than the norm. They like themselves, feel they are persons of value and worth, have confidence in themselves,

Table 13.1 Mean scores for several measures of the Tennessee Self Concept Scale for intending teachers prior to and at the conclusion of a tutoring experience

SELF-CONCEPT MEASURES	NORM	PRE-TEST	POST-TEST	PERCENT CHANGE
1. Total positive score	345.57	358.50	354.92	−1
2. Self-criticism	35.54	34.07	36.79	8
3. Identity	127.10	127.36	127.86	0
4. Self-satisfaction	103.67	111.29	106.36	−4
5. Behaviour	115.01	119.86	116.57	−3
6. Physical self	71.78	68.29	65.86	−4
7. Moral-ethical	70.33	74.71	74.29	−1
8. Personal self	64.55	68.00	68.43	1
9. Family self	70.83	75.50	73.93	−2
10. Social self	68.14	72.00	68.29	−5

and act accordingly. In only two areas were tutors slightly below the norm: self-criticism and physical self.

13.4 Analysis

In analysing this sample of reflective journals, several themes emerged: change in focus of concerns; career affirmation and role satisfaction; change in reflective viewpoints; and change in quality of reflection.

Change in focus of concerns

Students' reflections tended to mirror a progressive change over time in their concerns about children and teaching similar to Mackinnon's (1987) findings. A shift from being child-oriented, to teacher-oriented, to learner-oriented emerged. Table 13.2 shows the frequency of tutors' concerns initially and at the conclusion of the tutoring experience. Initially, tutors' descriptions of their tutees were highly descriptive and showed concerns about their relationships with children, anxiousness about the experience, and the process of 'getting to know' their 'study buddy'. Matt related he was 'the type of teacher who likes to form a relationship with my pupils'. Lauren felt 'it was easy to talk to Eddie and to help him review his work'. Only Joanna remained at the child-oriented focus of concern at the conclusion of the experience. Initially she reflected:

> The teacher I am is one that is afraid. I enjoy spending time with my study buddy because it allows me to get to know her feelings and how she views certain topics that have affected her life.

At the conclusion of the experience Joanna portrayed similar concerns:

> I am the teacher who misses Brenda whenever I cannot see her. I am the one who enjoys spending time with her.

Teacher-oriented concerns showed viewpoints of children as pupils who needed instruction. Classroom materials, teacher explanations and teaching methods became the major focus of concern. Sandra observed that 'the class was well managed but the pace seemed rushed.' Donna noted:

> I believe I am able to think on my feet and adjust a plan in midstream if it isn't holding children's attention – if they aren't comprehending what I thought they would.

Janis wrote:

> I found it very frustrating to see what happens to a child when he is not offered age-appropriate developmental activities. It is very hard for me not to be angry at the parents of this child and others like them.

Many of the tutors who shifted from a child-orientation to a teacher-orientation focus of concern at the conclusion of the experience, or showed no movement at all, began to refer to and incorporate concepts learned in the human development course. Donna related:

> I am confident that I can help children learn. I am sensitive to children's needs and flexible enough to try various approaches.

Susan became 'so much more observant about children. . .' and noted, 'I am able to use my knowledge of different theories to determine stages they are at or should be at'. Matt's reflection showed the same concern:

> I am. . .the type of teacher who pushes my students to learn, because if you set reasonable expectations they will work toward them.

Although Janis' reflections demonstrated no shift to the learner orientation focus, she reflected:

> I remain appreciative of his efforts. I praise Darien often and I bring him small rewards like new pencils or stickers which he really likes. I try to vary our activities and watch carefully for signs that he is bored with the current activity.

Only two intending teachers began the tutoring experience at the learner-oriented focus of concern where tutors tried to meet individual learner needs. Trudi demonstrated this orientation best:

I was pleased that I was able to recognise his ability level right away and so I concentrated on reinforcing the positive.

She continued to focus on learner-oriented concerns throughout the experience but became very frustrated:

The teacher I am is not very confident at this point. I feel that Juan was betrayed by the system. The teacher I am is understanding and I recognise the need for immediate help. This is so frustrating because the failure cycle was about to be broken and then just as things were going well, Juan was snatched away. I would have liked the opportunity to follow through with him. He seems to have lost enthusiasm. He started to trust and that trust was taken away. He started to have industry about his work and that was taken away. Inferiority was reinforced by not allowing Juan to have special help and succeed.

Sandra felt challenged with the recognition that her 'study buddy' had learning problems and reflected, 'The teacher I am is one that can comprehend from a child's point of view (that) things can get a little distorted at times.' Janis observed that she was alert to 'the signs that told me Joe was not feeling well.... Usually he is very attentive. He really wanted to continue despite not feeling well'. Mary realised that her attitude affected her tutees' learning and willingness to try:

They respond to me positively so therefore I must be doing a little right. My encouragement seems to increase their confidence. I believe the regularity and consistency of my visits has made them recognise my dedication to them was making them more dedicated as well. I am truly committed to becoming a teacher, and I think that commitment shows to the kids. I try to make them feel special and important because they are.

Career affirmation and role satisfaction

Tutors expressed confirmation and/or reorganisation of their cognitive structure of the role of teacher as a result of their experiences of tutoring. Janis confirmed role satisfaction when she wrote:

Table 13.2 Changing patterns of focus of concerns of intending teachers during ten weeks of tutoring at-risk students

	CHILD-ORIENTATION	TEACHER-ORIENTATION	LEARNER-ORIENTATION
Week 1	9	3	2
Week 10	1	6	7

I am so excited to see Charles make some real progress. If this is how it feels to teach, then I have picked the right career path this time. I hope that I will be able to help young children learn. What an important job!

Matt's belief that he possessed the ability to teach was reinforced:

To be complimented by Jose reinforced my belief that I am a good teacher. To watch the light bulb illuminate in a student like Jose is exciting. I hope to be the type of teacher who turns students on to learning. For Jose to turn from indignant to happy and thankful in a short amount of time is one of the most rewarding experiences I have ever had. I now realise what a difference a study buddy can make.

Other tutors pointed out they 'had not made a mistake in choosing a career in the field of education', or learned they had 'the ability to teach' and to be 'a good teacher'. Janis found it 'very gratifying to teach' and was 'pleased' that she 'appeared to have found a job she would enjoy doing'.

Two of the 14 tutors, Janis and Susan, experienced reorganisation of their cognitive structure of the teacher role. Although Janis knew early in the experience she wanted to become a teacher, she began to reorganise her 'teacher self' as a result of the tutoring experience:

I am really thinking about looking into getting a special education degree after I get my certificate. The study buddy programme has helped me recognise the need for these teachers and my own desire to give special help to special kids.

Susan changed the direction of her career:

I have decided to pursue a career as an at-risk teacher; teaching children with special needs is where I will feel needed. I learned that there is a world I have not really been impacted by until Jennifer, and that it would be selfish of me to deny what I can so readily teach.

Change in reflective viewpoints

Tutors became cognisant of their idealist viewpoints and demonstrated shifts toward more realistic perspectives. Two tutors, Janis and Susan, articulated these developmental gains in realism best. Janis stated:

I hope I will be able to maintain an enthusiastic and affirmative classroom. I would like to be able to motivate the children with my own attitude toward learning. Idealistic? Perhaps, but is it not important to strive for this even if it cannot be achieved?

Susan demonstrated this shift in perspective better than others. She described herself as a very enthusiastic teacher who:

> ...immediately wanted to teach Eric, open his mind and pour life into him. I had to refrain from hugging him; he just seemed so needy, and so did I.

Susan struggled throughout her tutoring experience and came to a more realistic perspective:

> I can see small steps as progress now instead of looking for big ones. I have finally started to feel good about each small step. I have realised that my small step for this child is a big step for him. What a revelation!

Changes in quality of reflection

One distinct impression surfaced upon the initial reading of the student reflections: almost all entries began as story commentaries which included specific details about the tutee and the environment in which the tutoring took place. Placing their experience within a context appeared to be necessary for tutors to experience before they could begin writing about the construct of the 'teacher self.' This observation finds commonality in Tann's (1993) research focusing on the personal theories of novice student teachers upon reflection of their lesson planning and evaluation activities.

All tutors indicated a sense of openness to new information relating to the experience of tutoring. Tutors became acutely aware of the need to learn more and become more knowledgeable about children and teaching. Mary related that she was 'dedicated and willing to be there for the children, but I know I have a lot of learning to do'. Joanna expressed this openness best:

> The teacher I am at the present is not the teacher I expect to be in two years. I am inexperienced with handling problems, and unsure of what is expected from me.

As various situations arose, tutors queried the professor, the programme coordinator and/or the tutees' teachers and collaborated with peer tutors. Tutors began to trust their 'teacher self' to discover and recognise problems in the tutoring experience. As a result, tutors began to explore alternative ideas and teaching strategies.

An increased receptivity to course instruction was heightened and long-forgotten memories of past teachers and learning situations were brought to consciousness. Reflections showed that tutors were attempting to find congruence and continuity of their past self, present self and future self in order to establish some level of comfort. Boyd & Fales (1983) believe this phase of the reflective learning process is the most productive period available for intervention by educators and counsellors.

As tutors progressed through the ten-week experience, their capacity to reflect improved. Lauren wrote:

> I was able to listen to Mary Ellen and I was sensitive to her need to talk. I'm glad she felt she could share her experience with me.... I was not able to deal with all the information she shared.... I could not write this immediately, but had to take time to think and put distance between the emotional impact and the analysis. I wanted to take Mary Ellen home and help her through this hard time.

Helen, who was taken by surprise when she discovered her study buddy had lied to her, wrote that 'it forced me to look closer at the teacher I am.... It really set me back a step and turned my thoughts to moral issues...'.

Evidences of self-affirmation were prevalent among all tutors toward the conclusion of the experience. Tutors felt good about themselves and were proud of the small achievements they attained as well as those of their tutees. Tutors tended to experience surges of positive energy and enthusiasm which enhanced their motivation. Susan wrote:

> I sometimes feel tired before I get to the school because of life and all its stress, but once I step into his class, those things are forgotten.

Trudi felt that 'the rewards for self outweigh what they learn.... The children's enthusiasm ignites you with energy'. Janis reflected that 'it was very exciting to see him respond to such a small amount of one-to-one help'. Marie related an 'aha' type of insight akin to Maslow's (1968) peak experiences while tutoring:

> I felt so good, because I felt like I am actually getting through to her. I felt useful and that made me feel so good. It really revitalised me. I am becoming more energetic and eager to keep going.

13.5 Evaluation: Impact of Programme

Interviews with the at-risk programme coordinator, principal and classroom teachers showed an overwhelming support and advocacy for continuation of the tutoring programme. Evaluation provided by the programme coordinator indicated that 62% (n = 29) of the tutees improved a letter grade or more in one or more core subject areas, while

19% (n = 9) maintained the same letter grade. Only 19% (n = 9) dropped a letter grade in one or more core subjects. The programme coordinator pointed out that 'maintained' grades should not be lightly dismissed. Most 'maintained' grades reflect a great deal of effort on the part of the student, especially as the year progresses. The consistency and commitment of the tutors to the programme appeared to positively affect students' grades, especially if the tutors consistently tutored twice per week.

Teachers reported dramatic decreases in school absenteeism. One student who missed nine days over the year and was tardy 10 times, had zero tardies and zero absences during the time he had a study buddy. Teachers also reported big improvements in attitude toward school as well as improved 'work habits' and industriousness. One teacher reported:

> I believe that the friendships that they formed with their 'buddies' was equally as important as the academic help. They knew someone cared about their progress in school. My children looked forward to their sessions. They worked hard with their 'study buddies,' as well as in the classroom – so that they had work to share with them when they arrived.

Another teacher pointed out that students were all doing 'beautiful work in class now with lots of self-esteem!' Others believed the programme helped build 'friendships' and taught 'socialisation skills'. An 'adult figure' who showed 'care and concern' and valued education and learning provided a positive role model other than the classroom teacher.

One teacher described the children's thoughts in this manner: 'I'm so special that my friend comes to school just to help me!' She went on to say the 'personal touch' of the programme was an added dimension: 'This is just great! The children feel 10 feet taller!' Needless to say, improvements in student self-esteem were noted by all teachers.

Tutors as well as tutees formed wonderful attachments throughout the experience and discovered it very hard to bring closure to the experience. Many found themselves 'dreading the end of a relationship with my student'. Several resolved to continue with the programme the following term despite the fact they had completed the course.

13.6 Conclusions and Discussion

Several themes emerged from the analysis presented here. Tutors, all intending teachers, demonstrated developmental shifts in their focus from the tutee, to teaching, to learning. Additionally, tutors showed gains in identity development, realism, reflectivity and motivation. Tutees tended to show improved grade levels, attendance, attitude toward school and self-esteem.

Tutors experienced little difficulty in writing their reflections. This may be attributed to the fact tutors were in the postconformist level of ego development and exhibited self-awareness and reflective capabilities prior to tutoring. However, there are many implications for future research. Since traditional age college students were represented in this sample, it was initially expected that some tutors would be classified in the conformist level of ego development as predicted by Loevinger (1976). Therefore, the question of whether conformist students approach the process of reflection differently than this group of postconformist students must be addressed in future research. Do tutors with lower self-concept approach reflection differently than tutors with a high sense of positive self-worth and direction? Does prior experience with children influence reflection?

Tutors experienced difficulty in articulating their expressions in professional terminology. Initially, observations were couched in collo-quial terms, making it necessary for the instructor to constantly provide feedback through conversation and class discussion in an attempt to address these needs. Attainment of a basic level of proficiency of educational language through additional tutor training would expedite reflection.

Reflective journal narratives proved an effective tool through which students could be made aware of their interpretative frameworks. Teacher educators can use students' interpretative frameworks to help individual students 'connect' with other theories, to 'clarify' and even 'challenge' their own theories about learning and teaching. When students begin to make connections between their beliefs and actions, a perspective change becomes eminent and can serve as powerful motiva-tion (Bruner, 1994; Henderson, 1992). Knowles (1993) discovered similar benefits in the use of life-histories as an effective instructional strategy.

Inherent within this study is the limitation which revolves around the strong female gender bias of the sample. Although all the participants were classified at the postconformist level of ego development, the question remains whether the results of the study would have been different if the sample had been inclusive of more males. Some readers may question the influence of availability of course credit upon the results of this study. The fact that these participants were at the postconformist level of ego development where high self-concept, reflectivity and self-directedness are inherent within the level, points to a negligible effect in this group of intending teachers. However, there is a need for a better understanding of the process of reflection tutors engage when tutoring children. What role do field experiences such as tutoring and student teaching internships play in encouraging a reflective stance? Once made aware of the process of reflection, do pre-service teachers continue to use this reflection-in-action in their professional employment? What additional experiences and classroom instruction will encourage reflection in intending teachers?

This study lends credence to the idea that students contemplating a career in teaching should be placed in field experiences as early as possible. A sense of tentativeness and uncertainty about the anticipated role of teacher suggests an openness to further examination among intending teachers. Appropriate and continuous opportunities to concurrently practise the skill of teaching and the process of reflection upon experiences can challenge intending teachers to learn from their pre-teaching experiences and to grow in the capacity to reflect upon their work. Grimmett (1988) reminds us of the paradox of learning that exists when intending teachers embark upon the journey of becoming professional teachers: they are attempting to learn how to become competent teachers, but have not yet gained a complete understanding of just what it means to be a competent teacher. Although this paradox exists, teacher educators must strive to provide intentional cultivation of reflective thinking practices in intending teachers. Instructional activities such as this tutoring programme, coupled with reflection upon the tutoring experience, can help intending teachers to learn from their experiences, to sustain that capacity to learn, and to grow in their work.

The author would like to express her grateful appreciation to the elementary school and teachers for allowing tutors to work with tutees. The names of all tutors and tutees have been changed to protect the anonymity of the participants.

Address for correspondence: Sharon H Harwell, Ed. D., Research Assistant Professor of Education and Associate for Education Reform, Institute for Science Education, University of Alabama in Huntsville, Huntsville, AL 35899, USA.

Chapter 14

STUDENTS AS TUTORS IN EARLY CHILDHOOD SETTINGS: THE ACQUISITION AND TRANSMISSION OF PROBLEM-SOLVING SKILLS

Margaret Shore

This chapter, part of a larger study, analyses the verbal discourse of an early childhood student as a tutor and her mentor, in a problem-solving situation with a child. Training in teaching and learning using seven abstract tools through the zone of proximal development (cf.Tharp & Gallimore, 1988; Wertsche, 1985) was provided to both participants. The tutor displayed a developing ability to scaffold the activity and decompose the process into distinct parts. However, the ability to hand over the task, when the child indicated he was capable of independent performance, was not apparent. Recitative questioning requiring predictable or yes or no answers, predominated (Hoetker & Ahlbrand, 1969). The implications of these results for tutors working in early childhood settings are discussed and the need to have realistic expectations of a tutor's abilities is emphasised.

14.1 Introduction

This chapter is part of a longer study involving seven early childhood students working as tutors with 0-to-5-year-old children for six months in early childhood development centres. The students worked under the supervision of mentors, some of whom were students themselves. The main purpose of this section was to assist students acquire problem-solving skills and develop the ability to transmit these to the children: formal and informal teaching and learning processes were involved. The programme is ongoing with students now placed as tutors with young children in community settings such as hospitals (paediatric and antenatal wards), schools, special education units, holiday resorts, recreational and activity centres, family day care and respite care situations.

A literature search on cognitive development and work-based learning involving mentors and tutors, was undertaken. I was looking for an effective method of assisting inexperienced students to gain the skills necessary to tutor young children effectively in early childhood settings. Prior experience with students as tutors had alerted me to the types of problems inherent when untrained people assist in programmes for young children. With this in mind, formal activities planned for assisting the development of problem-solving skills were not undertaken by the students until they had been working with the children one day a week for ten weeks.

As little has been written on caring for and educating groups of children under 4 years of age, the majority of references were drawn from early school situations. Newman *et al.*'s (1989) *The Construction Zone*; The Hawaiian Kamehameha Early Education Project (KEEP) programme conducted by Tharp & Gallimore (1988); and Rogoff *et al.*'s (1993) work with toddlers, all based on Vygotsky's zone of proximal development (ZPD), provided a theoretical base for cognitive development. Information on work-based teaching and learning was drawn from the cognitive apprenticeship model of Brown *et al.* (1989), the situated learning (SL) of Lave & Wenger (1991), and Chaiklin & Lave's (1993) work on legitimate peripheral participation (LPP). A post-technocratic model of professional training which combined theoretical and practical elements (George, 1992) was used as a framework.

From this background it was decided that students as tutors would need to develop specific abstract tools (cf.Bronowski, 1973) in order to assist effectively the development of children's higher-order cognitive skills and problem-solving strategies through the ZPD. Seven abstract tools were identified as necessary to be introduced:

■ observation – a diagnostic tool to assess needs for promoting higher-order cognitive skills and problem-solving strategies

- role modelling – a tool to demonstrate performance standards when promoting new behaviour
- contingency management – a tool to inform on the desirability of behaviour (does not promote new behaviour)
- feedback – a tool to provide information or motivation on standard of performance (does not promote new behaviour)
- instructing – a tool to provide information and knowledge when promoting new behaviour.
- questioning – a tool to challenge and extend existing thinking when assisting learning
- cognitive structuring – a tool to develop conceptual frameworks when promoting new behaviours.

Tutors, using these tools iteratively and skilfully within a scaffold (Wood *et al.*, 1976; Rogoff & Lave, 1984) of the whole task, also needed to be aware of the handover principle (Berk, 1991) which allows for learners to become increasingly independent. Tutors and their mentors were both instructed in using these tools through the ZPD by college lecturers.

Tutors were asked to observe mentors role-model problem-solving strategies with children using the ubiquitous jigsaw puzzle. As one of the earliest and easiest modes of assessing and increasing children's problem-solving capabilities in the socio-cultural setting of group care and education, the jigsaw is a familiar and non-threatening adjunct provided as part of the centres' daily activities. Mentors were audio-recorded while they performed the activity and two weeks later the tutors were audio-recorded as they performed the same activity with the same child.

Transcripts of the tapes were analysed against four criteria (adapted from Henze, 1992):

How is initiation into the activity accomplished?
How is the task of solving the problem structured?
What is the nature of the instructional interaction?
What is the relationship between the learner's zone of proximal development and instruction by a mentor or a tutor?

14.2 Discussion of the Findings

Initiation: Comparison of mentor-child dyad and tutor-child dyad

Although both mentor and tutor initiated the first interaction with the learner using an attention getter vocative, the mentor gave Max independent responsibility for the task by saying, 'OK. Let's see you put it back together!', while the tutor shared this responsibility by querying, 'OK, where're we going to start Maxie?' Both verbally scaffolded the activity, allowing the child to concentrate on individual elements as they formed part of the whole puzzle. However, while the mentor handed-over parts of the task to the child, limiting intervention and posing open questions as he explored various options in placing the pieces, the tutor maintained verbal control of the task using closed questions and direct prompts throughout the activity. This latter type of interaction diminished Max's opportunity to display independent problem-solving strategies and formulate new relationships between his existing knowledge and concepts arising out of the jigsaw and the socio-cultural setting.

When Max substituted the singular pronoun, 'I' in, 'No, I'm going to start', in response to the tutor's initiation using the plural 'we' in, 'OK where're we going to start?', he indicated his readiness to participate independently. However the tutor did not hand over to Max allowing him the responsibility of attempting an independent task solution; instead she initiated the continued sharing of Max's actions by using the plural 'we' in a subsequent interaction, '. . .OK. Who're we going to put next?'

A shared central focus was again initiated by the tutor when she challenged Max to identify the placement of specific people in the puzzle. In response to her question, 'Do you remember who – start with who. . .?', he replied, 'Gail, 'cause I know where that goes'. Although Max displayed existing knowledge of the problem, the tutor continued to prompt Max's actions with such predictable questions as, '. . .who's head's this?. . .' and, 'OK. What's Ben wearing?'

In contrast to these initiations by the tutor, an initiation two weeks previously by Max established a shared focus with the mentor:

Child: Do last my face. My face last.
Mentor: You want to do your face last.
Child: This won't fit in here.
Mentor: Do you think these two bits go together?

By repeating Max's words and using reflective questioning, the mentor shared and maintained the central focus, allowing Max to initiate the direction of his learning.

183

Task structure: Comparison of mentor-child dyad and tutor-child dyad

The structure of introduction and response to the elements of this problem-solving activity was shared almost equally in nine interpersonal interactions between mentor and child (5:4). Two weeks later the tutor dominated the activity, engaging with the child in seven interpersonal interactions (6:1). However, as Slade (1995:44) states, '...the flavour of thinking in a class is dictated by who is talking' and no longer should we have the symmetrical behaviour of teacher initiation, learner response and teacher evaluation. It is by practising on their mentors or tutors that learners must develop the critical and evaluative skills that typify the higher-order thinking necessary for effective problem-solving. The structure of the activity shows the various elements in these two different types of interactions:

Structure of activity: mentor-child dyad:

1.	Selects puzzle	M introduces	C responds
2.	Suggests strategy 1	M introduces	C responds
3.	Identifies problem	C introduces	M responds
4.	Suggests sequence	C introduces	M responds
5.	Suggests strategy 2	M introduces	C responds
6.	Introduces diversion	C introduces	M responds
7.	Redirects focus	M introduces	C responds
8.	Introduces diversion	M introduces	C responds
9.	Redirects focus	C introduces	M responds

The mentor introduced structural elements five times (56%). The following example illustrates the mentor's type of introductions:

Mentor: Six pieces – that's my face.
Child: Yes, watch out.
Mentor: I'd really like you to put my face back together.
Child: I'll do that right now – don't know where your face went.

The child responded to, and prepared to act on, the mentor's comments, the context in which the problems occurred and identified his own lack of knowledge. Assuming responsibility for introductions four times (44%), the types of verbal interchanges by the child were as follows:

Child: That one's a bit of shorts. Yes. Oh, oh, oh.
Mentor: You've got two that are matching.
Child: Yes cos ... got shorts on.

184

Mentor: So what do you think you should do with those two bits now that you've got them together?

Child: Put them together. . . .

These interpersonal interactions, according to Vygotsky (Wertsche, 1985), are internalised on the intrapsychological plane by the learner appropriating them into existing cognitive structures.

A diversionary interaction introduced by Max was related to a problem he perceived with the tape recorder: 'It's not coming on – the tape is – the tape's not coming on'. This statement was acknowledged by the mentor who elaborated on the operations of the tape recorder before she refocused him on the problem-solving activity. The second diversion, relating the number of puzzle pieces to Max's age as well as other environmental elements, was introduced by the mentor as an opportunity for cognitive structuring through the ZPD. Whenever the mentor redirected the learner's focus during the activity, she guided his orientation with an introduction to the next strategy: '. . .Was it this colour blue you were looking at or was it that colour blue?'

However, the structure of the tutor-child dyad showed a different pattern of interactions. Without the two diversions of approximately one minute to distract the learner's performance, the tutor-child dyad took six minutes, five seconds less to complete than the mentor-child dyad:

Structure of activity: tutor-child dyad:

1.	Selects puzzle	T introduces	C responds
2.	Suggests strategy 1	C introduces	
3.	Identifies problem	T introduces	C responds
4.	Suggests sequence	T introduces	C responds
5.	Suggests strategy 2	T introduces	C responds
6.	Summarises progress	T introduces	C responds
7.	Provides alternate puzzle	T introduces	C responds

The predominant type of introduction by the tutor was a series of direct, closed questions requiring convergent or factual answers:

Tutor: . . .Who is it?
Child: Evelyn.
Tutor: Evelyn, OK. You're doing this really well.
Child: Oh.
Tutor: Well who is. . . Great. . . have a look. . . Who's this here?
Child: Ben.
Tutor: OK. What's Ben wearing?

The tutor introduced 86% (six) of the interactions compared with 56% (five) introduced by the mentor. The tutor did not respond to the child's one introduction (14%), 'No I'm going to start', compared to the four introductions (44%) by the child to which the mentor responded.

The facility and speed which the child displayed in completing the problem-solving activity with the tutor, three minutes, 55 seconds, compared to ten minutes with the mentor, indicates that he may have appropriated strategies from the original problem-solving experience with the mentor and was using them successfully to complete the puzzle. The introduction of strategies by the tutor may not have been necessary.

Instructional interaction: comparison between mentor-child dyad and tutor-child dyad

While Louise (mentor) and Tracey (tutor) both scaffolded the problem-solving task, decomposing the whole puzzle into discrete elements, they displayed different levels of expertise in their use of various teaching tools. Louise observed Max's actions as he was placing the pieces in the puzzle frame while Tracey observed the puzzle to determine which piece was needed next. The tutor ignored Max's statement that, '. . .I'm going to start' and, '. . .I know where that goes', participating in each of his moves with instructions or questions such as, '. . .Have a look!' or, '. . .who's this here?' By observing without instructing or questioning, she may have discovered whether he could actually do this without her assistance.

The mentor used both open questioning – '. . .what makes you think it has to go in there?', and closed questions – 'Do you think those two pieces go together?' in 19 of her 28 interactions, (0.7 per interaction). This contrasted with the tutor's discourse which consisted of a series of 21 closed questions requiring factual, short or one-word answers – 'Who's head's this?' and, 'Do you know who that is?', in her 14 interactions (1.5 per interaction) with Max. Her use of the interrogative pronoun, 'who' or, 'who's' 19 times, illustrates her focus on Max providing factual information by identifying people and locating their places in the puzzle.

Conversely the mentor's questions focused on Max's ability in placing the puzzle pieces – 'You think it has to go in there'; whether the pieces were fitting where he placed them – 'Will that one fit?' and why he had placed a piece in a particular position – 'What makes you think it has to go in there?' These latter type of questions allowed Max to engage in internal self-talk, selecting from a variety of responses whilst assisting his reasoning and understanding of the relationships of the parts to the whole.

The mentor provided feedback to Max while the tutor relied on contingency management strategies to encourage continuance of behaviour. The mentor's feedback took the form of describing a correct action: 'You've got two that are matching', and questioning an incorrect one: 'But they're not fitting so is that the right piece for there?' to meet the standards required. Conversely the tutor used contingency management: 'Oh good one, great...' and, '...OK. You're doing this really well', describing the child's ability to perform rather than the standard of performance of the task.

The mentor role modelled cognitive structuring when she organised the 'raw stuff of experiences at hand and in like circumstances' (Tharp & Gallimore, 1988:65), by making a general statement on the numerical relationships between objects in the learning environment, Max's age, his future role as a pre-schooler, and the number of puzzle pieces he had placed:

Mentor:	So what do you think you should do with those two bits now that you've got them together
Child:	Put them together – these parts are very tricky – for a 3-year-old boy.
Mentor:	Tricky for a 3-year-old boy. How many's that? Let's count them.
Child:	One – two – three – four.
Mentor:	Are you 3 years old or 4 years old?
Child:	3 years old. I...
Mentor:	I'm looking at the birthday chart and the birthday chart says that you're 4. You've had your fourth birthday. Okay Dokes. You've got them in the puzzle now?
Child:	All I have to do is...
Mentor:	You are nearly a pre-schooler.

Conversely, the tutor drew attention to relationships within the puzzle itself, concentrating on the task components in isolation from the sociocultural surroundings. A monologue illustrates the type of discourse she used:

Tutor:	Oh that was good. You put the clown's head with the clown. OK. OK. Does that look like it would fit too?
	Look. What's this here?
	Do you know who this is?
	Maybe we could leave that piece and we could see – who's this here?

This recitation series of statements and questions are the most common types of interaction in schools: they seek predictable, or yes or no answers, are rarely responsive to student productions and rarely assist students develop more elaborate ideas (Hoetker & Ahlbrand, 1969).

The learner's ZPD: Comparison of relationship between mentors' and tutors' teaching

A shared focus on the same problem was apparent between Max and the mentor and Max and the tutor. However, the expert's and novice's differing skills in using assisted learning tools, and the higher-order cognitive skills displayed by Max during the second activity, influenced the verbal and non-verbal discourse and the length of time it took for the puzzle to be completed.

When the problem-solving activity was a new experience for Max, the verbal discourse showed many of his non-verbal actions to be inaccurate. After two minutes of trying to fit a piece into a certain place, Max introduced a diversion with a comment about the tape recorder:

Child: It's not coming on. The tape is – the tape's not coming on.
Mentor: No. The tape is recording now. That means you don't hear anything. Then I can rewind it then press the PLAY button and we can hear all the things we've been talking about and hear your voice.
Was it this colour blue you were looking at or was it the colour blue?
Child: That colour blue.

Max's diversionary comment about the tape was responded to by the mentor, through the ZPD, to increase his understanding of the operational processes of tape recording. His focus was then guided back to the task as she asked a direct question about the specific colour at which he had been looking.

Following this discussion, another minute passed and Max was still trying to fit the same piece in the same place. The mentor had presented various strategies before he responded to the following use of questioning combined with instructing to adopt a new strategy:

Mentor: ...Are you sure that's the bit that goes on there?
Child: Pretty sure. I have...
Mentor: I'm wondering if it is now because you've been trying for a long time and it hasn't fitted yet.
Child: Oh. No pieces.
Mentor: Try another one. ...

Max was not attempting to try different puzzle pieces even though the one he had selected did not fit. However, with the mentor's intervention of an open question and instructing through the ZPD, his problem-solving strategies were extended to include an alternate action and achieve the desired result. The length of time taken by Max to reach this point (three minutes), and his introduction of a diversionary comment, indicates the puzzle was proving too difficult for him and intervention by the mentor was essential for successful completion of the task.

Conversely, when working with the tutor, Max had no hesitation in placing the pieces and did not initiate any diversion, his focus remaining on the puzzle while responding to her direct questions accurately. Even allowing for the two interludes of diversionary discourse with the mentor (one minute), Max completed the puzzle with the tutor in less than half the time (three minutes, 57 seconds) of the initial attempt (ten minutes) with the mentor. He had not worked with the puzzle in the interim period.

14.3 Summary and Implications

While the tutor had acquired some skills to initiate Max into, and scaffold, the problem-solving task, she had not acquired the ability to hand over responsibility when he indicated he was ready. The task structure illustrates her control of the situation and, although there was a shared joint focus on the puzzle, her introductions guided the child's responses, allowing little freedom for experimentation or contribution. Conversely, the mentor's role-modelled behaviour allowed the child almost equal opportunity for joint task structuring, involvement and response.

Differences in using the abstract tools of observation, contingency management, feedback, questioning and cognitive structuring are also apparent in the two transcripts. The tutor's inexperienced and restricted use of these tools contrasts to the mentor's skill and competence in using them iteratively and relevantly to assist the learner acquire problem-solving skills. Although each observed the activity, their focus was on different elements. While the mentor observed and commented on the child's actions as he was placing the pieces, the tutor observed the puzzle and commented on which piece would be required next. Feedback was used by the mentor to describe whether actions met, or did not meet the standard required, while the tutor concentrated on contingency management to encourage continuance of the behaviour.

Working through the ZPD, the mentor extended the child's present level of development by open questioning requiring internal self-talk and selection of responses, while the tutor used closed, convergent questions which required factual or yes or no answers. Little instruction was provided by either mentor or tutor but cognitive structuring was provided by the mentor, pointing out various relationships between the activity and events in the socio-cultural environment. The tutor identified relationships solely within the puzzle itself.

While the learner's focus was on the problem-solving activity with both mentor and tutor, a temporary distraction which he initiated during the former experience indicated that he needed the mentor's assistance to perform the task successfully. The shorter time taken to complete the puzzle and the child's initial comments to the tutor also indicate that he may have acquired the necessary problem-solving skills when working with the mentor and was ready to proceed independently. However, the tutor did not introduce an avenue to ascertain this.

When children are not allowed to take responsibility for a task which they are able to perform independently, dependency or learned helplessness may develop. Knowing when to hand over a task to a learner requires analysis, complex judgement, appropriate action and reflection; a combination of strategic thinking and action, using assisted learning tools strategically. The skilful use of these tools takes time to develop!

Although this is only one case study, and the length of time it takes for learning and development to occur through the ZPD varies according to the person, their prior experiences and education, the findings demonstrate that the use of untrained or partially trained tutors in educational settings must be planned carefully. While the tutors may gain valuable experiences assisting young children in certain activities, this must not be at the expense of the learning and development of the child. Students as tutors must not be expected to have developed assisted learning tools to the same extent as skilled, experienced teachers; therefore the tasks they are expected to perform must reflect their developing capabilities.

Address for correspondence (and/or for a fuller version of this chapter): Margaret E. Shore, Community Services and Health Business Unit, Cooloola Sunshine Institute of TAFE, NAMBOUR, 4560, Queensland, Australia.

PART D: INSTITUTIONALISING STUDENT TUTORING AND MENTORING

Chapter 15

PEER TUTORING FOR ACADEMIC CREDIT

John Jones

This chapter argues that academic credit can validly be offered for courses appropriately organised around peer tutoring schemes in higher education. Evidence in support of this argument is drawn from literature relating to (a) student learning outcomes, (b) opinions of desirable outcomes in higher education, and (c) competency-based approaches to education. Three case studies from Auckland, New Zealand, are presented as examples of courses based around peer tutoring that carry academic credit. The cases involve law, science and business students respectively, all of whom are enrolled in degree studies.

15.1 Introduction

The benefits of peer tutoring have been documented in a number of publications (Goodlad & Hirst, 1989; 1990) and there is evidence (especially via attendance at conferences and the like) that interest in the approach is increasing. However, despite the evident benefits and interest, peer tutoring is still a 'marginal' activity – at least at the tertiary level which is the focus of this chapter – in that it is treated as a 'technique' where it is used at all, rather than as a central organising structure for a course or programme. It has rarely been absorbed into the mainstream of academic courses. The major argument of this chapter is that peer tutoring for academic credit is valid, and that it is possible to locate it comfortably within the usual academic arrangements. The argument can be summarised as follows:

- peer tutoring in higher education has the potential for facilitating:
  – significant academic learning on the part of the tutor (and those tutored)
  – desired generic outcomes that are frequently espoused by academics in terms of the aims of degree studies
  – 'competences' that are valued by potential employers of graduates
- given the significance of the potential outcomes listed above, peer tutoring can validly form the basis of university courses that carry academic credit
- three case studies are presented as concrete evidence that such credit-carrying courses are both feasible and valuable, and from these some tentative principles for the successful organisation of credit-carrying courses are drawn.

To begin, it is worth reviewing the kinds of rewards that are associated with peer tutoring in higher education, and this is best done within a broad categorisation of peer tutoring approaches. Projects reported on can be described under four headings, as follows.

Informal, interactive methods in classes

These methods consist of 'teaching tools', now used quite commonly in lecture classes, and involving arrangements where students learn from each other by interacting in directed discussion groups of one kind or another. Habershaw *et al.* (1993) give a good overview of the range of possibilities.

Formalised course structures involving peer tutoring

In these arrangements a significant amount of the substantive content of courses is presented or managed by students who are enrolled in that course. Perhaps the most common example is postgraduate or advanced level courses that are often based around student presentations of research or project work in which they are engaged, or of other material which is assigned to them for research and presentation. There are also other arrangements that have been put in place to deal with particular course demands and contexts: for one example, where students were trained to act as tutors in conjunction with computer-based learning packages, see Behrendorff & Marriott (1993).

Students at one level acting as tutors for those at another level in the same institution

Here the rationale is that 'competent' students are able to successfully teach 'less competent' students – usually at a less advanced stage of their studies. Two obvious examples of this, which many readers may have encountered, are the teaching assistant schemes common in the USA, and the laboratory demonstrator arrangements in the UK. There is a further – largely unstated – rationale that the arrangement is also useful in inducting the student tutors (many of whom will eventually teach in one way or another in tertiary institutions) into academic teaching. Other arrangements are possible apart from these 'conventionalities': Case Study 3, later in this chapter, describes one.

Students in one institution acting as tutors for those in another

As above, the essential rationale is that 'competent' (and more academically advanced) students can successfully teach those who are less competent. In addition, there is the potential for significant impact in terms of changing the attitudes and aspirations of the tutored students, and of facilitating the entry to tertiary education of social groups who are often under-represented. This aspect is picked up in Case Studies 1 and 2 below which describe arrangements of this kind; Jones & Jones (1987) have previously discussed some of the structural issues involved.

The first two categories of peer tutoring are similar in that they are both teaching or instructional strategies used within the boundaries of a 'conventional' course. As such it is similar to course demands such as sitting and taking notes in lectures, engaging in laboratory exercises, etc. At the end of the course the students who perform at the required level are awarded academic credit. It is less common to find the award of academic credit associated with peer tutoring arrangements that extend 'unconventionally' across levels within an institution, or across institutions. Where students have been involved in such schemes then the rewards, in any direct sense, have usually been either intrinsic or financial.

Intrinsic rewards come from the satisfaction of participating, in a voluntary capacity, in a worthwhile activity that has obvious benefits for those involved. The Pimlico Scheme (Goodlad *et al.*, 1979) is one example of such an arrangement.

Financial rewards are almost always associated with arrangements in which later year (usually graduate) students act as teachers in tutorial classes, or demonstrators in laboratories.

15.2 Peer Tutoring for Academic Credit

Within a conventional course in a tertiary institution it is perfectly feasible to set up arrangements by which students do almost all of the 'up-front' teaching of each other. I am aware of many graduate courses (and some at the later undergraduate level) where the major course activity consists of students being assigned or choosing a section of the substantive material of the course, and then being required to research this and present it in one way or another to the rest of the group. Students may be assessed in a number of ways: usually some credit is allocated to the teaching presentation, together with rewards for other assignments, test and end-of-course examination performance. This arrangement seems to be readily accepted within academic institutions. What is less common is to find cross-level peer tutoring arrangements within the same institution, or cross-institution peer tutoring that is incorporated into a course structure that attracts academic credit.

The three case studies described in the next section are examples of where this has been organised, in one way or another. Before presenting these case studies, a brief rationale or 'defence' of the use of cross-context peer tutoring approaches for academic credit is presented. This is necessary, I believe, as there is still considerable suspicion within academia of the essential structure. Evidence for the validity of the use of peer tutoring as a course rationale is drawn from three separate sources: first from literature relating to student learning outcomes; second from literature concerned with academics' opinions of the goals of a university education; and third from competency-based approaches to education.

Research into student learning in higher education

Over the past two decades a great deal of work has been carried out into student learning in higher education, stimulated by the early initiatives at the University of Gothenburg in Sweden (see, for example, Marton & Saljo, 1976 a and b). The broad thrust of all of this work has been to cast light on the ways in which students approach learning tasks and achieve different degrees or kinds of understanding of complex bodies of subject matter. As a result of this work, a basic distinction has been drawn between two different approaches to learning that students adopt; deep and surface. Descriptions of these approaches (based on Ramsden, 1992) are as follows.

A *deep approach* is associated with a meaning orientation, where a student attempts to understand material by relating the separate parts of a subject to each other, and also to integrate this subject matter with other knowledge and experience.

A *surface approach* is associated with a reproducing orientation, where the student's basic aim is to reproduce the symbols or words associated with a topic, in order to satisfy assessment requirements, without necessarily comprehending at any significantly meaningful level what those symbols signify.

A further broad conclusion to emerge from this work is that the nature of the tasks set in an educational setting will significantly affect the approach that a student chooses to take to learning, with consequent effects upon learning outcomes. If the student perception is that a surface approach (basically rote-memorising) is the sensible strategy to adopt in order to satisfy the assessment requirements, then that is the strategy that is most likely to be adopted. In this case the quality of understanding will be limited. Conversely, if the nature of the task demands that students 'really understand' the subject, then the chances of that occurring are that much greater.

There is a fairly obvious link between these broad conclusions and the very commonly expressed opinion that 'the first time I really understood the subject was when I had to teach it'. To teach something – in a tutorial setting as opposed to a didactic lecture setting – demands that one really come to grips with it, in order to render it meaningful to the learner. What is interesting is that this intuitive conclusion finds support in the research literature. The work of Pask (1976) and Novak & Gowin (1984) is pertinent. Underlying any body of knowledge is some kind of structure of concepts, facts, ideas and propositions that ties the whole together in a coherent way. Novak and Gowin describe the web of ideas that constitute a topic in terms of concept maps; Pask uses the term 'entailment structures'. In strictly formalised terms these are a little different from one another, but the essential principles underlying their construction are very similar. Most crucially for peer tutoring, one of Pask's fundamental premises is that learners have achieved understanding when they are capable of 'teaching back' the subject to someone else (possibly operating at a different level of intellectual development or experience) in a way that is mutually satisfying to both.

195

These ideas are also related to the SOLO taxonomy of Biggs & Collis (1982), which expresses learning outcomes in terms of the degree of elaboration and interconnectedness which a learner can validly bring to bear upon a set of subject matter. Again, it is a persuasive argument within their formulation that the ability to tutor someone successfully is a mark of understanding.

Expressions of desirable educational objectives

Educational courses and curricula aim to have students achieve 'valued' learning outcomes. Over the years there have been many descriptions, categorisations and expressions of opinion as to what these learning outcomes should be. For example Hall (1993) has reported upon a university staff perspective concerning the goals of a university educa-tion. These are: gaining a knowledge base in a subject; acquiring professional competencies; developing cognitive skills; developing re-search skills; personal development; and developing a value base. It is interesting too that staff articulated three 'enabling skills' for the achievement of these goals: communication skills; numeracy; and information technology literacy. The point which is being stressed in this present chapter is that teaching, via peer tutoring, can constitute a valid and effective vehicle for students to develop some of these skills, and move toward the achievement of the outcomes.

Opinions as to desirable outcomes are not confined to the ad hoc comments of academics! There is other work, derived from systematic literature survey, to back-up the broad expressions of opinion referred to above (eg, Allen, 1988). Particularly significant perhaps is Otter's (1992) work, in that it was based upon a series of workshops designed to collect various stakeholders' opinions of the desirable outcomes of higher education. One of the core learning outcomes identified was 'ability to communicate complex material to a variety of audiences'. This is consistent with the view of understanding discussed in relation to Pask's work, in the last section.

Competency-based approaches

Over the past few years, so-called 'competency-based' approaches to education have been a contentious issue in higher education and training, generating considerable debate in the UK (Burke, 1989) and Australasia (Bowden & Masters, 1992). Some of the major concerns expressed in connection with the approach centre on the tendency toward lengthy lists of reductionist and fine-grained competences, and the undue influence that the approach gives employers and professional bodies over the specification of educational outcomes. For all that, the work has generated some interesting research work and stimulated a focus on just what it is that higher educational programmes are aiming to achieve. It is arguable that it has led to an emergent recognition of the need for more 'integrated' outcomes that involve knowledge, skills and attitudes (see also Carter, 1985). In fact there is often a (surprising?) consensus among employers and academics as to the qualities that are desirable in a graduate. It is worth quoting Bowden & Masters (1992:107) on the views of employers concerning what it means to be a competent professional:

> All the respondents emphasised that a competent professional had to have technical or academic knowledge, (i.e. knowledge acquired through tertiary study), but also had to have other skills, competencies and qualities. Most commonly, these skills related to working with and communicating with people – be they colleagues or clients.

What has been argued in this section is that a proper 'deep' understanding of a subject comes with the ability to construct valid and elaborated conceptual maps of the knowledge domain, together with the ability to locate those maps in broader contexts. There is evidence to suggest that both the demonstration and the development of that understanding can be facilitated by peer tutoring arrangements. Moreover, the skills involved are central to those that are articulated by academics and employers as desirable goals for higher education. If we can accept that this is indeed the case, then the argument for organising peer teaching arrangements that carry appropriate academic credit becomes persuasive. The next section outlines three cases, all in Auckland, New Zealand, in which that course organisation has been accomplished.

15.3 Three Case Studies

1. Tutoring in schools by university law students

(This programme has been coordinated by Ann Jones, School of Law, The University of Auckland.)

Final-year students from the University of Auckland School of Law have been tutoring in local secondary schools since 1987. The aim was to make young people aware of their general rights and responsibilities. The rewards to the student tutors were intrinsic: they became involved because they thought that there was a need. From the outset, feedback from school teachers and students was very positive, and the demand for tutoring from schools was well beyond the resources available. By 1989 academic staff in the School of Law had become aware of the value of this experience for the law students. An evaluation carried out in 1988/9 revealed that law students felt they had learned a great deal from their tutoring. They had critically addressed a body of substantive law and had also acquired skills and values which would help them empower future clients to make their own decisions. These aspects led to the formalisation of the tutoring scheme as an option in the final-year practical component of the law degree. It is assessed on the basis of a report which students write, focusing on their critical reflections upon the tutoring placement. It has gained the reputation of a demanding but rewarding option to be undertaken by only 'the dedicated'!

The mechanics of the scheme involve having law students working with the same small group of (about five) school students for one session a week, over a period of a month. During these sessions the groups work on a variety of 'legal' issues (under-age drinking, hire purchase contracts, etc) that are of interest to the school students. A lawyer from the local community law centre visits the groups and becomes involved in discussions, after the law students have developed a rapport with their group over a week or so. This ensures quality control – and enables school students to meet with a real lawyer and take on board the notion of access to legal advice. As a preparation for tutoring in schools, an extensive orientation/training programme is undertaken. This involves aspects such as training in small group teaching, sensitisation to cultural differences, etc, as well as education about areas of the law that relate especially to young people.

The potential course-work credit is equivalent to 6% of a year's work: however, the 'impact' on students is almost certainly greater than this figure suggests. As described above, students are asked to write a report on their tutoring in the school, which gives feedback on their experience to the course organiser and is taken into account in awarding a grade for this component. The tutoring programme has been evaluated by gathering student feedback via a questionnaire that asks for both specific information (relating to course organisation, usefulness of the experience, etc) and open-ended comment. Tutors continue to report considerable intrinsic rewards. Many are from minority ethnic groups and have their own agenda of positive role-modelling. Others wish to work with people who feel alienated from the legal system and treat it with suspicion. They all reap the reward of feeling useful while learning themselves and of developing a relationship of mutual respect with school teachers and students.

2. Tutoring in schools by university science students

(This programme has been organised by John Jones, Higher Education Research Office, The University of Auckland, now at Educational Development Unit, Hong Kong Polytechnic University.)

For the last six years a paper has been offered in the science faculty at the University of Auckland entitled 'Tutoring in Science'. It operates at second-year level and represents about 15% of a student's annual workload. The whole of the paper is organised around a central core that involves university students tutoring in local secondary schools. In outline the paper is organised as follows:

Weeks 1 to 5:
   Orientation to tutoring in science (at university, two hours per week)
   This involved introducing students to some basic concepts of 'how students learn science', as well as addressing the skills of tutoring, team-building, etc.
Weeks 5 to 20:
   Tutoring in schools (in schools, two hours per week)
   Tutorials (in university, one hour per week)
Weeks 21 to 25:
   Reflecting on experience/report writing (at university, open-ended).

Students are assessed via three components: an on-course essay in the first term; a practical tutoring component; and an end-of-year report.

Enrolment in the course is limited to 20 students per year, who are divided into four groups for the 15 weeks of the tutoring component. Each group of five students is assigned to one school that they visit for a period of two hours on the same afternoon each week. During their time in school, students tutor – as a whole group – in two science classes, under the direction of the regular class teacher. One of the course requirements is that the university students produce a 'research/reflective' report based on their time in schools; to help facilitate that, and share information about activities in the different schools, a series of tutorial meetings is organised at university during the tutoring phase.

Prior to its adoption as a paper carrying academic credit, the tutoring scheme was operated as a research project, with student tutors paid for their work in schools. Evaluation of the project indicated that significant benefits accrued to both tutors and the tutored (Jones, 1990), and less formal ongoing evaluation has indicated strongly that these benefits have continued since the scheme has operated as an academic paper. The major benefits can be summarised as follows:

For school students
- a better understanding of science
- credible role-models in the form of university science students
- a boost in confidence that they can understand science.

For university tutors:
- consolidation and extension of subject knowledge
- trying out teaching as a career
- doing something useful with university learning
- developing communication skills and learning about other cultures.

Since the tutoring scheme was accepted as the basis for a paper carrying academic credit, it has been evaluated each year via university student responses to questionnaires issued at the end of each year. Students are generally very positive about it, and a significant outcome is the enthusiasm for the activity that most describe. They enjoy the experience – though they generally find the tutoring in schools to be demanding and exhausting. More especially, though, they learn a great deal. They learn more science, they learn about teaching science, and develop some useful skills associated with that; they learn about doing research. They generally put in considerable energy and effort and learn a lot, which is reflected in the good course grades that most attain.

3. Peer tutoring by polytechnic business students

(This programme is organised by Phil Ker, Student Services, Auckland Institute of Technology.)

For the first time, in the second semester of 1994, seven Bachelor of Business students at Auckland Institute of Technology had the opportunity to earn academic credit via a course based around peer tutoring. The paper represented one-sixth of a year's full-time work. Essentially it aimed to develop students as peer tutors in such a way as to provide them with the skills, knowledge and understanding necessary for supervisory/management positions in business. An important part of the justification for the paper is its vocational application – an aspect that has been recognised and supported by the NZ Institute of Management. Consistent with that emphasis is an explicit aim to develop students as critical thinkers and lifelong learners.

The course is divided into three sections.

1. An initial series of classes designed to introduce the conceptual underpinning for peer tutoring, together with the development of basic tutoring skills.
2. A practicum – consisting of the actual peer tutoring phase – during which students undertake work in either one, or a combination, of the following contexts:

    ■ one-to-one tutoring of students in a particular discipline
    ■ one-to-one tutoring of students in general study skills (literacy, numeracy)
    ■ assisting in the teaching of regular classes
    ■ managing small study/tutorial groups in a particular discipline.
3. A final feedback and reflection stage during which each student presents a review and analysis of one of their 'cases'.

Students were required to keep a reflective journal during their practicum, and to debrief at least once a week with an assigned academic supervisor. One of the rationales for the course is that of enhancing the provision of learning support in the institute, by providing a structure that supports the student tutors, develops their capabilities as tutors, and awards academic credit for appropriate achievement. Students were assessed on the basis of a 'portfolio' of written work (two learning resources and two case studies) together with an oral presentation concerning the 'cases' that formed the basis of the tutoring.

The course was evaluated by having a staff member from the institute's Centre for Professional Development meet with the students for a two-hour structured discussion. Substantively the feedback was very positive – though some suggestions for organisational modifications were forthcoming. Students found the course demanding and 'emotionally draining' on occasion but very worthwhile: 'a breath of fresh air' as one participant described it. An interesting spin-off that students reported on was the fact that they became much more critical of the way that other courses were run, and the way that they were taught!

15.4 Conclusions

There is considerable evidence to suggest that significant benefits can accrue from peer tutoring programmes. Benefits occur for tutors, for tutees, for teachers – and for the 'field' or context in which the tutoring takes place (Jones, 1990). What the case studies above demonstrate is that those benefits can take place within programmes that – very properly and validly, in terms of the arguments put forward earlier in this chapter – carry academic credit. In reflecting upon both the direct and vicarious experiences of the programmes I would suggest that there are a number of aspects which it is particularly important to address in organising peer tutoring programmes for academic credit. These are outlined briefly below:

- Expect a high standard of work from students, both in terms of written material and the 'professionalism' that they exhibit in their approach to tutoring. Associated with this, involve students in discussions about the criteria according to which their work will be assessed, and the standards expected. It is also important that students receive the training and support that enable them to achieve those high standards.
- Give students formative feedback on their performance, as regularly as possible. In practical terms this means:
  - regular contact with students during the practical tutoring phase of the programme
  - an opportunity (as a requirement) to submit draft written work, or engage in oral presentation, at an early stage in order to receive feedback and critique before final work is presented for assessment.
- For many students the business of tutoring is initially rather fraught and threatening. Those feelings can be reduced by allowing students to work together as a supportive team, and meet regularly to 'debrief' and share experiences and reflections with one another.
- Set up a well-organised structure and communicate this in writing to all involved – tutors, tutees, teachers, etc – so that participants' roles and responsibilities are clear to everyone
- As course organiser, practise what you preach! Especially, incorporate the elements of 'good tutoring' that you espouse in tutors' preparatory programmes into your own interactions with them.

202

■ Evaluate the course: systematically by means such as getting students to complete an end-of-course questionnaire; informally by staying as 'tuned' as possible to what is going on in the programme as it proceeds, and taking appropriate modifying action when necessary.

Note and acknowledgements

This article draws on a piece that first appeared in *HERDSA News*, 16, 3, in November 1994.

I gratefully acknowledge the contributions from Ann Jones and Phil Ker.

Address for correspondence: John Jones, Educational Development Unit, Hong Kong Polytechnic University, Hung Hom, Kowloon, Hong Kong. Tel. (852) 2766 6320. Fax (852) 2334 1569.

Chapter 16

RESPONDING TO STUDENT NEEDS IN A NEW ZEALAND POLYTECHNIC AND SECONDARY SCHOOLS

Peter Fisher and Jo Howse

Manukau Polytechnic is one of New Zealand's largest tertiary institutions and currently employs 50 peer tutors in the learning centre to tutor in a wide range of academic and technical subjects. Peer tutoring is now integral in the polytechnic curriculum and this model is being adapted to develop a programme with polytechnic students tutoring in local secondary schools. Research on student outcomes from peer tutoring will be shared.

At the end of this year, Manukau Polytechnic celebrates its 25th anniversary and it is timely to reflect on past, present and future initiatives.

Manukau Technical Institute, as it was then known, opened in 1970 located on one campus to the south of Auckland city in a semi-rural area. The immediate community was a low-cost housing area. Surrounding this were pockets of suburbs as well as areas of farmland. The primary role of Manukau Technical Institute was to provide training for engineering trades, technicians, and some basic-level business and secretarial programmes.

The past 25 years have seen considerable growth and an expansion to include academic and degree courses. To give an indication of its current size, the 1994 statistics were as follows:

Student enrolments	15,500
Equivalent full-time students (excluding overseas students)	4,200
Overseas students: 230 from over 24 countries	(160 EFTS)
Equivalent full-time staff	650
Full-time staff	450
Departments	16, organised into the four faculties of arts, business, health and technology
Campuses/sites	six.

The title 'polytechnic' has been used for some years in New Zealand. Over 20 institutions operate under the polytechnic regulations, but some have chosen not to use the word in their title. Today, they offer programmes at all levels of tertiary education and training: trades, community education, certificate and diploma courses, second language programmes, some teacher education as well as degree programmes. The range of programmes provided through polytechnics in New Zealand is enormous both in the spread of subjects and the variety of levels.

The New Zealand government has taken recent initiatives in tertiary education to develop a National Qualifications Framework. A recurring theme has been the need for 'staircasing' or a 'seamless' education system, where students may pass from secondary school education to a private provider, to a polytechnic or university, collecting transferable credits and building up a recognised qualification as they go. This framework classifies all tertiary level training on an eight-level scale and is similar to other models used elsewhere, such as the NVQ model in the UK. Units of learning are currently being written to describe the level of competence a student must have achieved in each subject at each level to gain credit. Level one includes qualifications that may be gained in the third or fourth year of secondary school as well as qualifications for speakers of other languages. At the other end of the scale, level eight describes postgraduate qualifications. Converting qualifications to the new framework and working through accreditation processes has been a major focus for polytechnics over the past three years.

Until the mid-1980s, every significant decision about polytechnics was made by a Department of Education. That Department has now been replaced by a Ministry, and polytechnics are bulk-funded and financially accountable according to an EFTS target which is negotiated with the Ministry. Policies to increase the number of places in tertiary education have resulted in student fees for a one-year business programme rising from NZ$130 in 1990 to NZ$1,530 in 1995.

Probably the greatest challenge has come in meeting the changing needs of the student population. Manukau Polytechnic's local area (South Auckland) is today characterised by :

■ high unemployment
■ a diverse multicultural population which includes Maori, Pacific Island and South East Asian cultures
■ a large number of refugees
■ workplaces mainly involved in light industrial activities.

While retraining and other programmes designed for mature adults will always be necessary, secondary schools are the source of about 30% of our EFTS. In recognition of this, partnerships with local secondary schools now offer innovative ways for secondary school students to link in with polytechnic programmes. Communication studies, for example, is a core subject in nearly all polytechnic programmes. With this in mind, a communications pathways programme has been introduced. This introduces the subject at school level and enables students to begin building credits towards national tertiary qualifications while still at school. Secondary school teachers are trained by polytechnic staff and carry out the teaching, while the polytechnic moderates their assessments. This year 20 schools will participate, involving over 500 students. The success of this model means that it will now be applied in other subject areas.

Secondly, foundation and bridging programmes have developed in many departments for students whose lack of basic qualifications or language skills or study skills would have prevented them from being placed directly onto a mainstream programme.

Thirdly, degree programmes and degree partnerships with universities in New Zealand and overseas have added a further dimension to our workload.

At the same time as our range of programmes has increased at both the lower and higher ends of the range, we have also had to be conscious of maintaining and developing the 'traditional' areas of trades, technician, certificate and diploma level courses.

Against this background of educational and administrative change, the learning centre and peer tutoring programme was established in 1992. On a pragmatic level, the learning centre was seen, in a time of rapidly increasing student fees and increasing competition from other providers, as an important ingredient in the total educational service we provide. Along with counselling, health and other services, it removes barriers to learning and enhances student achievement. Keeping students in the system is a sound strategy both from a customer service perspective and for the financial health of the institute.

Peer tutoring was founded to provide a learning support service to students on preliminary, certificate, diploma and degree courses. The peer tutoring programme provides learning assistance to all students across the curriculum of Manukau Polytechnic and the objectives are :

- to provide learning support to any student who is having difficulty with study or the academic requirements of their course
- to enhance the learning of all students
- to provide a range of tuition to meet the individual needs of students
- to provide a close working relationship with the programme leaders and the lecturers of all departments
- to maintain a supportive teaching environment conducive to quality learning.

During the inception, the manager initiated meetings with heads of departments, programme leaders and lecturers with an emphasis on information-giving and consultation so that the academic staff were stakeholders in the peer tutoring programme as it evolved. In 1994, 50 peer tutors were employed and trained to tutor students in most subjects across the polytechnic curriculum. The criteria for selection were:

- high academic performance in nominated subjects for tutoring
- excellent interpersonal skills
- a commitment to tutor for the remainder of the course/ programme
- a commitment to attend training sessions once a month.

On application to qualify as a peer tutor, students are required to complete an enrolment form and an interview with the manager or the administrator of the learning centre, as well as seek approval from the programme leader and the lecturer of the subject to be tutored. The learning centre staff spend considerable time matching the student with the tutor and the subject lecturer is notified (with the approval of the student requesting learning support) so that the necessary linkage and support with teaching resources is established. Peer tutoring is widely accepted by the academic staff of Manukau Polytechnic and a spirit of cooperation prevails between learning centre staff and the lecturers with the responsibility for the delivery of the curriculum in the classroom. This goodwill can be attributed to regular information-giving and communication, the hallmarks of the administration of such a large peer tutoring programme penetrating the whole polytechnic curriculum. The academic staff are encouraged to regard this as not only learning support for the students but also as a teaching support for the lecturers to enhance both teaching and learning, as the two are integral and should not be regarded as separate entities.

The peer tutor arranges a tuition time with the student and the time and venue are confirmed by the administrator who coordinates the timetable. The majority of students self-refer, although occasionally a concerned lecturer will accompany a student on the first visit to the learning centre. Self-referral is preferred as polytechnic students as adult learners respond well to personal choice, generally reflected in a higher level of motivation and successful outcomes.

The peer tutoring clientele (both tutors and students), in terms of the wide range of ages, academic levels, technical skills, ethnic groups and disabled students, reflects the continuum of the mainstream population of Manukau Polytechnic. Peer tutoring is open to all Manukau Poly-technic students with no restrictions, as some of the most academically competent require assistance with time management, exam technique or the writing of a research proposal. An emphasis is on process during the teaching session, although the peer tutor must be sound in subject knowledge as the two cannot be separated. Many students in their previous educational experience have failed to grasp the rudiments of writing an essay, the preparation for a test and often, because of low self-esteem and a lack of self-confidence, have not realised their full potential in their previous learning situation.

A compulsory training session for peer tutors is held every month and staff within the polytechnic are invited to train and to share their expertise and skills. The training covers sessions on Maoridom, Pacific Island focus, time management, essay writing, language of assignments and mind mapping. Peer tutors are granted the opportunity to share experiences and to socialise. It is particularly gratifying to see barriers removed between academic and technical courses. Training then con-tinues with peer tutors grouped into subjects meeting with the manager once a semester to enhance teaching skills within the context of a subject.

Peer tutors are competing favourably for employment in a tight market outside of the polytechnic and many won jobs at the end of last year.

In December 1994, a survey was conducted to gain student feedback on tuition in the learning centre. A sample of 55 students was randomly selected from over 2,900 students who were tutored in the learning centre in 1994, using a stratified linear technique. Letters of explanation and the questionnaires were posted to the students two weeks after course completion to allow time for the notification of final results. (The Privacy Act 1993, denies access to students' academic results.) It was disappointing that only 19 returns were received by January 1995 and three were returned as addresses were unknown. The 16 responses represented a 29% return rate and this eliminated the possibility of a detailed quantitative analysis. The sample was considered sufficiently random to be indicative of the whole sample but not sufficiently large to predict the population. The majority of respondents lacked confidence at the commencement of tuition, while a quarter indicated that they were confident and one student was very confident. The latter requested tuition in a specialist area in order to gain an A pass.

All students surveyed gained in confidence as a result of individual tuition in the learning centre:

> The learning centre gave me the confidence and slowed down the learning process to a pace I was comfortable with.

> The learning centre gave me what I lacked most: 'confidence'.

> The learning centre gave me more confidence in myself.

The majority of the students acknowledged an improved change in attitude towards learning while a quarter reported no change in attitude. The following are direct reporting of the students' responses:

> It made me determined to overcome problems.

> It helped me a lot after being out of school for over five years.

> The tuition has given me confidence in my work and attitude towards it.

> Spending time with someone who understood gave me the ability to see the basic principles and how to use them.

> It provided additional support and encouragement.

> Increased interest in learning.

> Given courage and warmth and patience.

> Boosted morale.

> I now enjoy learning.

> I can now tackle tasks and medication calculations feeling confident.

The number of hours of peer tuition ranged from two to 12 hours per student and the 16 respondents indicated that peer tutoring enabled them to understand the subject tutored, to complete the course work, to improve in grades and to gain personal support.

The learning centre and the peer tutoring programme are funded out of the mainstream Manukau Polytechnic budget and, in a cost-effective climate, it is heartening to see no charge for peer tutoring. The learning centre is fortunate to have the support of the Manukau Polytechnic Students Association to fund the refreshments made available to students. The organisational culture of the learning centre, with no charges, the new and colourful environment coupled with a warm and friendly atmosphere, is conducive to a successful learning experience and this is reflected in positive comments in the survey:

It is the most helpful system in Manukau Polytechnic.

Without this service, I simply couldn't carry on in class.

The learning centre is quite a saviour to those who want to get somewhere.

Is it possible to get more budget to increase the student tutorial hours in the future?

More of the same please.

It's nice to know you are there.

More time – I don't feel stress in here.

The current system is an excellent one.

It has helped my whole outlook on the course.

Thanks for your help, you're doing great.

Wonderful service.

Keep on the encouragement and good work!!

Although the sample was smaller than anticipated, the students' responses to the questionnaire were consistently positive and reflected for the majority an improvement in attitude towards learning, a personal gain in confidence and successful academic outcomes. Students indicated that they were helped most by:

- understanding the subject
- completing course work
- grade improvement
- personal support.

Three students requested additional tuition hours above the current two hours per week allocated. It is significant that all students finished the course and close to a third completed a degree, diploma or certificate in 1994. The majority indicated that they were returning to the polytechnic in 1995 to continue their studies.

Internal peer tutoring is now well established and accepted in the polytechnic and it is timely to consider an adaptation to extend the programme into local secondary schools in Manukau City, New Zealand.

It is government policy to encourage all New Zealanders to improve their skills and training, with a view to an overall upskilling of particularly young people as a means to secure employment, and the country's aim of becoming a high-tech, added-value manufacturer and processor. This policy is strongly supported by tertiary providers and the school system, but there are inevitably students who, because of their socio-economic background, have difficulty in developing their full potential under the current system. Manukau Polytechnic has identified the opportunity for polytechnic students to assist secondary students in this category. This will involve carefully selected and trained student tutors actually going into schools and working with students in the 'at-risk' category during their study periods in order to:

- help schools enhance learning for pupils by providing polytechnic student tutors
- raise pupils' aspirations and motivation for education and training beyond school-leaving age by providing positive peer role models
- give polytechnic students the opportunity to develop their social, organisational, problem-solving and communication skills in a practical context
- provide pupils' with learning support to raise self-esteem, to increase confidence and to improve performance in assignment writing, tests and exams
- provide learning support to pupils of all abilities.

Manukau Polytechnic has recently developed the communications pathways programme for secondary schools in South Auckland as part of a schools partnerships initiative. It is proposed to offer polytechnic students as tutors in secondary schools programme in conjunction with the pathways initiative. The students as tutors programme will be coordinated by the manager, Manukau Polytechnic learning centre, in partnership with communication studies, schools liaison and staff of the participating schools. A team of suitable student tutors will be enlisted and trained at Manukau Polytechnic and allocated to three selected secondary schools in the South Auckland region. It is envisaged that this programme will be implemented in the second semester of 1995. It is anticipated that an advisory group of representatives of the participating schools, the polytechnic and the sponsors will be established to review progress and to set priorities for activity as the programme develops and demand increases.

Education continues to be a sector of the economy which is vital to New Zealand's future development. Reinforcing the government initiatives, and highlighting the importance of upskilling at all levels within the workforce, this programme provides opportunities for young people who come from difficult backgrounds, with limited financial resource, poor family support mechanisms and low self-esteem.

The polytechnic students as tutors in secondary schools programme is designed to encourage secondary students to identify with poly technic student role models, to take advantage of special tuition, to improve their communication skills, to boost their confidence and to encourage them to seek higher education as a preparation for secure employment.

There are few programmes available within New Zealand that provide an opportunity in this way. Students learning from students is a proven educational technique. This programme formalises it into a recognised structure, and will provide significant benefits for secondary students, polytechnic communication studies students and polytechnic tutorial staff, and will provide the necessary linkage between Manukau Polytechnic and the local secondary schools.

Peer tutoring is well established and accepted at Manukau Polytechnic. Students' results have shown positive outcomes for not only the students but also the peer tutors in terms of an increase in confidence, raised self-esteem and the completion of course requirements. It is significant for the peer tutors that learning has been enhanced as knowledge is consolidated and extended with wider reading and additional research in preparation for tutoring.

Research assistant: Dr Brian Cusack, Learning Centre, Manukau Polytechnic.

Address for correspondence: Peter Fisher and Jo Howse, Manukau Polytechnic, Auckland, New Zealand.

PART E: THE WIDER SCENE

Chapter 17

FROM FRIENDLY VISITING TO MENTORING: A TALE OF TWO MOVEMENTS

Marc Freedman

One hundred years ago the Friendly Visiting movement in America set out to help poor children and families through engaging middle-class volunteers to forge personal relationships. The movement fell victim to inflated expectations about the effectiveness of volunteer solutions to the problems of poverty. Today, a movement based on many of the same principles – mentoring – is sweeping the United States. This chapter argues that there is much value to the contemporary incarnation, but that it is susceptible to some of the same pitfalls that undermined Friendly Visiting. However, if we adopt realistic expectations about mentoring, while strengthening the practice of mentoring, this movement can make a genuine contribution. Ultimately, it might even lead to a broader set of humanising reforms affecting the two institutions where young people spend most of their time: public schools and community youth organisations.

Volunteer movements often express as much as they address. They are significant as much as social phenomena, as social interventions. This chapter seeks to illuminate the mentoring movement that has gained considerable popularity today in the United States through examining it in a broader historical context. It is only through doing so that it is possible to understand the specific role students play within this movement, or to comprehend the lessons that the US mentoring experience might hold for efforts in other parts of the world.

17.1 Not Alms, But a Friend

More than 100 years ago, in the context of massive urban strife, a campaign with many of the features of the contemporary mentoring movement – the objective of helping poor children and their families, the reliance on middle-class volunteers and, most prominently, an emphasis on the power of personal relationships to uplift the poor – was promulgated in the major urban areas of the United States.

Spearheading this new movement was a British immigrant to Buffalo, New York, Stephen Humphrey Gurteen, a Protestant clergyman who had been deeply touched by social reform efforts in London while a university student. Gurteen's philosophy of charitable assistance was rooted in distrust of almsgiving, the welfare of the day. Writing in 1882, Gurteen instructed his followers, 'The chief need of the poor today is not almsgiving, but the moral support of true friendship' (Gurteen, 1882: 174).

Like mentoring, Gurteen's movement was optimistic in nature. Proponents promised a tidal wave of volunteers, sweeping over urban America, 'flooding every part with sweetness, and order, and light' (National Conference, 1887:132). Under the banner, 'Not Alms, But a Friend,' the Friendly Visiting campaigns aspired to big numbers – 100,000 new volunteers – and set their sights particularly on saving young people in poverty. One movement leader, Mary Richmond, explained to new recruits, 'We should not despair of the children, so long as we can attach them to us and give them a new and better outlook upon life' (Richmond, 1899).

'Attachment' was the operative phrase. The movement believed that befriending the poor would be what was required to eradicate urban poverty. But imparting this philosophy turned out to be more complicated than originally anticipated, and Friendly Visiting soon found itself facing a trio of difficulties.

First, it turned out to be hard to bridge the social gulf between middle-class volunteers and slum families. Even though both parties shared the same race, and sometimes the same religion and ethnic background, the poor showed a strong preference to turn to individuals in their immediate context – friends, neighbours, relatives – for guidance and support. They distrusted the often patronising outsiders.

If demand was a problem, so was supply. It turned out to be equally difficult to get sufficient numbers of sustained and committed volunteers. Instead of a hundred thousand, the actual turnout was a few thousand overall. The middle-class women recruited to be visitors faced numerous other competing duties in the home and found these time constraints greatly compromised the amount of hours they could serve. Furthermore, the work was hard, and few volunteers had the fortitude to stick with this enterprise. Increasingly, a group of paid agents who were hired to support the visitors were pressed into direct service.

Finally, the limits of the Friendly Visiting approach – focused on social support and relationship – were underscored by a series of depressions which pummelled the American economy in the 1880s and 1890s. While relationship had its virtues, so did employment. Poverty proved to be a stronger impediment to the poor achieving middle-class status than missing mores to be imparted by good-hearted volunteers.

In combination, these three issues undermined Friendly Visiting, and the movement soon took on, according to historian Paul Boyer, the familiar cycle of so many heralded movements in American social policy, proceeding rapidly from initial enthusiasm to baffled discouragement (Boyer, 1978:155).

The death of Friendly Visiting, as a discrete movement, was final. The charitable organisations set up to administer these campaigns disappeared. However, Friendly Visiting's demise turned out to be even more important as a turning point than as an end point. Out of the ashes of the visiting campaigns emerged the phoenix of social work. The paid agents hired to support the volunteers demonstrated the value of more formalised, intensive and reliable efforts in the area of social services – in other words, of moving beyond voluntarism.

However, in the opening decades of the 20th century the early social workers (among their leaders Mary Richmond and some of the pioneers of Friendly Visiting) succeeded not only in solidifying the place of paid staff and of relegating volunteers to ceremonial functions far from direct contact with the poor, but of doing away with the notion of personal relationship as a useful tool for fighting poverty. Instead, the new social workers pinned their hopes – and that of their profession – on the 'science' of case work. As Roy Lubove, an historian of early social work

215

writes, the new credo might well of been, 'Neither alms nor a friend, but a scientific service' (Lubove, 1965:150).

17.2 The Rise of Mentoring

One hundred years after the collapse of Friendly Visiting, at a juncture when urban strife is again widespread in the US and many argue that America has disintegrated into deeply-divided ethnic and economic factions, a movement with many of the same features as the 19th century crusade has emerged. Built upon the volunteer efforts of middle-class role models, targeted at poor children seen as isolated from the mainstream world, the new mentoring movement, like Friendly Visiting before it, is most fundamentally about the power of personal relationships.

Over the past decade, Big Brothers/Big Sisters and other established volunteer mentoring efforts have been joined by a new wave of one-to-one programmes aimed at assisting young people – particularly those young people growing up in high-risk situations – to improve school performance, develop social skills, improve access to the labour market and generally help these youths navigate the often treacherous course to adulthood. Dozens of corporations, universities, youth organisations and civic groups have launched mentoring initiatives. Nationally, organisations such as the group One-to-One have joined Big Brothers/Big Sisters in promoting the mentoring cause, and others, including the Public Broadcasting System, Proctor and Gamble, and the Rainbow Coalition (to name just a few) have promulgated mentoring schemes. A particular hotbed is college campuses. A 1989 study found more than 1,700 mentoring and tutoring programmes operating in institutions of higher education across the nation (Reisner *et al.*, 1990).

Federal government support for mentoring programmes ranges from longstanding efforts like the US Department of Education's Trio programmes, a $500 million initiative that includes mentoring and adult support elements, to more recent additions like the US Department of Defense's Navy Kids project, the US Department of Justice's Juvenile Urban Mentoring Program (JUMP), and a variety of job training projects emanating from the US Department of Labor.

Mentoring activity is also growing at the state and local levels. Rhode Island and New York have established statewide mentoring campaigns, while mentoring networks now exist in Boise, Boston, Minneapolis and dozens of other locations. Baltimore and Oakland have each established organisations to promote and support mentoring programmes.

Understanding mentoring's growth

Despite the cautionary tale of Friendly Visiting, and mentoring's outward similarities to this earlier movement, the contemporary phenomenon is, arguably, something we ought to cheer about. The forces of scientific method, professional expertise and bureaucratisation which grew in the wake of Friendly Visiting – despite some genuine virtues – have simply proceeded too far.

Mentoring constitutes a reaction to this trend. It is a diagnosis of what is wrong with our institutions for young people, and an acknowledgment that we have lost fundamental insights into what young people need to grow up into full human beings. Specifically, mentoring springs from the fundamental insight that adults in our society are not spending enough time with kids. A great many young people growing up in America today do not even experience one significant, close relationship with an adult outside their immediate family before reaching adulthood themselves.

The institutions we have relied on historically for the nurturance of youth have changed in ways that dramatically reduce their capacity to deliver it. There are fewer adults in families, for example. Today more than one in four children is born into a single-parent household, more than two out of three African-American children. The 1980s alone saw a doubling of no-parent households. Regardless of the number of parents in the household, changes in the nature of work make it far more difficult for adults to spend time with their kids; as research by Harvard economist Juliet Schor shows, since 1970 alone, the average American works an additional 164 hours a year (Schor, 1991). This shift is the equivalent of an extra month's work, a good part of it coming at the expense of time with children.

At the same time, the institutions that might compensate for these shifts – neighbourhoods and schools – are themselves far from nurturing places. A recent J. Walter Thompson poll shows that three out of four Americans do not know the person living next door; meanwhile, in many urban neighbourhoods, the fear of violence has driven community adults, once an important source of socialisation and support, behind barred doors. Community youth organisations, such as Boys and Girls Clubs and YMCAs have helped pick up some of the slack, but are often strapped for adequate staff and funding.

This problem is particularly acute in American public schools. Once bastions of adult guidance, these institutions today can resemble impersonal teaching factories, reeling in the aftermath of budget cuts.

Student–counsellor ratios commonly approximate 500 to 1 in urban districts. Class size is frequently 30 or 40 students, and the average teacher will often face 200 students in a single day. Even the most caring find it hard to connect with more than a few young people.

These figures are all the more troubling given the level of stress young people confront. Growing up has never been easy, but today's youth confront a bewildering array of temptations and choices. Those youths living in the inner city are particularly besieged, experiencing environments approximating war zones. Seventy per cent of inner-city children have witnessed someone being beaten by the age of 15, while nearly a third have seen someone being shot.

The combination of this stress and the erosion of natural institutions for adult support of youth is one reason promulgating the quest for new sources of mentors. There is widespread concern that we've entered a period where kids are not getting the adult support they need, at precisely the juncture they need it most.

The second reason for mentoring's rise is the perception that close relationships with unrelated adults can supplement the work of parents and make a vast difference in the lives of youth. While this sense accords with a broader cultural perception linking mentoring with success (one *Harvard Business Review* article proclaims, 'Everyone Who Makes It Has a Mentor'), it also squares with important research from the social sciences focusing on 'resilient' youth – young people who overcome poverty despite vast obstacles.

Research spanning a variety of disciplines suggests that mentoring relationships are linked to resiliency. In the most substantial of these studies, developmental psychologist Emmy E Werner of the University of California-Davis studied 500 children growing up in poverty on the Hawaiian island of Kauai. Examining these young people's lives over a 30-year period, Werner found that the youths who managed to make it, against the odds, could all count on the support of an adult mentor other than their parents (Werner & Smith, 1982). Sometimes this person was a grandparent or other relative, but usually it was a neighbour, teacher, coach or minister.

In another illustration, anthropologists William Kornblum of NYU and Terry Williams of CUNY followed 900 children in urban and rural poverty. In their book, *Growing Up Poor*, Williams and Kornblum conclude that 'The probabilities that teenagers will end up on the corner or in a stable job are conditioned by a great many features of life in their communities. Of these, we believe the most significant is the presence or absence of adult mentors' (Williams & Kornblum, 1985:108). These findings are reproduced in numerous other studies, across not only diverse disciplines but cultural circumstances as well.

Taken together, the erosion of adult support for youth and evidence suggesting the positive effects of its presence, have produced a vigorous search for ways to replenish this support, and fuelled interest in developing volunteer mentoring efforts for young people.

17.3 The Experience of Volunteer Mentoring

While the reasons behind mentoring's rapid rise to prominence are compelling, they raise basic questions. While resilience research links mentoring and success for young people in poverty, it leaves unexplained whether resilient youth do well because they find mentoring relationships, or whether these youth find mentoring relationships, and use them well, because they possess an inherent ability to overcome hardship.

This dilemma leads to the issue of whether it is possible for social programmes and policies aimed at providing more mentoring relationships, to reach youth beyond those with the internal wherewithal to cultivate such bonds on their own. (The resilient youth in Werner's work possess an uncanny ability to attract and recruit potential mentors.) Even if the answer is yes, the question remains whether these orchestrated relationships can generate the same benefits as with the natural bonds charted by Werner, Williams and Kornblum, and others.

The benefits of mentoring

Definitive answers to these and other issues remain forthcoming; however, returns from a set of research and evaluation efforts are beginning to uncover what mentoring can do to help young people growing up in poverty. Probably the most important of this research is being conducted by Professor Jean Rhodes and her colleagues at the University of Illinois (Rhodes *et al.*, 1992). Studying a group of girls attending an alternative school for teenage mothers in Chicago, Rhodes has succeeded in dividing the students into girls who have 'natural' mentors from the community, and those that do not. Through selective assignments of volunteer 'programme' mentors, she has created four groups for study: girls with both 'natural' and 'programme' mentors; girls with neither; and girls with one or the other.

Rhodes' findings confirm that those young women already demonstrating the ability to find and forge relationships with natural mentors are uniquely suited to make effective use of the 'programme' mentors assigned to them. Essentially, the rich do get richer in her findings. However, Rhodes' research also suggest that a substantial number of young girls without natural mentors are able to bond with – and benefit from – assigned mentors. The critical difference in connecting with these harder to reach girls appears to be the quality of persistence on the part of their mentors, dedicated volunteers who shrug off initial resistance and manage to build trust over time (Rhodes *et al.*, 1992).

Rhodes' finding that volunteer, programme mentors can reach, and make a difference, in the lives of youth appears to be supported by a range of programme evaluations. For example:

■ an evaluation of the Career Beginnings demonstration – which includes a number of components in addition to mentoring – shows students with mentors attending college on schedule at a higher rate than a control group (Cave & Quint, 1990);
■ research on Project RAISE (which includes students from two universities in its corps of mentors), conducted by Johns Hopkins University, finds RAISE students improving attendance and grades in English in comparison to controls (McPartland & Nettles, 1991);
■ a third study, of the Atlanta Adopt-a-Student programme, reveals young people with mentors more likely to enrol in post-secondary education (Stanwyck & Anson, 1989).

Other outcome research conducted by Public/Private Ventures of the Big Brothers/Big Sisters of America Program will not be available until 1996, and will provide the first glimpse of the effectiveness of the country's oldest, biggest and best-known initiative.

In addition to indications that mentors can help young people cope with difficult circumstances and make progress toward important goals like improving school performance, there is evidence that the benefits of mentoring are reciprocal. Some of these outcomes are in satisfaction, yet the potential runs deeper. Although the isolation of youth is a primary reason behind the creation of mentoring programmes – and a valid one – many of the middle-class adults recruited for these matches are just as isolated from the realities of poverty as participating youth are from the institutions and opportunities of middle-class life. At a time when statistics have lost their ability to shock, mentors are brought face-to-face with the unfair manner in which poverty affects innocent children. This education can build not only empathy, but advocacy on the part of the adults.

The significance of these results, and the wide level of interest mentoring has generated among adult volunteers, should not be underestimated in an age characterised by a precipitous decline in civic participation. For example, PTA membership in the US has dropped from 12 million to 7 million over the past generation, along with volunteer participation in a wide range of community organisations (Putnam, 1995). The rise of interest and participation in mentoring stands in sharp – and encouraging – contrast to these alarming trends.

The limits of mentoring

For all these positive indications, the overall scenario of the new wave of volunteer mentoring activity is mixed. The picture that emerges over and over again from research and other accounts is that this enterprise is hard, that volunteer mentoring based on formally matching adults and disadvantaged youth, one-to-one, is, in the overwhelming number of cases, a modest intervention.

Why is mentoring so difficult? The reasons are not surprising; in fact, they harken back to the issues that sunk Friendly Visiting a century ago. First, mentoring rests on a paradox around the issue of time. People come forward to participate in these programmes because they recognise that adults in our society do not spend enough time with kids. Unfortunately, the volunteers tapped for programmes quickly discover that they don't have enough time to mentor. They are the same individuals who are working an extra 164 hours a year, who are struggling to spend enough time with their own kids (this problem is exacerbated by the emphasis on recruiting successful 'role models' for these programmes – the lawyers, bankers and other professionals who tend to be the busiest people in society). The end result is that mentors are often better at signing up than showing up. This issue is particularly critical in light of Rhodes' research about the importance of persistence on the part of mentors.

Time is also a problem for college students functioning as mentors. A Public/Private Ventures study of the Campus Partners in Learning demonstration, which examined six programmes engaging university students as mentors to disadvantaged children and youth, found that these students 'typically perform a difficult balancing act', as they adjust to the challenges of college. Successful relationships were forged in fewer than half the matches studied (Tierney & Branch, 1992).

221

Sufficient time is critical for achieving the kind of persistence Rhodes extols, especially given another obstacle confronting mentoring programmes: social distance. Most mentoring efforts, as already suggested, focus recruitment on middle-class and upper-middle-class role models, individuals seen as exemplars of how to make it in the mainstream world. On the other hand, the youth targeted tend to come from the other side of the tracks. Vast differences exist in class, culture, generation, neighbourhood and, frequently, ethnic background. Many mentors and youth have never met anyone like their partner before. The opportunities for misunderstanding are considerable.

The paradox around time and the gulf of social distance, taken together with the artificiality of the one-to-one match (which one observer likens to 'blind dating as social policy'), can undermine persistence and produce disappointment. The last point raises the reality that mentoring, often portrayed as a win-win situation, can in fact be quite risky. When misunderstandings occur, or when mentors drop out, the result is frequently devastating. For youth who've been let down by adults in the past, it can mean that it will be that much harder to trust again. For adults, whose initial involvement is often motivated by a fragile sense of goodwill, the result is increased cynicism.

The obstacles facing mentoring and its inherent risks are made dramatically worse by an attitude toward this enterprise that might be called 'fervour without infrastructure', unrealistic expectations about mentoring coupled with naivety about what it takes to make mentoring work. Specifically, this perspective is evident in heroic fantasies about adult volunteers swooping in to save vast numbers of children from the ravages of poverty, combined with unrealistic notions that mentoring is cheap, easy and quick. It often takes the form of predictions of tens of thousands, or even millions of volunteer mentors, with little in the way of support.

Lessons for volunteer mentoring programmes

The experience of volunteer mentoring programmes over the past decade, while clear about the obstacles and limitations confronting these programmes, in no way counsels their abandonment, or the abandonment of other volunteer efforts in the important work of providing more adult support for youth. Rather, this experience suggests adherence to a set of basic lessons – for individual mentors, programme operators and policymakers – aimed at bringing this form of mentoring to its full potential. A number of such lessons are set out below.

222

Rethinking recruitment

Programmes have learned to exercise greater care in their recruitment tactics. Initially, many programmes emphasised 'screening in' potential volunteers in their quest to reach as many kids as possible, a practice that can lead to fanning romantic notions of mentoring in potential recruits. People would come to the programme, explains one programme director, 'expecting that they're going to save the world . . . and we fed them on that'. However, as his programme struggled through the first years and many of these individuals dropped out, this director shifted away from screening people in, to 'screening them out' – letting them know about the harder realities of mentoring from the start so that only those individuals genuinely committed would become involved. In retrospect he concludes, 'We lost some people – the total number of mentors we could claim in the programme went down – but the percentage actually performing went up'.

Creating a variety of roles

As programmes continue to gain experience, however, many operators are beginning to move toward a further correction. While 'screening out' has the advantage of discouraging volunteers unable to make the significant commitment mentoring entails, this strategy can result in turning away good people who might be able to help youth in other, more limited, ways. In response to this problem, some programmes have moved to provide a wider variety of roles for potential volunteers. The Philadelphia Futures programme, for example, offers a menu of volunteer options, including tutoring, role modelling and providing scholarship support, along with mentoring. The programme also works with interested adults in helping them select the role most compatible with their personality, time availability and resources.

Teaching the art of mentoring

Training is an essential part of preparing mentors for their job, especially as we learn more about the practices of effective mentors. For example, experience indicates that mentors who emphasise listening to youth early on in the relationship – and avoid the impulse to impose preconceived plans for the young person's improvement – are best able to establish trust and forge a connection. Later, these effective mentors are able to move toward balancing support with challenging the young person to move toward goals. One of the most effective strategies for imparting these and other lessons to aspiring mentors is through engaging experienced mentors who can share both triumphs and travails and provide an accurate glimpse of what it means to be matched with a young person.

Explaining before matching

It is just as important to provide youth with this advance glimpse of the mentoring process. Although mentoring is a familiar word to adults in the business world, for example, it is often a foreign term to inner-city adolescents. When told that they are being assigned a mentor, many youths are resistant or bewildered. Some undoubtedly wonder, 'What does this say about me – that I need help? That I am deficient?' These and other issues are best addressed before the young person is matched.

A variety of adults

Young people can benefit from contact with a variety of adults. Common ethnic and cultural ties do appear to be an advantage in forging connections, and these ties can mitigate barriers to trust and provide young people with models that look like them. At the same time, exposure to mentors of other backgrounds can help orient youth to individuals and situations contributing to the bicultural competence many inner-city youngsters must develop. Cross-ethnic matching can also contribute to the social development of the mentor, who learns about the young person's world through the mentoring process.

Matching by class

Although much attention focuses on the ethnic background of mentors and youth, class issues appear to play a significant role in relationship formation. Again, experience from mentoring programmes suggests that the most successful mentors are individuals who have weathered hard lives, often coming from the same neighbourhoods as the youth. Mentoring programmes, intent on finding successful 'role models,' might do well to recruit more individuals from such backgrounds. Recent ethnographic studies suggest that many working-class and lower-income exemplars of character and competence remain in our inner-city neighbourhoods and might potentially be reconnected with youth through the development of new mechanisms (Anderson, 1990; Duneier, 1992).

Integrating mentoring

One programme operator states: 'It would be wonderful if we could just put these two people together and tell them to relate, but it's not realistic'. In her experience, when mentors and mentees have something to do or work on together, it gives them more direction. Tasks can absorb initial nervous energy, provide a basis for conversation between partners, and diffuse the stigma of receiving help. The key is finding the right task – one that interests both parties. Stephen Hamilton of Cornell University argues that the workplace is ideal (Hamilton, 1990). Integrating mentoring into sports programmes, recreation programmes and other youth initiatives is also promising. Community service projects (such as the Boston University/Roxbury Middle School collaboration, part of the Campus Partners in Learning initiative) in which mentors and students are working side by side, can also provide an environment conducive to connection.

These points all conspire to the perspective that mentoring need not be a stand-alone strategy. In fact, it is both more likely that mentoring relationships will form, and that these bonds will have the desired benefits, when integrated in the broader context of youth development activities.

Supporting mentors

Although practitioners differ about the value of upfront training of mentors, most share an unequivocal belief in the importance of supporting mentors and the consequences of failing to do so. To combat the isolation in which much mentoring is conducted, some initiatives organise self-help groups for mentors to provide each other with emotional support, share experiences and develop solutions to common difficulties. Mentoring teams, where several adults share the job of mentoring several youths, also help reduce isolation in some programmes. As an added advantage, these teams help provide consistency for young people. When one of the adults cannot make it to a scheduled session, the young people can still expect to see one or two of the other mentors on the team.

Staff, the glue in mentoring

The most important source of support for mentors is also the most important single ingredient in successful mentoring programmes: field staff. These individuals are in contact with the kids, the mentors, school staff and families. Not surprisingly, in programmes where such staff are a full-time presence, the whole mentoring effort tends to revolve around them; they are the 'glue' in this process. Field staff assume many critical functions, from helping make sure that people show up, to brokering and interpreting for adults and youths, to serving as 'mentors to the mentors'. In part, these youth workers support young people, often with the advantages of social and physical proximity to them. Many come from socio-economic backgrounds similar to the youths and set up shop right in the schools or youth programmes the young people attend. Although some programmes attempt to subsist on volunteer coordination, experience suggest that employing full-time youth workers in this role is a far more effective path.

New sources of volunteers

As already stated, one of the great ironies of the volunteer mentoring movement has been its focus on recruiting the busiest people in society – middle-class, middle-aged, 'role models'. Mentoring programmes would do well to look at some new sources of potential volunteers, in particular older adults. Seniors are the fastest growing segment of the population, and there will be twice as many individuals over 60 in 30 years as there are today. Not only do many older people possess the time required to mentor (a substantial portion of Americans are now spending a third of their life in retirement), but their experience as citizens, workers and parents renders them a deep repository of the social capital so many youth require. Young people in well-supported initiatives remain a promising source of volunteers, despite difficulties to date. Some programmes even engage adolescents being mentored by adults as mentors themselves, pairing them up with local elementary school students. These so-called 'tripartite' programmes, such as the Young Leaders programme in Washington, DC, have numerous advantages. Not only do they support the elementary school children, they also provide participating adolescents with the experience of being mentors themselves. Furthermore, since many of these programmes match adolescents and elementary school children growing up in the same neighbourhoods, they can also be seen as community-development strategies.

Building infrastructure

While the lessons set out above can contribute to strengthening mentoring at both the relationship and programme level, institutional infrastructure is also required to support and sustain this activity over time. However, as one study of New York city programmes concludes, the mentoring field has been sorely lacking in this infrastructure, imperative for ensuring quality service delivery over time, building a track record of reliability, and developing ongoing sources of funding (Flaxman *et al.*, 1988). The biggest exception to this deficiency is Big Brothers/Big Sisters of America, which maintains a national organisation that provides standards, technical assistance, research and other supporting functions, and reveals one model of how solid infrastructure can enhance the practice of mentoring. Elsewhere, a number of cities and states have moved toward creating local organisations and networks to promote and strengthen mentoring efforts. However, these initiatives remain more the exception than the rule, and an effort to develop more local and regional mentoring centres is much needed.

Secure funding

Also required are consistent and long-term sources of funding. Too many mentoring programmes are launched amid an initial burst of enthusiasm (by private foundations, business collaborates, and civic groups alike) only to be abandoned after the start-up phase in favour of new fads arriving on the social policy landscape.

17.4 Youth Workers as Mentors

Adapting the lessons set out above will help volunteer mentoring programmes better address youths' need for adult contact and strengthen the support available to adults who provide that contact. However, it would be a mistake either to underestimate the extent of these needs or to overestimate the power of voluntary efforts alone to meet them. As one programme director warns, 'You're not going to have enough mentors. It's not going to work for a lot of kids. There will be a huge hole'.

The hole will continue to exist, even if responsible volunteer mentoring prevails, because the isolation of young people is a structural problem resulting from a set of fundamental changes in our society (for example, poverty serves in many and reinforcing ways to undermine natural support networks for young people). Rather than thinking of volunteer mentoring as a sufficient solution to the structural problem of youth isolation, we would do well to think of this important movement as a critical step in the right direction, one that highlights an unmet need, goes part of the way toward redressing it, and calls out for reinforcements.

From where might these reinforcements come? Mentoring programmes themselves provide essential clues, particularly in the staff roles discussed in the previous section. These paid youth workers tend not only to be mentors to the mentors but oftentimes to the young people as well. As the director of the Career Beginnings mentoring initiative explains, 'In a lot of Career Beginnings programs, the primary relationships are between the case managers and the kids, and only secondarily and maybe supportively, between the [volunteer] mentors and the kids' (Freedman, 1993). This insight comes from the 'I Have a Dream' project as well, where one report describes the youth worker who coordinates each project on a full-time basis as functioning 'more like a parent, aunt or uncle, or an older sibling than a bureaucrat', while an *Education Week* article describes them as being 'like guardian angels who provide the daily guidance and support needed to make sure the students have a shot at collecting on their sponsor's tuition offer' (Sommerfeld, 1992).

In this way, volunteer mentoring programmes – as well as efforts like 'I Have a Dream' – end up serving as back doors to traditional youth work; the need to administer the programme serves as justification for hiring adult staff who themselves come to provide the most critical mentoring delivered by the programme. Backdoor or not, the role many staff play underscores the basic insight that mentoring, while cast as a voluntary relationship, is by no means the exclusive province of volunteers.

Indeed, these youth workers are generally in a much better position than volunteers to mentor young people because their roles are structured for, and consistent with, fundamental principles about connecting with kids: namely, that a consistent and persistent presence is essential for successful mentoring. Because they are available to kids on a regular and intensive basis – because persistence essentially is built into their role – these youth workers are particularly promising sources of adult support. They are on hand, in the school or youth programme, day in and day out. When troubles arise in the youths' lives, they are not away on a business trip or even downtown in an office building. They can attend to the issue immediately. Many also come from the same neighbourhoods as the kids, thus minimising the social distance problem impacting many volunteer programmes focusing on middle-class professionals.

The individuals who come forward to fill these youth worker positions tend to combine the full-time, formal presence of a professional social worker with the sense of mission often associated with volunteers. Their role, with its focus on the provision of relationships, is often unique in the context of the schools and social programmes where they operate. As a result, these individuals are frequently overwhelmed by need as they become established and trusted. Young people flood their offices in search of someone to talk to or help them out.

Although some of these youth workers are finding opportunities to connect with youth through coordinator and other backdoor positions in a variety of mentoring programmes and related initiatives, an important next step for the youth development field is to open up more direct opportunities for these individuals to practise their intensive, full-time, persistent brand of mentorship – especially as evidence continues to accumulate that these youth workers are linked closely to the success of programmes. For example, recent research findings from the highly-effective Quantum Opportunities Program focused on adolescents from welfare families, identified these youth worker roles as critical to the programme's record of achievement. In the words of a March 1995 *New York Times* editorial, 'the adult supervisors . . . became not just mentors, but surrogate parents or family members, with roots in the same community' (Dugger, 1995).

Fortunately, there is evidence that programmes focused on engaging youth workers as mentors are becoming increasingly widespread. The Key Program in Massachusetts and Maryland's Choice initiative both follow this model. Another variation is the Friends of the Children project in Portland, Oregon. Endowed by a local financier with a longstanding interest in youth programmes, and supported by Portland's Meyer Memorial Trust, Friends of the Children 'employs full-time caring, loving adults who each work intensively with eight at-risk young children and their families'. The programme's goal is for these full-time mentors to become a substantial part of the children's lives 'from early childhood to young adulthood'. Beginning with second-graders already identified by teachers and school staff as headed for trouble, the Friends spend time in the classroom, become a bridge between school and home, essentially becoming surrogate family. Their focus is on developing life skills, including problem-solving, conflict resolution and character.

As evidence mounts about the significant mentoring role youth workers can play in a wide variety of settings and new initiatives of this type continue to be launched, a number of national leaders have called for the creation of new mechanisms for supporting such efforts. David Liederman, executive director of the Child Welfare League of America, urges establishment of a corps of inner-city youth workers, 'able to hit the streets and work directly with kids in their own neighborhoods'. He argues that these are the role models kids really need – not famous athletes on television, but caring adults they can 'see, touch, and talk to' (Liederman, 1990).

Liederman's vision of a 'small army of trained, committed youth workers talking about and developing positive values' may be in the process of being realised through two current programmes which underscore that this army might consist not only of salaried youth workers like the staff of 'I Have a Dream', but stipended national service participants. These are the AmeriCorps USA Program and the Foster Grandparent Program, both administered by the Corporation for National Service.

A significant portion of AmeriCorps' 20,000 national service participants (the majority of them high school graduates taking time off before college, college students interrupting their studies, or recent graduates) are working in direct and intensive mentoring roles with youth. In fact, after hiring four Friends through foundation and other private sources, the Friends of the Children programme was able to engage 20 more with AmeriCorps support. Taken together, AmeriCorps funding for this activity may well be on the way to producing the 'small army' of youth workers Liederman envisions.

The Foster Grandparent Program, a little-known initiative with roots in the War on Poverty, is itself a significant platoon in this developing army. Foster Grandparents worked one-to-one with 90,000 children last year, making it the biggest one-to-one programme in the US. These Grandparents are primarily low-income women over the age of 60, half of them members of ethnic minorities, who work half-time every day in schools, head start centres, and youth organisations. Their mandate is to work directly with disadvantaged or disabled young people, for which the programme's 23,000 participants receive a small, non-taxable stipend of $9.80 per day.

Taken together, these two efforts still remain relatively small – certainly in comparison to the need – yet point to ways in which policy can contribute to bolstering this important route toward providing enhanced adult support to youth.

17.5 Towards Mentor-Rich Environments

As we seek to develop more powerful strategies for supporting kids it is essential that we combine the efforts of volunteers and staff in ways capable of transforming the two institutions where young people spend the majority of their time outside the home: schools and community youth organisations. In doing so, we should seek to move beyond trying to locate any one 'supermentor' capable of singlehandedly meeting all the needs of a young person; rather, our goal must be to help construct a web of support, a portfolio of adults working together, as partners, to help out with the long-term, complex process of developing youth.

Ultimately, this approach dictates changing schools and community youth programmes so that these become places where youth interact with an array of caring adults. In creating such mentor-rich environments, we will need to fill them not only with volunteer mentors, who constitute one link in a continuous chain of caring, but also with youth workers, teachers, coaches, supervisors, counsellors and other adults who have the time and inclination to establish close ties with young people.

Young people exposed to mentor-rich settings are in a position to avoid many of the vicissitudes of formal, matched, volunteer mentoring. Rather than being assigned an adult and instructed to form a one-to-one bond with this elder, young people in mentor-rich settings would find ample opportunities for natural connections to develop. In such settings, youth are in a position to select the right mentor at the right time, pick mentors for different reasons, and experience aspects of mentoring from a variety of sources. In fact, a significant body of research suggests that the schools and social programmes with these features are most successful at reaching and developing young people.

As we go about trying to create adult-rich environments in these institutions – essentially 'stocking the pond' with interested adults in a variety of capacities – we might simultaneously work to develop the capacity of youth 'to fish', to develop their ability to make best use of the adults they find in their path. Doing so builds on the lesson from research that resilient youth – those young people who overcome the odds of poverty, at least in part through recruiting mentors from the surrounding community – possess a valuable ability to initiate relationships with adults. We might well strive to distil and teach these lessons to a wider spectrum of kids.

In the end, pursuing the three strategies set out above will not, in and of themselves, counteract all the social, economic and cultural forces undermining the ability of our communities to nurture and support their young people. This was not the case in the days of Friendly Visiting; it is not the case today. However, this combination of efforts should move us dramatically past those of volunteer programmes alone, and help us to begin reconstructing the social infrastructure our young people so desperately require.

Ultimately, I am hopeful that when historians look back a century from now – much as we do today with Friendly Visiting – they will see an important transitional movement, one culminating in sweeping institutional change. This time, however, I hope that they will find a transformation inspired by a volunteer movement's carefully cultivated success, not forged in reaction to its unhappy demise.

Address for correspondence: Marc Freedman, Vice President, Public/Private Ventures, 1422 Bonita Avenue, Berkeley, California 94709, USA.

Chapter 18

STUDENT TUTORING IN DEVELOPING COUNTRIES: PRACTICE AND POSSIBILITIES

Margaret Rutherford and Robert Hofmeyr

This chapter reports on a survey carried out to investigate student tutoring schemes in developing countries. There appear to be few if any programmes using tertiary student volunteers in schools. The reasons for this have been analysed and some tentative suggestions for possible interventions outlined.

18.1 Introduction

The brief for this chapter was to investigate student tutoring programmes in developing countries. The generic model was of tertiary level students being involved in activities in schools which were intended to provide role models for pupils, improve student communication skills and aid the teacher (cf the Pimlico Connection). Activities which could be classified as coaching or extra lessons or other forms of teaching (in the mode of imparting information) were excluded. Similarly the type of activity which might variously be classified as peer tutoring or mentoring or as supplemental instruction were not surveyed although several of these were reported. It can be seen therefore that the investigation was confined to activities where there was an age difference between the participants and where the older of these was not in a teaching role but was somewhere between the teacher and the pupil.

233

18.2 Investigation and Methodology

By its very nature the investigation is incomplete and there will undoubtedly be endeavours which are undocumented; indeed some were reported elsewhere at the IC/BP conference. In the initial phase of the investigation, letters or facsimile transmissions were written to about 30 universities in Africa, India, Pakistan, Papua New Guinea and Australia (this last enquiring about activities in the Pacific Rim countries). These enquiries requested information about either formal or informal programmes in which members of the respective institutions were actively involved. In addition, the institutions were asked to provide contact names and addresses for individuals or organisations which might be involved in such activities.

Responses were received from five institutions outside South Africa and from an additional five from within the Rebublic. None of these reported on a project similar to the Pimlico Connection. No responses were received from the remainder. Follow-up enquiries by facsimile or telephone to a sample group also elicited negative responses. It has been assumed that the lack of response on the part of the remaining institutions should be construed as indicating that there are no such programmes operative at, or in relationship with, those institutions.

We also made enquiries of 20 individuals based in developing countries and who through their employment or specialist areas would be in a position to know about programmes. Once again, the responses were negative.

Finally we interviewed eight individuals who had themselves been schooled in Sub-Saharan Africa, ranging across Ghana, Kenya, Swaziland, Zimbabwe, Zaire, Zambia, Mozambique and South Africa. These people had no knowledge of tutoring programmes but provided valuable insights into the social, economic and educational circumstances extant in the countries listed and which may throw light on the dearth of student tutoring schemes. We therefore concluded that although there might be some programmes of significance, they must at this time be on a small scale and lacking support and cooperation from major institutions and agencies in those countries.

To probe the reasons for the non-existence of such programmes, discussions were held with educationists in the specialist field of science education, not only in outreach activities but also in the fields of teacher training and educational sociology. From these varied sources it was possible to draw some conclusions regarding the factors militating against setting up such programmes and to suggest some of the circumstances necessary for the development and effective working of models which have proved themselves so valuable in other parts of the world.

Informal conversations at the International Conference on Student Tutoring and Mentoring in London in April 1995 elicited only one such programme in the developing countries (in Dar es Salaam), which is both new and small scale. In addition, the problems identified in the survey for implementation of such a programme were also mentioned by many delegates in both developed and developing countries.

The problems identified may be grouped into those relating to developmental level, to teacher status and training, to socio-economic matters, to logistics, to institutional concerns, to cultural matters, and to the divide between the two learning environments.

18.3 Developmental Issues

As far back as the late 1950s, concern was being expressed about the desire for and relevance of education in developing countries (see for example Ward, 1959; Curle, 1964). However, if one looks at the present state of education in many developing countries, one is forced to conclude that the majority of all schools are still in what Beeby (1966), for primary school systems, called the second stage of formalisation. These schools are characterised by, *inter alia*, a heavy stress on memorisation, one single textbook and rigid syllabuses. Whilst Beeby was considering only primary school systems, this is also true of many secondary schools in developing countries. As late as 1993, Palme, writing about education in Mozambique, claimed that pupils were passive receivers of information imparted by the teachers, and that they rarely contributed anything more than regurgitated answers to closed questions (Palme, 1994).

In developed countries on the other hand, schools are, in general, not only better physically equipped and resourced but have teachers trained in their subjects, with a broader perspective on the curriculum and a much wider range of teaching methodologies. This is characteristic of Beeby's stage IV (Beeby, 1966:72).

It therefore becomes clear that in the developed countries, teachers are less threatened by university students coming into their classrooms, whereas they are disempowered by the perceived better qualified students in most developing countries. Whilst this may not be a universal situation, it is certainly true that a large group of teachers (about 250) assembled to discuss possible outreach activities with the

University of the Witwatersrand in South Africa were primarily concerned with their own access to in-service education and would not welcome student activity in their classrooms without this support.

If this was the situation with secondary school teachers drawn from a 50km radius of an institution situated in the heart of probably the most advanced industrial area in Africa, it is likely that it represents the feelings of many teachers in developing countries. Teachers feel threatened by university students and have no experience of working with them in their classrooms.

18.4 Problems of Teacher Status and Training

Associated with the developmental level of a schooling system, is the position of teachers. In many parts of the developing world teachers have a somewhat uncertain status. Their qualifications are frequently at a level not much higher than the level at which they are teaching and, in mathematics and science particularly, may not even be in the same subject area.

In a report of a Round Table on Teacher Education convened by The Commonwealth of Learning, Kwapong amongst others cites the shortage of trained teachers, particularly in mathematics and science, as being a key issue in the educational process necessary for development (Kwapong, 1993). Where in addition the schooling system is socially and politically fragile, teachers are threatened individuals. Student tutors and mentors who have at least a grounding in the subjects may jeopardise their tenuous hold on classes. This is not universally so, for there are those under-qualified teachers who point their pupils towards enrichment programmes offered extra-murally which will help them. However, the more common experience is different, and understandably so, for teachers in knowledge-based areas feel the often uncertain relationship with their pupils under threat when more knowledgeable students intrude in that relationship.

18.5 Socio-Economic Considerations

It is a commonplace that many communities in developing countries are short of resources and in many areas operating at a subsistence level. Any student fortunate enough to even complete a secondary school programme is privileged and those few who manage to get to a university may well be the first in their community to do so. Community and parental support is a *sine qua non* when a community battles together for survival. For example, African society is based on *Ubuntu*, the people, rather than on individualism. In some rural societies, a child is sent to school as a representative of the group to discover and bring back the new knowledge. An individual career is not conceivable in this sort of situation since the future of the whole community has been mortgaged for the schooling of one individual. The student's obligations are towards this extended family and any spare time is 'owed' to them.

Obviously this will vary across socio-economic groups, with fierce competition on an individual level manifesting itself in urbanised communities. The fight for survival is there familial rather than communal. Nevertheless there needs to be an appreciation of why programmes requiring volunteer workers should be given any priority at all.

Many parts of the developing world have been and continue to be devastated by civil wars, with huge refugee populations exacerbating the already massive problem of rapid urbanisation. The social order which characterised the rural communities has often disappeared in the refugee camps and urban slums.

In the rural areas the modern vision of a school as an investment for the future makes no sense. For those farmers the concept of the future and of time is totally different. And why take a useful pair of hands off the land?

In the camps and urban slums there is a lively sense of the need to buy into the new culture of survival, but the choice is often not about whether or not to attend school but whether or not there is a school to go to! If there is, then the choice becomes one of whether the child becomes a street vendor or attends school.

Within this complicated socio-economic structure, a reward system is infinitely variable. The subsistence community, the student struggling to pay fees, the pupil under pressure to help with farming or with selling fruit in a street market: all these need to perceive a reward for sacrifice, some benefit in the present or immediate future.

All societies produce students motivated by a genuine desire to do what is good and helpful to others. In the more affluent communities the rewards for voluntary work are built into social norms. That is simply not true when resources are scarce. The young African student will, for the most part, have obligations which are primarily to family. He or she will often be eking out an existence on bursaries and other forms of financial aid. Time and employment opportunities are directed at survival and family success. Some students in fact try to send some of their bursary payments home to feed their families.

18.6 Logistical Problems

Even if students have the time and are not constrained to take part-time paid work, there are difficulties in actually making the physical link between schools and university campuses. It is a commonplace that there is a very wide range of experiences in the developing world, where urban, peri-urban and rural communities coexist and interact. There are modern transport systems alongside dirt tracks and footpaths. Universities tend to be a part of the 'modern world', while many students are impoverished and live across two worlds. Simply stated, students cannot with facility move from campus to village or informal settlement and back to campus. Money and time militate against this. It literally means walking and catching uncertain buses and hoping to make it back again to campus in time, for example, for the evening meal. This is a very different experience from the predominantly suburban campuses of the First World.

Obviously there are vast differences in student experiences across the developing world. The student in Johannesburg for example, who wants to become involved in a Soweto school has transport readily available. However, this can be dangerous and erratic – the famous or notorious Black Taxis, Toyota Hi-Aces for the most part – which criss-cross the cities and countryside, but not known for good tyres nor brakes and subject often to savage warfare between rival owner groups. Other countries have different problems but a common factor is the time-consuming nature of travel: a student travelling in South America quoted travel times in terms of days on a bus rather than the hours or even minutes considered normal for a student in a country with an advanced transport infrastructure. And the schools most in need of help from students, particularly as role models, are those least accessible.

Within the university system itself there are problems of calendars and timetables which are at best uncertain. A very large proportion of universities in Third World countries experience upheavals, closures and the extension of one academic year into the next in a way that is difficult to comprehend (Sawyerr, 1988). At the time of writing this chapter, there are upheavals on five tertiary campuses in South Africa, the University of Swaziland is closed; the same is true of universities throughout Nigeria and in Zaire. A climate of normality and predictability would, one would think, be necessary for establishing programmes which require careful coordination between the tertiary and the secondary systems. The university student who travels to the meeting place must know that the school pupils will be there: no programme will survive a series of ad hoc changes, no-shows and disappointments.

In many developing countries schools begin early in the morning and close in the early afternoon, whereas universities are in session for a full day, often with laboratory sessions in the afternoons. Timetabling therefore becomes a problem, since university students have no access to schools in the afternoons and programmes would be restricted to weekends. Integration of university and school activities is difficult and is exacerbated by the poor communication systems, including a lack of telephones at many schools.

Venues similarly prove problematic. Reference is made later to secondary school pupils coming to a university campus and in many instances the established campus would serve as an appropriate venue for a programme. Whilst some school buildings and community centres could also be used, these are frequently ill-equipped and lack fundamental requirements such as a desk for each pupil or even window glass. However, there are factors which conspire against the use of university campuses, since the administrations of such campuses, with very constrained budgets, are becoming reluctant to permit the use of facilities at no cost. In addition, security is a major concern, especially where equipment is being made available. Perhaps more significant in terms of the need for outreach, is the paucity of such facilities: they simply do not exist in rural settings.

In brief, we are constrained to look at a world often without telephones, without bus services and without the type of infrastructure that the developed world takes for granted. In addition we are looking at a world without running water, without laboratory facilities, without electricity, much less overhead projectors, and without money.

18.7 Cultural and Societal Issues

We are dealing with a post-colonial world. There are some quite wonderful studies of universities as implants in the developing world: Singh (1992), has spoken of flowers on a mudbank. Less poetically, Sawyerr (1988) speaks of a foreign/European bias and a departure from traditional ways, thus exacerbating the social distance between the university and the rest of society.

Whilst schools are more closely related to societies, they likewise are, in Africa at least, an import. In addition, unlike the coherence perceived in developed countries between schools and universities, there is, in the developing world, little relationship between them. The far-flung community schools in rural areas and their relationships with the universities is tenuous at best. In South Africa a very small percentage of African pupils will complete a curriculum of more than eight years. Even fewer will contemplate university entrance examinations. Many teachers have taken a non-university route in their training. The result is a real lack of coherence at a personal level since the teachers have no conception of university activities.

There is a further problem in the gulf between the activities considered to be of value in the universities – the search for 'truth' as an academic exercise – and those of importance to the wider communities, and this is manifested not only in the content and interpretation of natural events but also in the language used to describe them.

The cultural issues attendant on science education in particular have received some attention and there has been a move to 'de-Westernise' science. The debate centres on 'whose knowledge is important?' Unless there is a coalescing of what is taught in schools and what is believed and practised by the community in which the pupil spends his or her life, the knowledge will continue to be rote learned and without significance: 'a ritual imposition of cultural hieroglyphs . . . because the culture, language and experiences . . . are constantly suppressed.' (Palme, 1993).

The teacher is a mediator in that situation, and needs to integrate two worlds. (There are enormous requirements for training: the teacher will in many instances revert to rote learning and a mechanistic approach to the learning process.) Rajput (1993) has listed some of the competencies required of teachers in such situations: they include the development of an holistic view of science; appreciation of both social and ethical aspects of science; interpretation of new ideas and technologies to the community; perception and utilisation of the relationships of science to health, agriculture, industry, nutrition and other aspects of day-to-day living. The implications for student endeavours are enormous. It is difficult enough for the professional teacher; how much more for the volunteer who is spending a valuable free afternoon or weekend on a programme.

The student moving back into such situations is more than likely to repeat his or her own experiences and encourage rote learning, the means to his or her own success in the school situation. Youngsters who

240

have been in impoverished schooling situations tend, on going back into those situations, to perpetuate what happened to them. They went through the system with a degree of success and will take the next generation along the same route. Even if a tertiary student is prepared to volunteer, the training aspect is time-consuming and therefore expensive. A major problem is that the students have (generally) become proficient in the second language which is the medium of instruction in developing countries. They have learnt much of their science in a language with a vocabulary and register foreign to the majority of the population and cannot translate since this will frequently change the meaning (even if, nominally, the words exist in the local vernacular).

The problem of different cultures is of course highlighted dramatically in the two learning environments: the student will for the most part be learning in an environment which is technologically advanced. The university laboratory and lecture theatre are far removed from the classroom in an impoverished community.

Students perceive it as extremely difficult to reinterpret scientific concepts in the 'other world' because of lack of facilities there. 'How can I teach science without the means by which I was taught it?' Physical constraints, lack of equipment and lack of resources will nullify good intentions. These are very real reasons for not volunteering.

The student who has learned about photosynthesis in a laboratory somehow believes it is something that can be learned only in a laboratory and not on a windowsill and in the veld. (And, of course, we have to accept that there will be rooms without windowsills!)

The knowledge base at universities is seldom sensitive to communities; curricula remain 'Western' and tuition is individualistic. Students buy into a system which is in effect insensitive to schools and especially to schools which are rurally-based.

There are no incentives to students to become involved in mentoring and tutoring, except in so far as there are employment opportunities (eg, in Kenya) and in teacher training. The average student derives no perceived benefit and in fact his or her university training is disabling rather than enabling to that purpose.

So far the situation has been reported as inconducive to the type of student tutoring described by Goodlad (1995a). Is this in fact the case or are there possibilities concealed in the report? It may be that a different type of intervention is called for but, as Goodlad states, this should not be for its own sake but to address a specific problem. Let us look at an endeavour which has, over the last eight years, done just that.

18.8 The STEP Project

A case study

STEP is a voluntary student–pupil programme. The funds raised are used to hire venues and provide written materials. Some 70 university students from all the major faculties at the University of the Witwatersrand give up their Saturday mornings to teach pupils from the surrounding township schools (mainly Soweto and Alexandra). Some 1,200 pupils enrol in a typical year. The courses taught include not only the usual school subjects but also such things as street law and drama.

Here the intention is to highlight the features which relate specifically to the problems enumerated above.

What are the specific problems (and perceived needs) addressed by STEP?

1. The disruption of the schools in South Africa over the past 20 years.
2. The poor qualifications of many school teachers.
3. The perceptions of parents and pupils that education is a way out of the poverty trap (mentioned also by Beeby, op cit).

How have they recruited their volunteers?

Despite reports to the contrary, there are sufficient students who for various reasons do not require payment for their activities. Many of the students are on university or other bursaries and live on campus where the classes are held. In addition, since the classes are on campus and not in the schools, students from the more affluent sectors of the population are able to participate (until recently, it was dangerous for anybody not known in the area to venture into the townships). When classes are held in vacations, the students are paid for their participation.

What about the teachers?

The difficulty with teacher status has been avoided since the pupils themselves choose to attend, although in 1995 for the first time the STEP organisers have deliberately targeted certain schools in their publicity and recruitment.

The use of the university campus also means that adequate facilities are available and that the pupils have experience of a very large urban campus.

18.9 The Way Forward

In summary, the problems are, *inter alia*:

- *logistical*, ie, poor infrastructures, poor communication systems, lack of venues, uncertainties within the tertiary system itself, lack of amenities and lack of money;
- *sociological*, ie, the status of teachers under threat; the problems of mediating between two worlds, and of easy reversion to an impoverished schooling system; lack of resources and incentives for communities and individuals;
- *different learning environments*, ie, the university laboratory and the primitive classroom; medium of instruction and the common language; lack of coherence between the schooling system and the tertiary sector.

It becomes evident that these are not simply obstacles to the successful running of tutoring programmes: they are problems which bedevil the education process itself in developing countries. While we cannot pretend to address the whole of education policy in the course of this chapter, it is worth highlighting some of the issues.

The debate on the meaning of science and technology in a developing community is recognised as being of national importance. It is an unfinished debate. As Kwapong has said, the global divide is moving from a rich vs poor country dichotomy to one between 'haves' and 'have-nots' in terms of knowledge (Kwapong, 1993).

The problem though is that, in creating a small élite which divorces itself from the communities from which its few individual members are drawn, the communities are themselves further impoverished. Science, technology and mathematics need to become part of the life of the community itself.

The very act of escape impoverishes the student. He or she takes nothing with them into the university situation. They have not been enabled by their schooling to bring with them any of the wealth of the community. There is no valid interaction. He or she becomes increasingly alienated from their origins.

The question to ask is, 'Is student tutoring appropriate in this setting?' I believe that the answer is 'yes' but, following the STEP approach, in a very focused way. Some of the specific problems which might be addressed by student tutoring activities are:

- the dearth of role models and the low expectations of pupils
- the lack of practical activities in school science
- rote learning vs meaningful learning
- the gap between university and community/school.

This would require an institutional awareness which would promote interaction and appropriate curricula encouraging a more relevant approach to science and mathematics at both school and university level. Students would then have the background to help in appropriate ways. One view is that mathematics in schools fails because frequently the culturally-framed ways of counting and calculating – very often a base five – are denied any application value in school. The models and principles of the textbooks are incomprehensible to many pupils and even to some of the teachers (Kilborn, 1993).

At another level, there must be incentives for students to take back the new concepts and work them out in the community context, mediating, teaching and learning. Their own understanding would be enhanced by the activity and their own effective interaction with the community increased. This would ideally be in the form of credits towards their final qualification rather than in financial terms.

In addition, some in-service opportunities for teachers are seen as essential. One mode could be to provide new resource material for use in the classroom where the student and teacher work together to implement the activities. In this way neither the teacher nor the student tutor has a monopoly of expertise.

It is important that any such scheme is manageable. The travelling should not eat up most of the volunteers' free time. It may be that a concentrated effort during university holidays when the student goes home is the most appropriate type of interaction (as in the Perach endeavour). Alternatively, a science club in out-of-school hours could serve the same purpose.

In addition, the activities must be closely related to the official school syllabus since the objective in most schools is simply to 'get the pupils through the examinations'. Anything which detracts from this is given cursory treatment.

Are there alternative solutions?

Looking at the problems stated above, we need to ask if alternative interventions would be more appropriate. To provide role models, one-to-one mentoring may be more effective, although a tutor in a classroom will reach more pupils. Practical activities require both apparatus and confidence in using that apparatus – the use of university campuses is probably easier than trying to take equipment into schools. Rote learning is endemic in developing countries (and not unknown in developed ones!). Teacher education is required to move from this mode to one which emphasises understanding. The familiarity with university campuses necessitates some activities on campus.

The conclusion therefore must be that, depending on the problem considered to be the most pressing, the intervention or outreach endeavour will vary. For role models and classroom assistance, monitored student tutoring with INSET is probably the most appropriate, whereas for practical activities and familiarisation with tertiary institutions, on-campus activities would seem most relevant. In all cases some form of reward for students is needed.

There are already prototypes. Some universities and technical institutes give credits to students who take their work into impoverished communities and relate it to village or slum conditions. Water supply, agriculture and other facets of life, including law and health-care, become points of interaction between the community and the campus. The tertiary institutions themselves may create incentives for such outreach, not only in the form of optional credits, but also required credits. Teachers can be brought onto campus or into distance-learning situations which offer qualification-related courses which will integrate their teaching with the student initiatives.

Students will need training in their roles as junior partners in the process. They should not run cram sessions in preparation for examinations; nor can they supplant teachers, but rather assist them. An intervention would therefore be appropriate at primary school or the lower levels of high schools, rather than the senior levels. An important aspect of their work would be to act as role models. They must encourage pupils to learn rather than expect to be taught.

We would encourage a symbiotic relationship between the parties: teachers must themselves become lifelong learners; pupils must become learners rather than passive recipients; students must be mentors and role models in this important aspect of schooling; universities must provide the back up and training.

The teachers benefit in this scheme: they are given access to resources, such as teaching aids, the assistance of the students in setting up experiments and providing technical expertise; and they will have easier access to campus and distance education systems.

The universities will benefit and the endeavour must be regarded as an important outreach. Better prepared school-leavers will make a very considerable difference to the recipient institution.

We cannot pretend that this model will answer all the problems raised. They are too vast. In all honesty there is no intervention at the level of a single institution which can make a national difference. What each can do is provide a model, applicable to other universities and other schools, believing that it is worth doing.

Address for correspondence: Margaret Rutherford and Robert Hofmeyr, University of the Witwatersrand, Johannesburg, South Africa.

Chapter 19

GUIDANCE BY STUDENT TUTORS AND MENTORS

Sir Christopher Ball

Good morning ladies and gentlemen, I'm glad you stayed, and I hope you will be. This is a daunting audience to address. It's hard to follow three such competent speakers as Sinclair Goodlad, Marc Freedman and Margaret Rutherford, each of whom has impressed me (and you) so much over the last two days. I found them instructive and inspiring; and that combination is hard to match.

I've not felt so challenged as a speaker since I addressed a rotary club in a country (which I won't name) about as far away from the United Kingdom as you can get. I addressed them over lunch. They didn't stop eating while I spoke so there was the clink of glass and of silver on good china as I addressed them. At the end the Chairman thanked me and (rather to my surprise) gave me an envelope. I was sitting at a table and so I covertly opened it to see what was inside while he went on with his thanks. There was a cheque for the equivalent of five pounds. I was slightly disappointed!

So I put it back in the envelope, stood up as the Chairman finished and gave it back to him, saying into the microphone, 'Chairman, I'm sure this contains a most generous cheque, but I couldn't possibly accept it. I would like to give it back to your rotary club for charitable purposes.' I got my best round of applause – and there's an important message here: you should stop when you're ahead! Because I went on foolishly to ask: 'It would be interesting to know how the rotary club will spend the (no doubt) princely sum inside this envelope?' Well the Chairman was up to the challenge. He leaped to his feet and said, 'Thanks to your generosity, Sir Christopher, we shall be able to reward appropriately many more speakers of the quality you have shown today.' So you have been warned.

My presentation falls into three parts. I want to talk about the challenge of lifelong learning. I want to talk about the nature of good guidance for learning and work and I want to draw some conclusions from our conference. Professor FitzGibbon urged me to tell you (and I promised I would) that my paper would be largely speculative and inevitably not based on a lot of empirical research, since it deals with a fast-changing world and with an uncertain future. You have been warned again.

The motto for my address is drawn from a 15th century English morality play called *Everyman*: 'Everyman, I will go with thee and be thy guide. In thy most need to go by thy side.' I find, and have for many years found, these lines inspiring. The words are spoken by a character in the play called Knowledge, who is the sister of Good Deeds. Student tutoring and mentoring seems to me to be a combination of knowledge and good deeds – indeed, to be the best sort of guidance.

But first let me say something about the challenge of lifelong learning. I am a SIF. You may not all know the term – it means a single issue fanatic. I believe that all problems (and this is how single issue fanatics start sentences!) – I believe that all problems can best be tackled by learning. Learning is the best route to a better life both for individuals and for our nations. And I suspect that in saying this I am preaching to the converted. I would be surprised if any of you disagreed with the broad thrust of that claim. Health, wealth and happiness, the traditional definition of the good life for humans, can all be best achieved, or at least enhanced, by the process of learning. Learning is a better solution than crime, drugs, dependency, whinging, stoicism or revolution. I was going to say, I should know: I've tried them all – but that isn't quite true.

In Europe since the middle ages we have had a succession of what are called paradigm shifts. In the middle ages in Europe you find a society which seemed to behave as if religion were the most important subject in life. Religion was Europe's 'big idea' at that time. It was something to die for, something to kill for. People behaved as if they thought that if you could get your religion right, all would be well. And that is perhaps what we mean by medievalism.

Well, if you study the history of Europe it's interesting that at a certain period (when we think modern Europe develops) that big idea seems to be gradually set aside and replaced with a second big idea. Politics became all important. Europe grasped the new big idea that if we could only get the constitution right, if we could only get the government right,

248

then all would be well in society. Of course, in Europe and elsewhere in the world today we still live in the 'political era'. Against all the evidence, we seem to believe that if only we could select a new government, somehow society would be made perfect. Soon there will be a general election in the UK. But society will not be made perfect thereby. You know that. I know that.

I think we are trembling on the brink of the third big idea, a better one than religion or politics, the idea of learning. The world is now ready to grasp the principle that learning is the big idea that really works.

You can put the point another way. In the past, power and wealth resided in land and property. Then, as industrialised societies developed in many parts of the world, we realised that land and property (though important) were not as important as energy. Coal and oil (as BP shows) have been the sources of wealth in the modern world. But that is changing. We are entering a world where the source of prosperity is applied intelligence. Applied human intelligence is the function of learning. Invest in that, and you will do better than investing in land and property or in coal and oil. The new 'big idea' is applied intelligence. The good news is that we have all got some.

A recent study of the newly industrialised countries of South East Asia, like Taiwan, Singapore and Korea, has suggested in broad terms that the secret of their success resides in three factors. What they have, what we need, what perhaps we once had in the UK and must recover, are the ethic of hard work, the habit of learning and a strong family tradition. It appears that nations that have those three factors are prospering in the modern world. It appears that nations that lack those three factors are in trouble.

This is of course not a new idea. You can find it in traditional Scottish thinking. Or you can look to traditional Jewish practice worldwide to see just how important those three factors have been in the past – but particularly are now in the later 20th century. Learning is vital. Now these ideas I am putting to you are a commonplace in the world today. I imagine most of you know them and live by them already. But the thirst for learning puts a strain on our traditional provision for education and training and on our national resources to meet this ongoing and increasing demand for opportunities to learn.

In the UK the school-leaving age when children were allowed to (and did) leave school, has risen in three generations from 13 to 15 and (in practice today) to 17. My grandparents lived in a world where the school leaving age was 13. My parents lived in a world where the school leaving age was 15 and I am living in a world where the effective school leaving age is 17 in this developed country. Over three generations we've generated a need for 50% more teachers by that simple process. It will continue, because we know that in Japan more than 90% of children stay on in full-time schooling until the age of 18. And this creates an enormous demand on our national resources.

In a recent conference held last November in Rome on lifelong learning, an action agenda was developed for the 21st century. I want to quote from that report to give you a sense of the way people are now thinking about the main thrust of learning for the future:

> The main finding is clear enough. It is that our traditional and inherited systems of education and training have failed to create learning societies in which everyone is motivated and enabled to practise lifelong learning. A world containing almost nine hundred million adult illiterates is not the learning world which is our vision. What we have created so far is not good enough. Existing systems of education and training tend to favour an élite of fast learners, to focus on teaching, rather than learning, and to over-emphasise initial education at the expense of lifelong learning. What is required is not more of the same. If we are to reach the unreached and include the excluded, more must mean different.
>
> In consequence we are calling for major reform and restructuring of the provision for education and training to enable every person to develop their human potential as fully as possible by means of lifelong learning. This is because in the 21st century those individuals who do not practise lifelong learning will not find work. Those organisations which do not become learning organisations will not survive. Those schools, colleges and universities which do not put their students first will not recruit. Learning pays. In a world which increasingly rewards learning, it provides economic, social and personal benefits which are in principle available to all.
>
> The key principle governing provision in the future must be the primacy of personal responsibility for learning, encouraged and enabled by the support of the whole community. Although the world is obviously made up of faster and slower learners, everyone is capable of further useful learning and people can learn to learn faster. We have in the past underestimated the human potential for learning. A generation ago in many developed countries fewer than 5% of young people went into university-level education; today the figure often exceeds 30% and is still rising. The essential feature of learning is not ability, it is not even resources, it is motivation. When people take responsibility for their own learning and encourage one another the learning world becomes a realisable vision.

I see considerable sympathy and overlap between the conclusions of the Rome conference and the work of this conference in London. Let me briefly develop three ideas from this report: the claim that learning pays, the suggestion that we have underestimated the human potential for learning, and the principle of personal responsibility – encouraged and enabled by community support.

I will not dwell for long on the idea that learning pays. We live in a world which rewards learning. Learning provides economic, social and personal benefits to nations, companies and individuals. There is considerable evidence, and the evidence is mounting, that each of those claims is substantially true. I find as I travel round the world that there is very little dispute about them, except in one country, and sadly that's my own. Only in the United Kingdom are we still debating the issue of whether or not learning pays.

Of course learning is also fun, or it ought to be, and learning sets us free. I know that from my own experience, and as a teacher. But I must emphasise the economic argument, because for most learners in practice that is the most powerful motivator. Only those whose economic needs are met can afford to talk about 'learning for its own sake'.

Each of the speakers at this conference has chosen a teaching aid. At this point I want to hold up my teaching aid which is not a chain, like Sinclair's, but the conference folder which we were all given at the beginning of the conference. I expect, like me, you have enjoyed exploring it (almost like a Christmas stocking) to see what was inside. The more I explored it, the more depressed I became – because I found that the folder was made in Taiwan, the little note pad inside the folder – although called 'tartan notes' and therefore suggesting that it came from Scotland, was made in France and the calculator is also made in Taiwan. That gives you some direct sense of the challenge that we in this country face. Why have we failed to learn how to make these things at a competitive price and quality for ourselves? Why has BP had to go to Taiwan and France to provide us with the essential tools of this conference?

That is the challenge to our learning. And one reason for this state of affairs is that we've underestimated the human potential for learning in the past. We can and we must aim higher. I quote from one of the exhibits at the poster session – 'youth is getting more intelligent day by day'. My own impression is also that youth is getting more intelligent day by day, but of course it's a slightly puzzling idea. How can that be so? I don't really think that youth is getting more intelligent; it is just that young people have more opportunities, higher aspirations, better motivation to develop their intelligence day by day.

When I went to my university as a student 40 years ago, barely 4% of my age group entered higher education in the United Kingdom. Fifteen years ago when I was teaching in a university some 12% of the 18-year-olds in the United Kingdom entered university-level education. Today about 30% of our 18-year-olds do so, and there is no reason to think that the increase will stop there. It is funding, not intelligence, that is holding up the expansion at present.

No one believes themselves incapable of further useful learning. They are right. I should think there would be very few people in this room who could identify someone they know well, and care about, who they would judge to be incapable of further useful learning. And here I have clearly in mind the disabled as well as the fully able. We are all capable of further useful learning during our lives.

In a world where resources were readily available to expand university education to meet the demand of all people who wanted advanced learning and who could benefit from it, how many of us would have the capability to share in the experience of university education at some appropriate point in our lives? Where do you think that the limits of the human potential for advanced learning will be found as we develop educational opportunities further and more widely in the 21st century? I'd like you to think of your family, your friends, your colleagues, your students and your neighbours and calculate from that group a percentage of people who could benefit if they had the opportunity of some university education at an appropriate point in their lives. Remember that we are carrying out a sort of national experiment on just this question in the UK, a rich developed nation: the figure has risen from about 4% to precisely 31% over the last 40 years.

Each of you should by now have seen the force to the question and should have a rough percentage in your minds. It might be 4% if you thought that my experience was the right one 40 years ago; it might be 30% if you thought that the UK had just about reached the limits of useful learning; or it might be a different figure. I will prompt you no further. You should each now have a figure in your mind.

[A member of the audience: 'Can I ask a question? Can we in this imaginary situation assume that the nature of what we consider to be university education is able to adapt to increasing demand?'

Answer: 'Of course. More means different. Assume that we can develop an appropriate form of advanced learning for the potential students you're thinking of.'

Guidance by student tutors and mentors

Note: In a show of hands delegates responded with propositions ranging from below 60% to above 90% of the 18-year-old age group, with an average level of about 75%.]

I am struck both by the high average level and the remarkable range of your responses.

This is a very disparate and varied audience of people from many different countries from all over the world so one wouldn't expect complete coherence of response. On the other hand we're all broadly in the same sort of business with the same sort of interests and yet you've given figures that range from below 60% to above 90%. The conclusion I draw from that is not that your peer groups are all vastly different from one another, but that none of you has the faintest idea of the right answer to the question! Nor do I, because nobody in the world knows the limits of the human potential for learning.

What we do know is that for many centuries we have badly underestimated what people could learn, and we're just beginning to explore what's possible. In the United Kingdom our Confederation of British Industry (CBI), employers, has proposed that 40% of the 18-year-old age group should graduate from universities by the year 2000. That would require our universities to recruit in 1997 for the traditional UK full-time three-year degree a proportion of the age group which I calculate to be something between 46% and 48% (to allow for drop out and deferral). And since at the moment we recruit 31%, we have a long way to go in two years if we are going to meet the demands of the employers.

But those figures pale into insignificance when you see what other countries are planning to do. Korea and France are each seeking in their national plan to ensure that no less than 80% of their 18-year-olds should be qualified for university entrance by the time we reach the turn of the century.

These arguments – that learning pays and that the human potential for learning is unexhausted (and possibly inexhaustible) – create a world-wide demand for opportunities for education and training – for lifelong learning – for all people. It cannot easily be satisfied by conventional means and at conventional costs. Teachers are too expensive and too few. And in developed as well as developing nations, we're running up against a major resource problem as we try to extend traditional models of education and training to meet this massive and ever-increasing demand for more learning.

253

So we need to replace a dependency model of learning with the principle of personal responsibility for learning, encouraged and enabled by the support of the whole community. At its best, student tutoring and mentoring represent the ideal form of community support for the responsible learner.

The task is to develop a world where everyone practises lifelong learning. The problems we face are of motivating people to take responsibility for their learning, and of providing the required resources. Which is the greater problem? Both are very serious challenges: to motivate and to provide resources for learning. I note with interest that in developed countries it is motivation that is seen as the key issue. The United Kingdom is considering mounting a 'national campaign for learning' in order to encourage those people in our society who haven't yet understood the value of their own learning to take more action to learn. A generation ago, Earnest Bevin used to talk about the 'poverty of the aspirations of our people', a sad comment on our culture. In developed countries it is often the case that motivation is seen to be the prime problem. But I know that in developing countries motivation is not nearly so serious a problem as the lack of resources. Remember Margaret Rutherford's haunting image of the need for 'flowers on the mud bank' in developing countries. We need more resources, and we need keener motivation.

What can be done? Well, we might consider – though I wouldn't want to – Stalin's solution. When he came to power in the Soviet Union, Stalin discovered that more than 50% of Russian adults were illiterate. This is a great problem if you're trying to maintain a revolution, because revolutions depend on slogans and posters – and people have to be able to read them. Literacy is a vital tool for the revolutionary. Stalin therefore decided that a massive literacy campaign must be one of his first acts as a leader. So he called the teachers together and ordered them to teach people to read – and the graph of literacy moved slowly upwards in the way it does when educators are asked to try harder. Stalin wasn't satisfied. He decided to make illiteracy a criminal offence. He announced that after a year or two any adult who was illiterate would be sent to prison. What's more the whole village was to be sent to prison too because literacy is a community responsibility.

Now, there's some good thinking there, though I'm not sure I like the method. The implication of taking very seriously the learning of a whole society and laying the responsibility for success on the community is something that we might ponder. We might also ponder on the results of

254

Stalin's plan – which was one of the most successful literacy campaigns the world has ever seen.

My own proposal for dealing with these problems is that every adult should be encouraged to have a personal learning plan. I have a personal learning plan (I'm sure many of you have one too) related to my objectives in life and work, written down and supported by a mentor. My mentor is somebody who I've chosen to encourage me in a friendly way. I wonder how many people in this room have something like this, a personal learning plan written down and supported by a mentor? Can I have a show of hands? Congratulations to those holding their hands up – perhaps ten, perhaps a dozen, not many of us yet!

This is a conference of student tutors and mentors and those responsible for them. We've not heard the voice of the mentees as yet. I want to ask each of you to turn yourself for a moment in imagination into the role of the mentee, because, if there is a weakness in this conference, it is that while we've heard reports from the student mentors, and we've heard from all the experts, we have not yet heard what the mentees think. What have they to tell us? Nothing direct as yet. So I'm now going to transform you into mentees and listen to what you say to me.

What I want you to do is this. Imagine you have decided to create a personal learning plan at this very moment. What single item do you most want to learn? How would you most like to learn it? And who would you choose as your mentor, if you were following my practice of having a written personal learning plan supported by a mentor? Three questions – what do you most want to learn? How would you most like to learn it? And who would you want as your mentor? Please discuss this for a moment or two with your immediate neighbour.

[After a moment's astonished silence, the audience began to discuss the three questions with growing interest for about seven minutes.]

It's easy enough to start such an exercise, but it's more difficult to bring it to an end! Thank you very much. If you remember nothing else from my address in a year's time I hope you'll remember this exercise, and what you found out about yourselves. I hope you'll act on it.

[On a show of hands the participants responded roughly as follows to the three questions put to them:

(i) Do you (a) most want to learn something work-related?   (40%)
or (b) most want to learn something life-related?   (40%)
or (c) think those are silly questions?   (20%)

255

*(ii) Do you (a) want to learn it formally (on a course of study
with a teacher)?*   *(10%)*
or (b) want to learn it informally (at home or work)?   *(70%)*
or (c) think those are also silly questions?   *(20%)*

*(iii) Do you (a) want as your mentor a professional educator
(qualified teacher)?*   *(10%)*
or (b) want as your mentor a friend or colleague?   *(70%)*
or (c) think that those are yet again silly questions?   *(20%)*

Please note the high score for life-related learning: for many of us this kind of learning is highly motivated. For some it provides the only effective route into work-related learning. Please also note the extraordinarily high scores for informal learning and non-professional mentors. What would happen to formal education and training if we ever took notice of what the clients say they want? Those of you who thought that I asked silly questions probably did so because you wanted both work-related and life-related learning, a mixture of formal and informal learning, and mentors who were both friends and professional teachers.

Most adults learn best if they're in control of the subject, the time, the place, the pace and the duration of their learning. That is exactly the opposite of what is happening now, since I am in control of all those things, not you. As a learner, I am an extreme example of such an adult. I simply refuse to learn unless I am in full control of all those things. (How I managed to get through my childhood education, I still don't know.)

I want to urge you to trust informed student demand. One of the few moments in this conference when I found myself frowning was when Russell Seal said that BP wants to influence the subjects chosen for study. I would urge BP to be more cautious. In a rapidly changing world, learners are as likely to know what is best for them as their teachers, or their employers. I am somebody who believes strongly in the principle that we should trust in informed student demand. (But the word 'informed' is absolutely critical. Don't trust in uninformed student demand.) In other words, mentors need to be humble if they're to do the job well.

So what is the nature of good guidance for learning and work? Well, it is very similar to the qualities that I grew up believing were the qualities of a good teacher: helping people to discover their aptitudes, helping people determine their own goals, and helping people change themselves through the process of learning – because learning is changing.

Guidance by student tutors and mentors

Few countries today can guarantee full employment through government action – certainly not the UK. But we can, I think, define employability, the qualities that make people work-ready. Moreover, we can offer it as a condition in principle accessible to all except the most severely disabled. In theory, I think 100% employability is achievable.

What do I mean by the characteristics of employability? Well here I must give a UK answer, though I think it's a European answer as well. (It may not work for other parts of the world.) In the UK you need to achieve the appropriate level of learning, the appropriate quality, the habit of learning, and mobility.

The level has to be what we call A level or level 3 learning – roughly equivalent to US graduation from high school, the kind of learning that people of average learning speed achieve by the age of 18 or 19 in developed countries with systematic education. Without that level of learning today, you're in trouble. In that sense the world has changed since I was a boy, because my generation of young people could (and many of us did) leave school at 15 or 16 and get good jobs. That world has gone forever. The experts tell us that in the next century the level of learning will rise again. If you want to be employable, you will have to achieve the qualities that today we expect from graduates.

The quality of learning is the second feature. In this country we have national learning targets. One of our targets, known as Foundation Target 4, says that we should develop 'self-reliance, adaptability and breadth'. I'd like to call those three words the alternative National Curriculum, because I think they're so much more – and so much more comprehensible – than our full National Curriculum. Without those qualities, even if you've got level 3 learning you're in trouble. They're not easy qualities to achieve or retain. Many of us relinquish self-reliance, lose our adaptability, and abandon breadth as we work through our life of employment.

We also need the habit of learning, continuing education, (for example) my suggestion of an active personal learning plan. People who don't maintain the habit of learning will become unemployable over time – even if they have been employed earlier. And you also need mobility, the capability of moving to where the work is, if the work doesn't come to you.

In Europe those people who achieve and retain these four conditions will not (and do not) long remain unemployed. But the characteristics of employability are rising generation by generation. People need good guidance to help them understand this and find the appropriate actions

257

to develop (or redevelop) this condition of work-readiness that I'm talking about. Responsible adult learners need mentors. I do. I argue that you do. If, in principle, we're seeking to develop a learning world in which everyone practises lifelong learning, then we all need mentors. And we all are potential mentors. The City University of New York claimed on one of its posters that: 'everyone is a tutor'. Alec Dickson has taught us: 'each one, teach one'. I think that means us. Perhaps the quality of a good mentor could be summed up (not entirely frivolously) by suggesting that no one should be one who hasn't got one. To be a good mentor you need a mentor.

I'm arguing that the findings and experience of this conference, and the influence of the international mentoring and tutoring project, offer us the best available answers to the challenge of developing lifelong learning for all in a learning world. That what we have been talking about and what you are all doing in your lives is better than Stalin's inhuman solution of criminalising illiteracy. It's a better solution than the information technology revolution which is proving too expensive (and inhuman in a different sense) to meet the needs of lifelong learning for all people. It's a better solution than attempting to expand indefinitely our traditional models of education and training, because that is proving far too expensive and demands more teachers than the world can possibly produce to meet the explosive demand for learning.

The mentoring and tutoring movement may turn out to be not just a useful adjunct to 'business as usual' (which perhaps some of you see it as) but the shape of things to come in the learning world of the future. Perhaps I'm making a higher claim for this movement than you would want to make yourselves. But I want you to consider it seriously.

I shall leave this conference much inspired, much better informed, much more hopeful, but also conscious of an agenda of work that remains outstanding. The richness, variety and fervour of the conference has been remarkable. As examples of what I have been especially impressed by, I note: 'the Buddy system' from Singapore, the Perach project (Israel), Ikhonki (South Africa). The latter is the Xhosa word for 'chain' – and brings the conference full circle, since we started with Sinclair Goodlad's chain two days ago. I could have adduced so many more equally impressive examples of worldwide endeavour and achievement. Perhaps others, like me, will have been particularly struck by the statement of the students who spoke collectively just before this final session of the conference of their personal commitment to tutoring.

The serious self-questioning evident in so many of the sessions and presentations is equally remarkable and admirable. In attempting to summarise outcomes, I identify seven critical issues.

1. **Evaluation**: how can we best evaluate student tutoring and mentoring? Is it cost-effective? There seem to be problems not only with finding reliable forms of measurement, but also with our own attitudes to the ideas of measurement and evaluation. There is also (perhaps in consequence?) a paucity of sound research available at present. Professor FitzGibbon's presentation made a strong and persuasive case for a method using 'random sampling' techniques. As for cost, I was struck by two figures revealed to the conference: a UK statement that student tutoring cost about £4 per hour to deliver, while from Belgium we were told of students receiving payment of about £8 per hour. My own view is that the governing principle should be 'those who benefit should pay' – and that we therefore require a much more rigorous analysis of the question: 'who benefits?'.

2. **Persistence**: it has become clear from a range of presentations that it is essential to attend carefully to the selection, training and sustaining of tutors and mentors. There appears to be a wide variation in the expected and actual degree of personal commitment. Since from the point of view of mentees 'persistence' is vital, there is a real opportunity for the international movement to study and learn from 'best practice' in this respect. (I was especially impressed by the French GENEPI organisation for student tutoring in prisons.)

3. **Welcome**: there is obviously a pervasive problem with the attitudes of schools, and of teachers. Unless carefully handled, student tutoring and mentoring can be seen as a threat to the professionalism of teachers. It is essential to organise schemes so as to deliver real benefits to all participants – including the 'host schools' and teachers. Where the welcome is less than warm, the effectiveness of student tutoring and mentoring is much diminished.

4. **Dependency**: I shall never forget Marc Freeman's provocative equation: 'required helpfulness' + adult mentor = resilience. Schemes of the kind reported to this conference can easily generate dependency in the recipients, unless careful measures are taken to maintain and enhance individuals' personal responsibility for their own learning. Among other factors needing attention is the issue of closure – the planned withdrawal of support which is an essential feature of all communal help for learners. As I thought about the many presentations given at the conference, one question occurred to me repeatedly: 'Why don't we ask people what they want and need?'

5. **'Minute particulars'**: the English poet William Blake used to say that 'he who would do good to another, must do it in minute particulars'. Margaret Rutherford told us to 'start small'. Sinclair Goodlad suggested that student tutoring needs to offer 'solutions to specific problems'. The devil is in the detail. Keith Topping's observation was that 'you will get what you plan and structure to get'. Alexander Pope wrote:

> For forms of government let fools contest;
> Whate'er is best administered is best.

To which we might reply –

> Of forms of mentoring let fools contest;
> Whate'er works most effectively is best.

6. **Developing and developed countries**: in the week in which UK schoolteachers are thinking about going on strike if class sizes exceed 30, we have heard tell of a South African class of 120 pupils. The conference has repeatedly been made painfully aware of the disparity of material resources in the developed and developing world. What can we do about this? I stand with Shakespeare's Viola, who said:

> O Time, thou must untangle this, not I;
> It is too hard a knot for me t'untie.

But we can be clear about the nature of the true resources of the international student tutoring and monitoring movement. It is, of course, the intelligence, knowledge and commitment of students – knowledge and good deeds, the best sort of guidance. Those seeking help, in both developing and developed countries, are young people who do not have 'enough caring adults in their lives', for 'it takes a whole village to raise a child'.

7. **The role of leadership**: throughout the conference we have been reminded of the importance of sound leadership. Success seems to follow when good leaders can unite fervour with a well-organised infrastructure. We should not forget Russell Seal's emphasis on the task of 'managing change'. Existing systems produce existing results, so if you want something different you must change the system. Only in heaven is the status quo good enough – and so sustainable. On earth, it is our duty constantly to challenge it in the unremitting search for something better.

And so we all acknowledge, and express our gratitude for, the leadership of BP – and (in particular) of John Hughes. The sponsors of the international student tutoring and mentoring movement have a critical role to play in providing leadership, encouragement and pump-priming funding. But they, too, must beware of creating the habit of dependency. Pumps should not require repeated or indefinite priming.

But my thanks are addressed above all to you, the many participants in this memorable conference. You have provided me (and each other, I am sure) with an inspiring learning experience. You have demonstrated in your enthusiasm, your seriousness of purpose, and your deep commitment, the qualities that are implied in my motto for the whole conference:

> Everyman (and every woman) I will go with thee and be thy guide,
> In thy most need to go by thy side.

Go forward; guide well; and persist. Thank you for your attention.

Address for correspondence: Sir Christopher Ball, 45 Richmond Road, Oxford OX1 2JJ.

Appendix A

SETTING UP A TUTORING SCHEME:
The links in the chain

Define aims

- What problem(s) are you trying to solve?
- Is the activity a substitute for, or a complement to, something else?
- Decide objectives for tutors/mentors.
- Decide objectives for tutees/mentees.

Structure the content

- Base on the skill-needs of tutees/mentees
- Plan a systematic sequence of tasks
- Specify clearly procedures to develop independence in tutees/mentees.

Define roles and logistics

- Time and duration of sessions
- Space – including noise problems
- Meetings – frequency, purpose
- Selection of tutors/mentors
- Selection/matching of tutees/mentees
- Role of sending teachers
- Role of receiving teachers
- Role of coordinator
- Documentation/materials.

Get secure finance

- Identify a suitable source

- Calculate amount precisely (including overheads)
- Plan for continuity: be clear what will happen when start-up funds cease.

Train the tutors/mentors in how to:

- Start a session
- Know the content of the syllabus
- Give praise
- Avoid doing the work for tutees/mentees
- Cope with trouble
- Vary the content of sessions
- End individual sessions
- Keep records
- End the tutoring/mentoring arrangement.

Support the tutors/mentors

- Give them good written materials
- Build into their curriculum
- Devise appropriate assessment/reward.

Evaluate the scheme

- Keep basic records of who did what
- Use rating scales for specific items
- Collect reflective anecdotes
- Measure what is measurable
  BUT
- Don't hassle people.

Appendix B

SHORT NOTES ON A VARIETY OF SCHEMES

(Note: these are arranged alphabetically by the name of the person to contact)

Title of scheme: Israel: PERACH

Overall purpose of scheme:
1. To cultivate and enrich disadvantaged children from deprived areas.
2. To bring different groups of the society together.
3. To deepen students' involvement in social and communal life.
4. To assist students by offering a partial scholarship.

Tutors/mentors: University students. About 18,000 annually.
Aims for tutors/mentors: To become a better person and more involved in his/her surroundings.
Tutees/mentees: Mostly primary-school children. About 45,000 annually.
Aims for tutees/mentees: To take at least one step further (higher) in the direction of their needs.
Subject/substance of work: With every child according to his/her needs.
Date of start of scheme: 1974.
Duration of each cycle: Nine months – at least 34 weeks. Twice a week: two hours each session.
Type and length of training: Seminars, school meetings, one-to-one with coordinator: three to four hours a month.
Outcome measures: Questionnaires to all involved (yearly) about everything concerning the activities.
Source and nature of finance: $22,000,000. Government, universities, municipalities, funds, donors. . .
Report(s) available: Yes. Free.
Person to contact: Amos Carmeli.
Address: Perach, Wiezmann Institute of Science, Rehovot, PO Box 26, Israel.
Telephone: 972 8 343426   **Fax**: 972 8 343468

Short notes on a variety of schemes

Title of scheme: UK: Grampian Student Tutoring Scheme at the University of Aberdeen

Overall purpose of scheme: Student tutoring is a voluntary scheme which involves students going out into local schools to work with pupils under the supervision of a classroom teacher. Locally the scheme is managed jointly between the Centre for Educational Development at the University of Aberdeen, and the Customer Relations Unit at the Robert Gordon University. Students tutor for one full morning/afternoon in either a local primary or secondary for the duration of eight to ten weeks.

Tutors/mentors: Any second, third or fourth year undergraduate students can take part; 105 this year.

Aims for tutors/mentors: To develop skills such as communication, time-management, organisation, problem solving. Increase self-confidence; 'do something different'; find out about teaching as a career.

Tutees/mentees: Pupils of local primary/secondary schools. All years are covered.

Aims for tutees/mentees: Enable work in smaller groups; more individual attention possible; enable wider range of activities to be undertaken; to raise aspirations about moving on into FE/HE.

Subject/substance of work: Varies between schools and classes.

Date of start of scheme: October 1992.

Duration of each cycle: eight to ten weeks; sessions run October – December, February – April.

Type and length of training: One evening for a couple of hours. Students can air concerns; issues which they may expect to face in the classroom are covered; former tutors share their experiences.

Outcome measures: What tutors/teachers like most and least about the scheme; any comments; record of learning is completed with the tutors. Evaluation forms for tutors and teachers. This year videos have also been taken in the primary schools asking the pupils about their tutors.

Source and nature of finance: Up until next year, BP sponsorship, £2,000; pays travel costs for students.

Report(s) available: No.

Person to contact: Miss Nicola Coole/Mrs Brenda Holohan.

Address: Centre for Educational Development, Edward Wright Building, Dunbar Street, Aberdeen AB9 2TY.

Telephone: 01224 273499   **Fax**: 01224 273671
     Email: edvO15@aberdeen.ac.uk

Students as tutors and mentors

Title of scheme: UK: University of Strathclyde: BP Tutoring

Overall purpose of scheme: To raise aspirations of pupils by providing role models, ie, students who help in a practical way in subject classes but take opportunities to introduce pupils to the idea of continuing in education. (Fairly straightforward BP ACE model.)

Tutors/mentors: Total since inception – 280. Ninety students, mainly second or third year, mainly science or engineering, but also small numbers of arts and social science students and business students.

Aims for tutors/mentors: To increase confidence, develop interpersonal skills, enhance CV.

Tutees/mentees: Large age range. Forty primary and secondary schools.

Aims for tutees/mentees: Enhancement of learning, extra help and encouragement, increase enthusiasm for particular subjects, increase self-esteem.

Subject/substance of work: Subject classes – science, maths, technology, languages, English, geography. Primary School – some general, most concentrating on technology.

Date of start of scheme: 1992 Pilot scheme.

Duration of each cycle: 12–18 weeks (mostly from date of first visit; October/November till end of Spring term).

Type and length of training: Half-hour presentation; two-hour training session; induction visit to school; regular contact with experienced tutor; one-hour recall meeting midway.

Outcome measures: Evaluation forms sent to tutors, teachers and pupils.

Source and nature of finance: Mainstream – BP paying travelling expenses plus £500. Alumni Fund £1,000 for general expenses. Islands – BP Island travel expenses. Education authorities £500 for Island tutoring. University provides technology kits for Island.

Report(s) available: Report will be available for 1994–5 session. Cost not yet decided.

Person to contact: Imelda Devlin.

Address: University of Strathclyde, Graham Hills Building, 50 George Street, Glasgow G1 1QE.

Telephone: 0141 552 4400 Ext. 4248   **Fax**: 0141 552 7362
Email: i.devlin@strath.ac.uk

Short notes on a variety of schemes

Title of scheme: Belgium: Tutoring Programme ULB Secondary Schools (Brussels)

Overall purpose of scheme: Help disadvantaged pupils (SES, immigrants, low achievers) to bridge the gap of the scholar, weaknesses or failures, to develop higher expectations, for some of them to successfully attend higher education.

Tutors/mentors: 85 undergraduate and postgraduate university students.

Aims for tutors/mentors: Teaching experience; sharing of own experience; information about higher education.

Tutees/mentees: 800 secondary school pupils aged 14–18.

Aims for tutees/mentees: Pedagogical help/role-modelling.

Subject/substance of work: Cognitive skills (pairs – improvements).

Date of start of scheme: 1989.

Duration of each cycle: One academic year/two cycles a year.

Type and length of training: Short tutors' training (six hours).

Outcome measures: 1993–4 provided evaluation of the academic improvement for the tutees (average 20%).

Source and nature of finance: Regional Ministry in Brussels, yearly.

Report(s) available: Yes.

Person to contact: L De Vos/A Medhoune.

Address: University Libre Bruxelles, 50 Av. F.D. Roosevelt C.P. 160/11, 1050 Brussels, Belgium.

Telephone: 32 2 6502408   **Fax**: 32 2 6502264

267

Students as tutors and mentors

Title of scheme: Australia: Star

Overall purpose of scheme: To create a greater mutual awareness of science and technology among high school students (and where possible their parents); to have those students raise their educational/career aspirations – specifically in science and technology; to provide tutors with an experience that will enhance this commitment to science and technology, and develop their 'transferable' skills and improve their employability; to bring schools, higher education and industry closer together and to provide the opportunity for worthwhile, long-term partnerships based on mutual understanding and respect for their contributions to science and technology.

Tutors/mentors: Currently 30 tutors. University science students (second year upwards).

Aims for tutors/mentors: To provide opportunities for developing/improving 'transferable' skills – virtually ignored by the university (though now being addressed as a matter of extreme urgency as part of a national quality assurance – outcomes programme). To provide stimulus for the students' own studies and encourage them to enjoy community service.

Tutees/mentees: High school science students (Years 8–12, aged 13–17). Approximately half in schools of low post-secondary participation and in areas of high youth unemployment; 700.

Aims for tutees/mentees: 1. To stimulate a greater awareness of science and technology by providing academic tutors who are also good role models. 2. To encourage tutees to continue studies in science and technology at high school. 3. To raise their aspirations to study science and technology beyond high school at either a college or university.

Subject/substance of work: Science and technology tutoring; with access to the workplace to strengthen the 'weak' link – ie, where do science and technology graduates get worthwhile, stimulating jobs and careers?

Date of start of scheme: February 1994.

Duration of each cycle: Each peer tutor is contracted to the programme to provide a half-day a week in a school for a full semester: 12–13 weeks. More contract for a full year.

Type and length of training: Personal interview and one-day group programme in communications skills (written and verbal; listening skills); questioning techniques; classroom etiquette; potential problems and how to handle them; student/tutor relations; teacher/tutor relations.

Outcome measures: Questionnaire and interview at end of school year. 1995–6 will see study of transfer of tutees to further and higher education courses.

Source and nature of finance: Government's National Priority Fund grants and corporate sponsorship (BP).

Report(s) available: Yes. Cost: postage only – depending on where in world.

Person to contact: Russell Elsegood.

Address: Murdoch University, South Street, Murdoch, Western Australia 6150.

Telephone: 9 360 2894　　**Fax**: 9 310 4233　　**Email**: elsegood@csusun1

Short notes on a variety of schemes

Title of scheme: UK: Wales: Trinity College Student Tutoring Programme

Overall purpose of scheme: To enable BA (humanities) and BSc (rural science) students to get school-based experience so as to share information with pupils (primary/secondary) and tertiary students.

Tutors/mentors: Since inception: 70–80. BA humanities and BSc rural environment students.

Aims for tutors/mentors: Offer/give opportunity to undergraduates to sample 'school life' with a view of improving communication skills, etc.

Tutees/mentees: Infant, junior, secondary and tertiary students in West Wales.

Aims for tutees/mentees: To offer an opportunity for students to assess whether or not they wish to apply for a PGCE course (primary or secondary).

Subject/substance of work: History, geography, maths, science, language (Welsh and English).

Date of start of scheme: 1993.

Duration of each cycle: One term.

Type and length of training: One half-day each session.

Outcome measures: Carried out by local Education & Business Partnership (Dyfed).

Source and nature of finance: BP and local TEC. West Wales TEC to 1995.

Report(s) available: Yes. Progress reports as submitted to managing agents BP and University of Glamorgan (Danny Saunders).

Person to contact: Tom Evans.

Address: Trinity College, Carmarthen, Dyfed SY 23.

Telephone: 01267 237 971

Students as tutors and mentors

Title of scheme: UK: Student Tutoring/Mentoring at Oldham College

Overall purpose of scheme: To meet community needs/raise profile of college and strengthen links by: (a) Students from FE college into secondary schools acting as positive role models. (b) Students on a 'resit GCSE course' into primary schools as role models and to boost their self-esteem. (c) Bilingual students into primary/secondary schools to assist one-to-one those pupils with little English. (d) Receiving HE students as positive role models.

Tutors/mentors: (From above) (a) 30 students (all ages) 18plus on advanced/ higher level courses; (b) 15 students aged 17plus; (c) 15-plus bilingual students (all courses, first level to higher); (d) 23 HE students mainly from science, maths, IT. Since inception, total number = over 100.

Aims for tutors/mentors: Increases confidence and social/communication skills. Seen as a valuable community service and good for their CV!

Tutees/mentees: See above – from primary, secondary and FE students – all being tutees or mentees.

Aims for tutees/mentees: More individual help with a positive role model; lessons more interesting and enjoyable; increases aspiration to further education and training.

Subject/substance of work: See information above.

Date of start of scheme: 1992 start of Student Tutoring Pilot project.

Duration of each cycle: Registration one hour plus information; training session two and a half hours; student recall and certificate presentation, two hours.

Type and length of training: Training involving BP video and involvement of school teachers and past student tutors. Mixture of formal and informal.

Outcome measures: Students: completion of log book/questionnaires/final report and 'debrief'. Teachers: questionnaires on scheme and each tutor. Pupils: questionnaire 'Having student tutors in my class'. Annual report published.

Source and nature of finance: TVEI; Oldham Compact; Oldham TEC; Oldham College. Total 1994/95 = £5,000.

Report(s) available: Yes. Annual report 1993/4 available. 1994/5 from end of May. Cost £15. Student log book £20. Disc with these documents £5 (with permission to copy above). Postage for reports: UK £1; Overseas £3.

Person to contact: Patricia Eyres.

Address: Oldham College, Rochdale Road, Oldham, Lancs OL9 6AA.

Telephone: 0161 624 5214 Ext. 1903   **Fax**: 0161 626 9059

Short notes on a variety of schemes

Title of scheme: USA: I Have A Dream Foundation (Colorado) (part of a national US programme)

Overall purpose of scheme: Reduce drop-out rates by selecting whole classes of elementary students for programme which incorporates nine to ten years of tutoring, academic enrichment, college preparatory, and mentoring and culminates in a small scholarship.

Tutors/mentors: Approximately 75% of group (currently 200 students) have one or both.

Aims for tutors/mentors: Improve grade levels in subjects, provide life skills and opportunities for exposure to things outside own culture.

Tutees/mentees: 200 'at-risk' minority inner-city students.

Aims for Tutees/Mentees: Reduced drop-out rates.

Subject/substance of work: School studies.

Date of start of scheme: 1988 – chose first class – graduates 1995. 1990 – chose second class – now grade 9. 1992 – five chose two more classes.

Duration of each cycle: Nine to ten years per class.

Type and length of training: Minimal tutor training. Formal recruitment, screening and training and ongoing monitors for mentoring.

Outcome measures: Number of high school graduates, number of pregnancies, number of drop-outs, number of college/secondary school enrolment.

Source and nature of finance: 100% private (corporation, foundation, individual) funding – raised annually.

Report(s) available: Yes. Write for information.

Person to contact: Kelly Felice, Executive Director.

Address: Colorado I Have A Dream Foundation, 3801 Martin Luther King Building, Denver, Colorado 80205, USA.

Telephone: 303 320 6214   **Fax**: 303 320 5703

Students as tutors and mentors

Title of scheme: UK: Bristol: CSV Learning Together

Overall purpose of scheme: To encourage pupils to stay on at school post-16 through positive role models of student tutors.

Tutors/mentors: 16 years, from FE and HE institutions, the majority being undergraduates. 250 student tutors 1994–5 (started 1992–3).

Aims for tutors/mentors: Increased confidence and communication skills, enriched CV, personal satisfaction.

Tutees/mentees: Pupils in primary, secondary, and special schools and further education colleges.

Aims for Tutees/Mentees: Help with learning. Growth in awareness of education/career opportunities.

Subject/substance of work: Cross-faculty and special needs.

Date of start of scheme: October 1992.

Duration of each cycle: Ten weeks of two hours a week minimum.

Type and length of training: Group training sessions – three hours approximately – preceded by personal interviews – BP Handbook.

Outcome measures: Feedback questionnaires from teachers and students.

Source and nature of finance: CSV principal partners finishing this academic year.

Report(s) available: Yes. Bristol Connection Annual Review. Bath Connection Annual Review.

Person to contact: Dorothy Field, Avon Coordinator.

Address: CSV, 7–10 Lawford Street, St. Philips, Bristol BS2 0D4.

Telephone: 01179 552968

Short notes on a variety of schemes

Title of scheme: UK: Nottingham: William Crane School – Mentor/Achievement System

Overall purpose of scheme: To raise the academic achievement of pupils assessed as having the ability to be high achievers and to provide progression routes so that pupils will go on to further educational or training opportunities.

Tutors/mentors: Vice-Principal from the College of Education, staff from the local TEC and staff employed by Boots the Chemist, Raleigh Cycles and local community leaders.

Aims for tutors/mentors: Providing (1) a role model to motivate the pupil and encourage growth and achievement; (2) to provide opportunities for work placement, or work shadowing throughout the pupils' final two years; (3) broaden pupils' perspectives and sharing valued skills.

Tutees/mentees: Two parallel groups of 30 pupils entering their final two years (Years 10/11).

Aims for tutees/mentees: Contracting to high expectations of attendance/ behaviour and a commitment to twilight sessions designed to enrich academic/social/emotional development.

Subject/substance of work: Target setting, team building, presentation skills and work designed to give pupils appreciation of the relevance of learning and to bring about a change of attitude.

Date of start of scheme: September 1994.

Duration of each cycle: Two years, one twilight session every two weeks for enrichment programme.

Type and length of training: Mentor support with support from class teachers attached to groups.

Outcome measures: Pupils attaining five or more A–C passes at GCSE with subjective reporting from mentors.

Source and nature of finance: School-based funding.

Report(s) available: No.

Person to contact: Mrs S Fitton/Mr J Watson.

Address: William Crane School, Minver Crescent, Aspley, Nottingham.

Telephone: 01159 293100

Title of scheme: USA: A New Peer Tutoring Design for Disadvantaged Students

Overall purpose of scheme: The aim of the programme was to minimise the unequal hierarchical structure that exists between the tutor and the tutee to increase tutees' motivation to learn and have an impact on their learning. Three programme features were introduced in three randomly assigned treatment schools: (1) tutees met with tutors jointly for planning, training, sharing and assessment; (2) tutees were given an opportunity to become tutors the following semester; (3) tutees were provided with a stipend for participation in group meetings.

Tutors/mentors: 42 high school students in six low SES schools with high drop-out rates; 21 in three treatment schools; 21 in three control schools.

Aims for tutors/mentors: To learn effective tutor skills to enable them to successfully tutor within the programme.

Tutees/mentees: 126 high school students enrolled in six low SES schools who were identified at high risk of dropping out of school; more than half were ESL students.

Aims for tutees/mentees: Have them remain in school, have more positive attitudes toward school, achieve higher grade point average for the semester, and pass the course in which they were tutored.

Subject/substance of work: Tutees were tutored in subjects (major academic, eg, English, maths, social studies) which they identified as those they needed help with.

Date of start of scheme: September 1993.

Duration of each cycle: Two semesters. Different cohort of students was tutored each semester. Tutoring took place for one hour, three times a week.

Type and length of training: Four hours pre-service in tutoring skills, eg, communications, building relationships, tutoring in content areas. Weekly (one hour) in-service training over the semester.

Outcome measures: Treatment tutees had higher programme attendance, significantly higher grades, and higher rates of completion in tutored courses.

Source and nature of finance: WK Kellogg Family Foundation $150,000.

Report(s) available: Yes – no cost.

Person to contact: Audrey Gartner.

Address: Peer Research Laboratory, CASE/City University of New York, 25 West 43rd Street, Room 620, New York NY 10036.

Telephone: 212 642 2929   **Fax**: 212 642 1956

    Email: gar@cunyvms1.gc.cuny.edu

Short notes on a variety of schemes

Title of scheme: UK: UWE Bristol: Student Tutoring – The Bristol Connection

Overall purpose of scheme: Raising aspirations for inner-city pupils in junior and secondary schools.

Tutors/mentors: 50 (undergraduates, all disciplines except education).
Aims for tutors/mentors: Exposure to inner-city schools and development of core and transferable skills.
Tutees/mentees: School pupils aged 6–18, approximately 500.
Aims for tutees/mentees: Raising of aspirations, awareness of HE as possible option.
Subject/substance of work: Various one-to-one literacy skills – group projects.
Date of start of scheme: November 1992. Scheme runs November – Easter break.
Duration of each cycle: 15 weeks – two hours per week.
Type and length of training: Three hours – programme structure and process skills. (Includes link teachers.)
Outcome measures: Group evaluation: student awareness of personal growth; student understanding of the wider world, and of the implications of commitment.
Source and nature of finance: CSV/National Power.
Report(s) available: No.
Person to contact: Chris Croudace/Brian Gay.
Address: UWE Bristol, Frenchay Campus, Coldharbour Lane, Bristol BS16 1GY.
Telephone: 0117 9656261   **Fax**: 0117 9750422

Students as tutors and mentors

Title of scheme: UK: Scotland: The 'Accessible Curriculum' Project

Overall purpose of scheme: To develop a means of entry into higher education via a wider access strategy (not an access course) that interconnects the institution with socially/educationally disadvantaged sections of the community.

Tutors/mentors: Final year students in management/social sciences combined studies. Seven mature students from similar backgrounds to tutees.

Aims for tutors/mentors: Improve communication/self-confidence but mainly encouraging 'trailblazers' to become role models.

Tutees/mentees: 12 students (all mature) from educationally and socially disadvantaged backgrounds.

Aims for tutees/mentees: Improve levels of subject understanding with study skills; institutional orientation; also encourage them to become future tutors and role models.

Subject/substance of work: Psychology – sociology – two hours work with two students each.

Date of start of scheme: February 1995 (first year of operation of scheme. Second year programme).

Duration of each cycle: 15 weeks.

Type and length of training: One hour per week plus ongoing contact (email/telephone).

Outcome measures: (1) Evaluation of project via interviews with participants; (2) evaluation of project via assessment exercises (exams and coursework).

Source and nature of finance: £500 BP Pilot for Student Tutor Programme.

Report(s) available: Yes. Cost £5.00 (including postage), October 1995.

Person to contact: Philip Gillies-Denning.

Address: Queen Margaret College, Clerwood Terrace, Edinburgh EH12 8TS.

Telephone: 0131 317 3383   **Fax**: 0131 317 3256

   Email: dnden@uk.ac.qmced.ic

Short notes on a variety of schemes

Title of scheme: UK: Sussex University Student Mentoring

Overall purpose of scheme: To use university students as mentors to provide academic and social support for 14–16-year-old pupils at local secondary and special needs schools.

Tutors/mentors: Students any year, any discipline; 25 currently.

Aims for tutors/mentors: (1) To develop personal transferable skills; (2) to reflect on and improve their own study skills and learning strategies.

Tutees/mentees: Mentees between 14 and 16.

Aims for tutees/mentees: (1) Inspire in coursework, attendance, punctuality and social skills; (2) learn more about higher education and discuss future career and training plans; (3) to develop communication skills and increase self-confidence.

Subject/substance of work: Help provide support for mentees and work towards mentees' individual goals.

Date of start of scheme: April 1994.

Duration of each cycle: One academic year.

Type and length of training: Three two-hour sessions focusing on what mentoring means, the role of a mentor and the expectations of mentees, and developing communication skills, passing on listening and questioning techniques.

Outcome measures: Evaluation for mentors and mentees. The scheme is evaluated by meetings and questionnaires for students, pupils, and teacher coordinators.

Source and nature of finance: Sussex Enterprise Unit/TEC, Sussex.

Report(s) available: Yes. Free.

Person to contact: Tessa Gooderson.

Address: Enterprise Unit, D421, Sussex University, Brighton BN1 9QN.

Telephone: 0273 678543   **Fax**: 0273 678466

Students as tutors and mentors

Title of scheme: USA: National Society of Black Engineers Pre-College Initiative

Overall purpose of scheme: Our purpose is to develop young black students' interest in maths, science, and therefore engineering. We also intend to create productive community citizens by raising their awareness and aspirations.

Tutors/mentors: Case Western Reserve University, undergraduates – 25 university students.

Aims for tutors/mentors: Community involvement.

Tutees/mentees: Collinwood High School: ages 14–18; 150 students.

Aims for tutees/mentees: Development of critical thinking skills, self-awareness, self-confidence and communication skills.

Subject/substance of work: Algebra.

Date of start of scheme: August 1994.

Duration of each cycle: Whole school year (August–June).

Type and length of training: None.

Outcome measures: Grades, attitudes towards coursework, self-respect.

Source and nature of finance: Corporate and university sponsorship.

Report(s) available: No.

Person to contact: Leija Green.

Address: 1862 Farmington, E Cleveland, Ohio 44112.

Telephone: 216 721 8545   **Fax**: 216 368 4715   **Email**: Iggcpo.cwru,edu

Short notes on a variety of schemes

Title of scheme: UK: University of Sunderland Mentoring

Overall purpose of scheme: To offer an opportunity for Level 3 students (mentors) to facilitate small groups or individual Level 2 students (usually from franchise colleges). The group aims to alleviate problems and promote a positive experience in learning, for example, improving study skills.

Tutors/mentors: Level 3 students on health studies programme at the University of Sunderland (School of Health Sciences).

Aims for tutors/mentors: To give an opportunity for mentors to develop interpersonal skills, guidance skills and practise reflective learning.

Tutees/mentees: Level 2 students on health studies programme (School of Health Sciences) at the University of Sunderland.

Aims for tutees/mentees: To be part of a small group/individual who has opportunity to develop a relationship with their mentor in order to share experiences.

Subject/substance of work: Basic counselling skills, study skills, adult learning and problem-solving.

Date of start of scheme: Week one of 15-week semester (approximately end of September).

Duration of each cycle: 12 weeks.

Type and length of training: One day training in June followed by a ten credit (hay module); 15 week by one and a half sessions as part of the module.

Outcome measures: Three assessments in the module. Qualitative evaluation from mentors and protégés (mentees).

Source and nature of finance: Two-year funding from Enterprise in Higher Education.

Report(s) available: No.

Person to contact: Barbara L Griffin.

Address: School of Health Sciences, University of Sunderland, Sunderland, Tyne and Wear.

Telephone: 0191 515 1565

Students as tutors and mentors

Title of scheme: UK: Wakefield EBP Mentoring Scheme

Overall purpose of scheme: To widen aspirations, boost the self-esteem and confidence of Year 10 students in areas of Wakefield which have been worst hit by recent coal mine closures.

Tutors/mentors: Currently 20, expanding – adults who live/work in the local area.

Aims for tutors/mentors: Increase confidence and communications skills of their student.

Tutees/mentees: 20, expanding. Year 10 students from a range of abilities unlikely to achieve to their full potential.

Aims for tutees/mentees: To gain as many experiences as possible.

Subject/substance of work: Topics decided by the student.

Date of start of scheme: March 1995.

Duration of each cycle: One academic year – 45 minutes per week.

Type and length of training: Initial half-day briefing.

Outcome measures: Evaluation by teacher, student, parent and mentor feedback forms.

Source and nature of finance: Coal regeneration funding.

Report(s) available: No.

Person to contact: Pip Guilding.

Address: Wakefield EBP, Prospect Corner, 9 Market Place, Pontefract, Yorks.

Telephone: 01977 602022   **Fax**: 01977 602023

Short notes on a variety of schemes

Title of scheme: UK: East London Connection – Student Tutoring Scheme

Overall purpose of scheme: Raise aspirations among young people by providing positive role models (and raise the profile of local FE/HE institutions). Provide pupils with additional curriculum support. Provide teachers with an additional resource.

Tutors/mentors: Student volunteers from local colleges and universities. All levels and disciplines in 'A' levels, BTEC National, undergraduates and postgraduates. Since inception: 1,020 student tutors.

Aims for tutors/mentors: Personal development: social, time keeping, presentation, etc., CV enhancement and work experience. Greater understanding of local community.

Tutees/mentees: Tutees from primary, secondary, special schools and colleges. Since inception: 30,600 tutees (business studies, IT, engineering, homework clubs – all subjects, sociology).

Aims for tutees/mentees: See 'Overall purpose' and confidence building.

Subject/substance of work: Tutorial support, mostly classroom-based, but some work takes place at a local nature park.

Date of start of scheme: 1990.

Duration of each cycle: Two hours/week for ten weeks. Two and a half hours training, one hour review session (mid-way) and one hour debrief.

Type and length of training: Standard training session lifted straight out of BP research pack (two and a half hours).

Outcome measures: Pupil, teacher and student tutor evaluation (BP resource pack) and recently reading literacy tests (Suffolk Reading test).

Source and nature of finance: £24,000 this year – BP Oil.

Report(s) available: Yes. Free except for postage.

Person to contact: Meenal Gupta, Project Coordinator.

Address: Tower Hamlets Education Business Partnership, Toynbee Hall Site, 28 Commercial Street, London E1 6LS.

Telephone: 0171 377 9497   **Fax**: 0171 375 2323

Students as tutors and mentors

Title of scheme: USA: 'Tutoring in Urban Public Schools: Theory and Practice'. An academic, for credit, university course involving tutoring at the University of Pennsylvania

Overall purpose of scheme: To deepen and improve the tutoring experience by combining it with academic work for credit. To combine theory and practice around tutoring. To provide tutors with an opportunity for students to engage in academically-based service.

Tutors/mentors: 25 students at the University of Pennsylvania.

Aims for tutors/mentors: Integrate tutoring and academic work, theory and practice. Improve quality of tutoring; provide opportunity for reflection. Experience of tutoring someone from a different background.

Tutees/mentees: 25 pupils in local elementary schools in Philadelphia.

Aims for tutees/mentees: Increased success in school, increased self-esteem, improved academic work, experience with a university student role model.

Subject/substance of work: Pupils' school studies.

Date of start of scheme: September each year.

Duration of each cycle: One semester.

Type and length of training: One semester.

Outcome measures: Student journals, research projects and exams.

Source and nature of finance: Instructor salary, paid by university (as adjunct).

Report(s) available: Yes. Syllabus at $3.50.

Person to contact: Linda Hansell.

Address: Graduate School of Education, University of Pennsylvania, 3700 Walnut Street, Philadelphia, PA 19104–6216, USA.

Telephone: 215 898 2497   **Fax**: 215 898 1089
      Email: LindaH@nwfs.gse.upenn.edu

Short notes on a variety of schemes

Title of scheme: UK: Westminster Connection Student Tutoring Scheme

Overall purpose of scheme: To place students at the University of Westminster in primary and secondary schools local to the university to act as student tutors. To encourage lecturers at the university to see student tutoring as a valid student activity. To give school students access to higher education via role models.

Tutors/mentors: Average 55 university students per year, aged 18-plus.

Aims for tutors/mentors: Experience tutoring and to experience 'live' primary and secondary education.

Tutees/mentees: Varies depending on schools involved. Tutors normally work in small groups.

Aims for tutees/mentees: To have access to students in higher education. To consider further and higher education as a real option.

Subject/substance of work: Depends upon school, type of activity.

Date of start of scheme: 1992.

Duration of each cycle: Academic year.

Type and length of training: Voluntary between ten and 15 weeks, one session per week.

Outcome measures: Voluntary – feedback from schools and tutors.

Source and nature of finance: CSV, University of Westminster.

Report(s) available: Will be soon – free.

Person to contact: Mike Healy.

Address: University of Westminster, 32–38 Wells Street, London W1.

Telephone: 0171 911 5000 Ext. 2314   **Email**: healym@wmin.ac.uk

Students as tutors and mentors

Title of scheme: UK: University of Westminster: Student Tutoring in Primary and Secondary Schools

Overall purpose of scheme: To place university students as tutors in primary and secondary schools; to provide an environment to develop a range of transferable skills; to enable school students to have access to students in higher education; to provide an alternative learning experience for university students.

Tutors/mentors: Up to 20 – new module aged 18-plus.

Aims for tutors/mentors: To pass a 30-credit module, to act as tutors, to develop a range of learning skills.

Tutees/mentees: Variable.

Aims for tutees/mentees: To have access to university students and to consider further/higher education as a viable option.

Subject/substance of work: University students to act as tutors with small groups.

Date of start of scheme: New module will start October 1995.

Duration of each cycle: Academic year – one session per week.

Type and length of training: Preparatory workshops – three to four three-hour sessions; mid-term reviews; on-site assessment.

Outcome measures: Formal academic assessment by way of (1) project; (2) portfolio of work; (3) presentation.

Source and nature of finance: Funded as per normal module.

Report(s) available: Not yet – will be next year.

Person to contact: Mike Healy.

Address: University of Westminster, 32–38 Wells Street, London WC1.

Telephone: 0171 911 5000 Ext. 2314   **Email**: healy@wmin.ac.uk

Short notes on a variety of schemes

Title of scheme: UK: BP Student Tutoring Programme (Scotland)

Overall purpose of scheme: To motivate more young Scots to continue their education and training. Student tutoring can also enhance teaching and learning in the classroom. There are also demonstrable benefits for the participants.

Tutors/mentors: Student undergraduates – universities and FE colleges; more than 1,000.

Aims for tutors/mentors: To act as positive role models and assist teachers and pupils.

Tutees/mentees: School pupils; approximately 15,000.

Aims for tutees/mentees: To think more about educational opportunities after school.

Subject/substance of work: Variety of subjects from drama, art, English, science, technology.

Date of start of scheme: 1991.

Duration of each cycle: Eight to 15 successive weeks.

Type and length of training: Ideally joint training with teachers and students.

Outcome measures: Quality assurance framework plus process available for self-evaluation (indicators of good practice).

Source and nature of finance: BP plus local consortia, LEAs, universities, colleges, EBP.

Report(s) available: Yes. Free from BP Educational Services.

Person to contact: Joe Hogan, BP Student Tutoring Fellow (Scotland).

Address: 134 Eldar Street, Greenock PA16 7RS.

Telephone: 01475 786116

Title of scheme: UK: University of Exeter: Peer Tutoring within an Engineering Framework

Overall purpose of scheme: Second-year engineering students undertake a module entitled 'Independent Study'. The aim of this module is to give students the opportunity to study a subject of their own choosing and hence practise the skills of setting their own targets and deadlines, assessing their own performance and preparing themselves for self-directed learning and project work in the advanced courses which follow. They also acquire a wide range of personal and transferable skills plus the skills associated with their individual assignment.

Tutors/mentors: Whilst the majority of students undertake an engineering-based project or study, over the last six years some six to ten students have opted to be involved in peer tutoring schemes with local schools. This has been in conjunction with all age groups from 5 to 16 years and has involved a wide range of activities.

Aims for tutors/mentors: Setting targets and deadlines; assessing their own performance; increased range of personal, transferable and pedagogic skills.

Tutees/mentees: School pupils aged 6 to 16 in local schools.

Aims for tutees/mentees: Increased range of classroom activities. Use of peer tutors as 'roving teams'. Provision of role models.

Subject/substance of work: Studies of specific topics. CDT projects on design and construction. Use of peer tutors' particular expertise.

Date of start of scheme: Trinity term each year.

Duration of each cycle: Eight to ten weeks.

Type and length of training: Introductory visit to school.

Outcome measures: Questionnaire.

Source and nature of finance: Internal.

Report(s) available: No.

Person to contact: Dr R M Hooper.

Address: University of Exeter, School of Engineering, Harrison Building, North Park Road, Exeter EX4 4QF.

Telephone: 01392 263661   **Fax**: 01392 217965
    Email: R.M.Hooper@exeter.ac.uk

Short notes on a variety of schemes

Title of scheme: Tanzania: BP Student Tutoring Scheme

Overall purpose of scheme: To encourage secondary school youth, especially girls, to take the science subjects and/or remain in the science streams and science, technical and engineering fields.

Tutors/mentors: Four students (two females and two males): Advanced Diploma in Engineering students of Dar-es-Salaam Technical College.

Aims for tutors/mentors: To help and encourage pupils, especially girls, aspire for science and engineering fields (acting as role models).

Tutees/mentees: Four science streams of form three pupils of Zamaki Girls' Secondary School (about 120 of between 16–19 years).

Aims for tutees/mentees: To remain in the sciences and courses in the engineering fields.

Subject/substance of work: Doing tuition in sciences and mathematics.

Date of start of scheme: 21 March 1995.

Duration of each cycle: Twice a week visits for about ten weeks. Each session takes two to two and a half hours.

Type and length of training: Only one day training workshop before starting the scheme.

Outcome measures: None yet.

Source and nature of finance: BP (Tanzania) Ltd and British Council. TSH 3000 per session per tutor = 240,000 – £300 for 10 weeks.

Report(s) available: Not yet.

Person to contact: Mrs Alodia K W Ishengomia.

Address: The Technical College, POBox 2958, Dar-es-Salaam, Tanzania – or c/o BP (Tanzania) Ltd.

Telephone, Fax, Email: None but BP (Tanzania) facilities can be used (c/o BP (Tanzania), BP Student Tutoring Project).

Students as tutors and mentors

Title of scheme: UK: University of Surrey/Surrey Compact Student Tutoring and Student Mentoring Programme

Overall purpose of scheme: To encourage school pupils to think about science and engineering at FE/HE by providing positive role models in the form of science and engineering undergraduates as tutors. Also, to encourage tutors to develop their personal transferable skills in a 'real life' environment.

Tutors/mentors: University of Surrey undergraduates. Approximately 80 in 1994–5 academic year.

Aims for tutors/mentors: To develop their personal transferable skills in a 'real life' environment.

Tutees/mentees: Pupils from 15 local primary and secondary schools and sixth form colleges.

Aims for Tutees/Mentees: To be exposed to a role-model from higher education and to get help with their academic work from a different perspective.

Subject/substance of work: A wide variety of subjects but with an emphasis on science and engineering.

Date of start of scheme: Scheme started in academic year 1992–3.

Duration of each cycle: Tutors in school for ten weeks. From next year they will tutor for six months.

Type and length of training: Two-hour sessions in the evening of an interactive nature led by scheme coordinator.

Outcome measures: Evaluation forms. Moving towards Records of Achievement, self- and peer assessment.

Source and nature of finance: £7,000 from Surrey Compact; £2,000 from EHE at Surrey; £2,000 from University of Surrey Foundation fund.

Report(s) available: As of July 1995.

Person to contact: Rob Jackson.

Address: Student Enterprise, Room 2, Hut 10, University of Surrey, Guildford, Surrey GU2 5XH.

Telephone: 01483 259920　　**Fax**: 01483 300803

Short notes on a variety of schemes

Title of scheme: USA: Indianapolis: Student Mentor and Resource Center

Overall purpose of scheme: The student mentor programme focuses on providing academic and personal support to university students in high-risk courses (any course with a D, F, W rate of 30% or above). Academically and socially successful students facilitate collaborative learning sessions weekly, reinforcing both course material and study skills. Students helping students works.

Tutors/mentors: Traditionally third and fourth year undergraduate students working with first and second year. Current staffing is at 50 with 16 courses.

Aims for tutors/mentors: Provide students with role models, encouragement, support and academic assistance.

Tutees/mentees: 1,100–1,500 students per week throughout the two full-time semesters Spring and Fall.

Aims for tutees/mentees: To increase their knowledge of course material to a deeper level, but more importantly to share experiences and build community.

Subject/substance of work: Maths, sciences and economics. Developing a deeper understanding to course concepts through collaboration.

Date of start of scheme: August 1991.

Duration of each cycle: 16 weeks Spring and Fall.

Type and length of training: Three days beginning of each semester. Two hours every other week throughout semester.

Outcome measures: Student feedback, instructor feedback, graduate analysis comparing those that attend mentoring and those who do not (traditionally one to two full letter grades higher).

Source and nature of finance: University, grants, departmental support.

Report(s) available: Yes. $5.00.

Person to contact: Christine M. Jakacky, Programme Coordinator.

Address: 815 W Michigan Street, Lybio, Indianapolis, Indiana 46202 5171, USA.

Telephone: 317 274 2369   **Fax**: 317 278 6284
Email: CJAKACKY@UEC.IUPUI.EDU

Title of scheme: UK: University of Wolverhampton: CSV Learning Together Student Tutoring Scheme

Overall purpose of scheme: To raise pupils' aspirations and motivation for staying on in education and training beyond the age of 16. (Providing a positive role model.) To give university students the opportunity to develop their personal and transferable skills in a practical context. To help make schools' lessons more interesting and provide extra stimulus to pupils of all abilities and greater flexibility to teachers in planning pupils' activities.

Tutors/mentors: Students at Level 2 plus education students at Level 3. Any student from any discipline. This year 251 students in 94 schools; nearly 700 tutors to date.

Aims for tutors/mentors: To gain personal and transferable skills. To pass the module, the scheme is accredited (standard 15 credit independent study module).

Tutees/mentees: Infant, primary (junior), secondary, sixth form, FE colleges, special schools. Community centre. We have realised thousands of tutees.

Aims for tutees/mentees: To be provided with someone to look up to. To gain in their education if they are struggling, excelling or just for more attention.

Subject/substance of work: Any student from any subject/discipline.

Date of start of scheme: Second semester 1991–2 academic year.

Duration of each cycle: Twice a year (one each semester); two weeks training, two weeks placing, then 10–13 weeks tutoring.

Type and length of training: Two three-hour sessions run by the faculty of education. Seminars and lectures full of details/information.

Outcome measures: Assessed by the faculty of education. Students must keep a diary of objectives (40%), a presentation (40%), a link teacher assessment (20%) and a self-assessment profile (pass/fail).

Source and nature of finance: Coordinator post funded by University of Wolverhampton (£7,000); £2,000 for two years secured by CSV donated by GKN.

Report(s) available: Not yet.

Person to contact: Mr Peter Jaworski, Student Links Officer.

Address: University of Wolverhampton, Corporate Enterprise Centre, 183 Stafford Street, Wolverhampton WV1 1ND.

Telephone: 01902 322337   **Fax**: 01902 322704

Short notes on a variety of schemes

Title of scheme: UK: Students as Tutors as a modular degree credit programme in the University of Sunderland

Overall purpose of scheme: To enable students from a range of degree courses in science, technology, Information Technology, computing and business studies to attain modular credit points towards their degrees by tutoring in local primary, secondary and FE institutions in their subject specialism.

Tutors/mentors: 1992 – 15 (engineering and advanced technology); 1993 – 38 (engineering and advanced technology); 1994 – 89 (engineering and advanced technology – computing and information systems).

Aims for tutors/mentors: To tutor pupil groups from all phases of education in their subject specialism with the objective of developing skills in problem-solving, organisation, planning, communication.

Tutees/mentees: Pupil groups from 36 primary, eight secondary, two tertiary colleges.

Aims for tutees/mentees: To enhance their learning attainments in science, technology, IT and computing by working with subject specialist tutors.

Subject/substance of work: Topic-based work in the range of subjects offered by tutors.

Date of start of scheme: 1992.

Duration of each cycle: One semester (15 weeks), half-day session per week.

Type and length of training: Half to one-day training session, module guide, supported initial visit to school with university coordinator to arrange topics for tutoring, follow up visit by subject tutor and university coordinator.

Outcome measures: Assessment of skills by teacher in school/college – 30%. Summative assignment – 30%. Log book – 15%. Individual presentation – 25%.

Source and nature of finance: Teaching, assessment and student support from HEFCE mainstream student funding. Student travel to schools and college – funded by Wearside Business Education Partnership.

Report(s) available: Yes.

Person to contact: Anne Johnson.

Address: Centre for Continuing Education, University of Sunderland, Green Terrace, Sunderland SR1 3PZ.

Telephone: 0191 515 2931   **Fax**: 0191 515 2928

Students as tutors and mentors

Title of scheme: UK: Newstead Wood School: Curriculum Enhancement Projects at two Levels: primary and secondary

Overall purpose of scheme: The scheme offers an opportunity for very able student tutors to take responsibility for an enrichment programme with able and gifted primary school tutees. It is designed to enhance conceptual understanding of subject areas for the student tutors and to facilitate differentiation in the primary schools.

Tutors/mentors: Year 11 (16-year-olds) tutors at the end of the Summer term when they have taken their GCSE examinations. Between eight and 15 each year.

Aims for tutors/mentors: To develop understanding of concepts relating to their chosen subject area and of the skills specific to each subject. To develop leadership skills.

Tutees/mentees: One to four per tutor.

Aims for tutees/mentees: To enrich a curriculum area in which they have been identified as very able.

Subject/substance of work: Subject is chosen by the tutor, as an area of particular interest (I then ask primary heads if they have pupils with needs in that area).

Date of start of scheme: 1987.

Duration of each cycle: Five morning sessions, wholly devoted to the project.

Type and length of training: Training in writing a scheme of work/lesson planning/evaluation process by Christine Lloyd in consultation with subject teachers in the secondary school (ie, Newstead Wood).

Outcome measures: Evaluation by (1) tutor questionnaire; (2) tutee questionnaire; (3) debrief by Christine Lloyd. Focus is on the development of conceptual understanding and skills relating to the subjects studied, both for tutors and tutees, and on development of leadership skills in the student tutors.

Source and nature of finance: I have a small curriculum enhancement fund – for materials/photocopying. No great finance needed at present. Since it takes place in the second half of the Summer term, Newstead Wood staff have some 'spare' time as they lose exam classes, so can support.

Report(s) available: Not yet. There is a lot of data going back to 1987 which have not been published yet. There are sample schemes of work and evaluation sheets.

Person to contact: Christine Lloyd.

Address: Newstead Wood School for Girls, Avebury Road, Orpington, Kent.

Telephone: 01689 853626   **Fax**: 01689 853315

292

Short notes on a variety of schemes

Title of scheme: Malta: University of Malta: Learning Support Scheme (LSS)

Overall purpose of scheme: The Department of Education (Malta) has run a student tutoring scheme for both primary and secondary school pupils attending state schools in Malta and the sister island of Gozo. The pupils attend on a voluntary basis. The university students tutor the pupils in the basic school subjects on a one-to-one basis or in small groups.

Tutors/mentors: About 250 university students per year.
Aims for tutors/mentors: To enhance communication skills and to obtain 'tutoring' skills.
Tutees/mentees: Approximately 750–1,000 per year.
Aims for tutees/mentees: To receive support in the basic academic subjects of Maltese, English, mathematics.
Subject/substance of work: Basic school subjects.
Date of start of scheme: July 1991.
Duration of each cycle: Ten weeks (two hours per day, ten hours per week) over the Summer vacation.
Type and length of training: Introductory sessions and relevant courses on BEd(Hons) degree programme.
Outcome measures: Diagnostic tests in language and numeracy skills.
Source and nature of finance: Department of Education (Malta).
Report(s) available: No.
Person to contact: Dr Charles L Mifsud.
Address: Faculty of Education, University of Malta, Msida, Malta MSDO6.
Telephone: 00 356 32902931   **Fax**: 00 356 317938
    Email: cmifs@unimt.mt

Students as tutors and mentors

Title of scheme: New Zealand: Te Tari Awhina, Unitec Institute of Technology, Peer tutoring/tuakana-teina scheme

Overall purpose of scheme: An additional mode of delivery within a flourishing learning support centre for students enrolled at the institute. Two-fold purpose within parallel scheme: (1) peer tutoring: to provide support in programme content; (2) tuakana-teina: to provide holistic support (which may include peer tutoring) for Maori students.

Tutors/mentors: Year 2 and 3 students (13).

Aims for tutors/mentors: To support other students in their department, to consolidate own knowledge and gain additional skills and confidence.

Tutees/mentees: Year 1 students (40-plus).

Aims for tutees/mentees: To realise academic potential; to increase retention rates.

Subject/substance of work: Programme content.

Date of start of scheme: 1994.

Duration of each cycle: Variable; 18 or 36 weeks.

Type and length of training: Six hours paid training (coaching skills, cultural differences and learning styles). Ongoing monthly support groups – feedback and problem-solving.

Outcome measures: Evaluations from peer tutors, peer students, tuakana-teina and departmental academic staff. Programme results.

Source and nature of finance: Institute (Unitec).

Report(s) available: No.

Person to contact: Diana Nicholson/Yvonne Hawke, Programme Coordinators, Te Tari Awhina.

Address: Te Tari Awhina, Unitec Institute of Technology, Private Bag 92025, Auckland, New Zealand.

Telephone: 09 849 4180

Short notes on a variety of schemes

Title of scheme: UK: South West Regional CSV 'Learning Together'

Overall purpose of scheme: To encourage pupils in schools to stay in education post-16, by using students from FE and HE colleges as role models in classrooms.

Tutors/mentors: Ranging across South West (Reading to Plymouth) from FE and universities. Grown since 1992/1993 from 'A' level, BTec to postgraduates: 200–500 this year.

Aims for tutors/mentors: To give university and college students an opportunity to develop their interpersonal skills and to get involved in the local community.

Tutees/mentees: 2,500 pupils in primary, secondary, and tertiary institutions.

Aims for tutees/mentees: Improved understanding of class work, increased knowledge of opportunities available for further education and raised expectations.

Subject/substance of work: Cross-faculty and special needs – primary to sixth form college.

Date of start of scheme: October 1992 (Reading, Swindon, Bath); three new schemes started January 1995 (Plymouth, Street, Weston-Super Mare).

Duration of each cycle: Ten weeks plus.

Type and length of training: Three hours group training based on BP Handbook.

Outcome measures: Questionnaires and feedback sessions.

Source and nature of finance: CSV Principal Partners initiative – pump-prime lending – ends July 1995.

Report(s) available: South West register to be produced 1995.

Person to contact: Sheila Parsons, SW Region Coordinator.

Address: c/o National Power, Windmill Hill Business Park, Whitehall Way, Swindon SN5 6PB.

Telephone: 01793 892440   **Fax**: 01793 892454

Title of scheme: UK: Student Tutoring in Science, Lancaster University

Overall purpose of scheme: To enable science students at Lancaster to help in local schools – mainly primary schools; hence to develop student skills and support/develop science teaching and to encourage young people to become scientists.

Tutors/mentors: Mostly second year science students (ten in 1994/5) plus some third/fourth year and postgraduates (five in 1994/5).

Aims for tutors/mentors: Develop experience in teaching/develop communication and scientific skills.

Tutees/mentees: Mostly top two years of primary schools (six schools, 180 pupils); also secondary pupils (one school, 100 pupils).

Aims for tutees/mentees: Engender enthusiasm and understanding of science.

Subject/substance of work: Science tutoring in area of relatively low population density (Lancaster and Morecombe each have populations of 40,000 and a rural area of 40,000 over 150 square miles).

Date of start of scheme: September 1993 pilot.

Duration of each cycle: 10 weeks but some continue over 20 to 30 weeks.

Type and length of training: Two hours introduction to tutoring; one to three hours induction in school.

Outcome measures: Anecdotal reports; school and student returns, etc.

Source and nature of finance: Start-up grant from CSV; now grants from Royal Society of Chemistry, NW Acolytical Division.

Report(s) available: No.

Person to contact: Dr Colin Peacock.

Address: Chemical Sciences Division, School of Physics and Chemistry, Lancaster University, Lancaster LA1 44A.

Telephone: 01524 593717   **Fax**: 01524 844037

Short notes on a variety of schemes

Title of scheme: Student Tutoring – An Indian Experience

Overall purpose of scheme: To do voluntary service while in the university and to gain the benefits of the student tutoring programme. According to the student tutors they gained a lot of experience in different areas, besides being useful to the school system in many ways.

Tutors/mentors: M Ed I Technology students – 12.

Aims for tutors/mentors: As a voluntary service, to gain benefit from the programme.

Tutees/mentees: Middle and primary school children – 480.

Aims for tutees/mentees: Individual attention and enriched experience.

Subject/substance of work: Different work – at different schools (12 in number).

Date of start of scheme: August 1993.

Duration of each cycle: One semester on all Wednesday forenoons.

Type and length of training: Orientation given for five days.

Outcome measures: Assessment of the skills of tutors and tutees.

Source and nature of finance: BP has given an initial pilot scheme fund.

Report(s) available: Yes.

Person to contact: Dr G Subramonia Pillay, Professor and Head, Department of Education.

Address: Madurai Kamasaj University, India.

Telephone: Madurai, India 625021

Students as tutors and mentors

Title of scheme: UK/Netherlands: Hogeschool Holland/University of Wolverhampton Tutoring Scheme

Overall purpose of scheme: Personal development tutors. Classroom assistance teachers. International tutors for tutees: Dutch students tutor at UK schools, UK students tutor at Dutch schools.

Tutors/mentors: English and education/English teacher training, Level 2 – 70.
Aims for tutors/mentors: Personal development, first step towards teaching.
Tutees/mentees: Netherlands: secondary school pupils of English (5 – 10); UK secondary school pupils, subjects vary.
Aims for tutees/mentees: Netherlands: to gain experience in communicating in English and to receive extra help.
Subject/substance of work: Netherlands: classroom assistance.
Date of start of scheme: September 1994.
Duration of each cycle: One semester.
Type and length of training: Three three-hour sessions reflecting on various aims, establishing personal goals and discussing classroom practice.
Outcome measures: Logbook, presentation and line-teacher assessment.
Source and nature of finance: Module is part of curriculum.
Report(s) available: Not yet.
Person to contact: Greem Popma.
Address: Hogeschool Holland, PO Box 261, 1110AG Diemen, Netherlands.
Telephone: *31 20 495 1576   **Fax**: *31 20 495 1920

Title of scheme: UK: University of Kent: Peer Tutoring for Management Science Students

Overall purpose of scheme: To support first year management science students at the University of Kent by offering one-to-one help, on a voluntary basis, from second year students. This is primarily intended to enable students with varied mathematics backgrounds to succeed in the maths and stats 'service' course; help with other aspects of the degree programme is a bonus.

Tutors/mentors: Second year Management Science students; about ten each year; eight on any given occasion.

Aims for tutors/mentors: Reassure and help first year students. Consolidate their own understanding of mathematics and other skills. Earn a little money.

Tutees/mentees: First year management science students; up to 100 each year; six to 20 on any given occasion.

Aims for tutees/mentees: Non-threatening encouragement and support in understanding maths and stats and other aspects of the course.

Subject/substance of work: Based around set exercises (covered elsewhere by lecturer), often requires explanation of mathematical or statistical concepts.

Date of start of scheme: October 1991.

Duration of each cycle: 25 weeks, two hours each week tutoring, one year (October–May).

Type and length of training: Brief discussion of importance of letting tutees do talking and writing. Constantly available support from lecturers. Now, tutors have all been tutees.

Outcome measures: Course evaluation (and other) questionnaires to tutees and tutors.

Source and nature of finance: Departmental part-time teaching budget. Approximately £1,000 annual cost.

Report(s) available: Yes. Cost (including postage) about £1 domestic (or sea mail). *Peer tutoring: an evaluation* (third year student project, 1992).

Person to contact: Beatrice Shire.

Address: Institute of Mathematics, University of Kent, Canterbury CT2 7NF.

Telephone: 01227 764000 Ext. 7762 or 01227 827762   **Fax**: 01227 475453
    Email: B.J.Shire@ukc.ac.uk

Students as tutors and mentors

Title of scheme: UK: CSV Learning Together, Merseyside

Overall purpose of scheme: To allow students to gain new skills – interpersonal skills, communication skills, confidence-building, etc. To enable schools to have access to an extra pair of useful hands in the classroom.

Tutors/mentors: Any FE or HE student from institutions on Merseyside (250 during the last year).

Aims for tutors/mentors: To work alongside professionals and gain new skills.

Tutees/mentees: Pupils from secondary, primary and special schools on Merseyside. Also some FE students are tutees.

Aims for tutees/mentees: To receive more individual attention.

Subject/substance of work: Varied, including reading, lunch-time clubs, art-work.

Date of start of scheme: April 1994.

Duration of each cycle: Ten two-hour sessions.

Type and length of training: Half-day training (informal group work) before placement.

Outcome measures: Subjective.

Source and nature of finance: BT, to June 1995. After that, hopefully the Merseyside Education Business Partnership.

Report(s) available: Not until September 1995.

Person to contact: Sue Reed, CSV Student Tutoring.

Address: Liverpool John Moores University, 4 Rodney Street, Liverpool L1 2TZ.

Telephone: 0151 231 3159

Short notes on a variety of schemes

Title of scheme: UK: Student Tutoring (at University of Kent)

Overall purpose of scheme: To offer students opportunities for involvement in the local community, enhancement of communication skills, and an enjoyable break from studies. To offer hard-pressed teachers an extra pair of hands and schoolchildren contact with their local university.

Tutors/mentors: Initially second year chemistry students, now open to students in any year, any faculty; 40 this year; total 90 in three years.

Aims for tutors/mentors: Extra dimension to skills described in their CVs. Tutors prefer the work to be extra-curricular.

Tutees/mentees: Children between 5 and 19 in local primary and secondary schools and also at Canterbury College (FE).

Aims for tutees/mentees: Increased opportunities for project work, individual support and conversation. Friendly role models.

Subject/substance of work: Several tutors work in primary (8–11 years) language teaching offering French conversation (supporting a Kent Education initiative). Others help in science, IT (computing), art, drama and psychology.

Date of start of scheme: October 1992.

Duration of each cycle: First year 15 weeks, two hours per week in school. Present commitment – some 15 weeks, some ten weeks (because of teaching practice by local PGCE students).

Type and length of training: One hour introduction for all tutors. One hour, half with link teacher, introducing students to school.

Outcome measures: Reports (questionnaire responses) from tutors. Brief reports from most link teachers.

Source and nature of finance: Initial year, BP; second year £3,000 from Enterprise Kent. Now £5,000 from Kent TEC.

Report(s) available: Yes. Cost (including postage): 25p. Annual summaries of schools and subjects involved.

Person to contact: Beatrice Shire (David Scally, Chemistry, UKC until June 1995).

Address: Institute of Mathematics, University of Kent at Canterbury CT2 7NF.

Telephone: 01227 764000 Ext. 7762   **Fax**: 01227 475453
    Email: B.J.Shire@ukc.ac.uk

Students as tutors and mentors

Title of scheme: UK: Teaching and Training Skills, City of Stoke-on-Trent Sixth Form College

Overall purpose of scheme: To raise educational and career aspirations in the local area; to offer experience for prospective teachers.

Tutors/mentors: Around 70 out at any one time. Tutors are from our 16–19 cohort; they mostly help in the primary sector, but around 20% work in secondary.

Aims for tutors/mentors: Increased self-confidence; interpersonal skills; communication skills; career-specific skills.

Tutees/mentees: Over 100 schools registered (one nursery; 14 infant; five junior; 60 primary; 21 secondary; two special).

Aims for tutees/mentees: Improved progress; increased career and educational awareness.

Subject/substance of work: Varied – flexible according to local needs within the conurbation.

Date of start of scheme: September 1993.

Duration of each cycle: Minimum of 12 weeks; in practice many tutors stay on for more. Some do more than 36 weeks.

Type and length of training: Only distance learning packages at present but should be part of the taught curriculum for volunteers from September 1995.

Outcome measures: Evaluated by both host schools and tutors. Accredited via the Open College Network from September 1995.

Source and nature of finance: None at present – hoping for Open College Network accreditation followed by FEFC funding; 1994–5 – sponsored by Staffordshire TEC.

Report(s) available: Yes. No standard cost – just telephone and ask.

Person to contact: Paul Swinhoe.

Address: City of Stoke-on-Trent Sixth Form College, Victoria Road, Fenton, Stoke-on-Trent, Staffs ST4 2RR.

Telephone: 01782 48736 **Fax**: 01782 717456

Short notes on a variety of schemes

Title of scheme: USA: Ravenswood Stanford Tutoring Program (RSTP)

Overall purpose of scheme: RSTP links Stanford University students with elementary school-aged children for after school tutorials. The programme's focus is the development of language skills (reading, writing, and self-expression) through the use of children's literature.

Tutors/mentors: University students are recruited as tutors. About 120 volunteers each academic year.

Aims for tutors/mentors: Establish a relationship with the student, learn about the school and community, and develop strategies that engage students in their learning.

Tutees/mentees: Elementary students (grades 1 through 6). One or two students per tutor (usually the same number of tutors).

Aims for tutees/mentees: Develop greater appreciation for the written word, develop confidence and self-esteem, and develop a relationship with a college student.

Subject/substance of work: Primarily reading (through children's literature) but not limited to it. Tutors may also work on maths, homework or educational games.

Date of start of scheme: The programme began in 1987.

Duration of each cycle: Tutors make a two-quarter commitment (minimum), eight weeks in each quarter, three quarters in an academic year.

Type and length of training: One hour orientation to the programme; one hour 'training' (logistics, expectations, basic protocol, suggestions for beginning the relationship).

Outcome measures: Tutor logs and teacher evaluations.

Source and nature of finance: University funds for full-time staff person, six student coordinators and programme costs.

Report(s) available: Tutor manual – $10.

Person to contact: Anne Takemoto, Program Coordinator.

Address: Haas Center for Public Service, Stanford University, 558 Salvatierra Walkway, Stanford, California 94305 8620.

Telephone: 415 723 5786   **Fax**: 415 725 7339
        Email: cr.ast.@forsythe.stanford.edu

Students as tutors and mentors

Title of scheme: USA: East Palo Alto-Stanford Summer Academy (Epassa)

Overall purpose of scheme: Epassa is a summer day camp and academic year tutoring/mentoring programme for middle school-aged children (ages 11 –13 years). The programme provides an academic, cultural and social environment for low-income youth from the surrounding communities of East Palo Alto and Redwood City, California.

Tutors/mentors: A summer staff of six university students, who act as 'counsellors'. Up to 30 tutors/mentors for individual pairings with students during the school year.

Aims for tutors/mentors: Summer staff design all 'non-academic' portions of the programme, develop relationships with students and their families. Tutors must establish rapport and assist with school work.

Tutees/mentees: Up to 30 students. Mostly Hispanic, African-American and Pacific Islanders – ages 11–13 years.

Aims for tutees/mentees: Strengthen academic skills, explore their own identities and those of others, become comfortable on a university campus, and become active students.

Subject/substance of work: Provide students with academic skills and opportunities to mature in a supportive environment.

Date of start of scheme: 1987 as a summer programme.

Duration of each cycle: Six weeks summer day camp, followed by an academic year tutoring programme, which meets on Saturdays.

Type and length of training: Summer staff take an education course designed to provide them with theoretical understanding of adolescents and the reality of the community.

Outcome measures: Whether students remain in school and continue in high school.

Source and nature of finance: Grants from foundations and corporations and individual contributions.

Report(s) available: Annual programme report – $10.

Person to contact: Anne Takemoto, Program Coordinator.

Address: Haas Center for Public Service, 558 Salvatierra Walkway, Stanford, California 94305 8620.

Telephone: 415 723 5786　　　**Fax**: 415 725 7339
　　Email: cr.ast@forsythe.stanford.edu

Title of scheme: South Africa: University of Fort-Hare Computer Literacy Programme

Overall purpose of scheme: The aim of the project is to promote computer literacy to high school students and teachers. Computer science is not offered as a course at high school level and therefore most if not all of the students that the university admits have never used a computer.

Tutors/mentors: Senior students doing computer science as a course.

Aims for tutors/mentors: To assist and teach high school students and teachers the basics of using computers.

Tutees/mentees: Matric students.

Aims for tutees/mentees: To familiarise themselves with how to use computers.

Subject/substance of work: Computer science basics taught to high school students.

Date of start of scheme: May 1992.

Duration of each cycle: One year.

Type and length of training: No training as they (tutors) are computer science students.

Outcome measures: Assessment of introduction of computer studies to local schools.

Source and nature of finance: University funded; limited funding for administrative purposes. There is a need for more funding as the university is under-resourced.

Report(s) available: Yes.

Person to contact: Lennox Tshwete/Mike Matibe.

Address: University of Fort Hare, Private Bag x 1314, Alice, South Africa.

Telephone: 0027 404 22488   **Fax**: 0027 404 31669

      Email: Tshwete@ufhcc.ufh.ac.za

General comment: We would like to broaden the project to include other subjects, especially science and technology but funding is a constraint in this regard.

Title of scheme: UK: Aberdeen University Summer School for Special Entry, Link Programme with Target Schools

Overall purpose of scheme: Raise awareness of special entry scheme and 'open door' policy for those schools. Encourage aspirations for HE by example of ex-students from each school. Develop coping skills for personal/ practical obstacles through mentors' experience. Develop study skills to cope with academic obstacles using mentors'/tutors' experience of this as a successful means of gaining/sustaining entry to HE in summer school. Build on growing goodwill between schools and university to change perceptions and practice, where students provide compelling evidence of the factors instrumental in their success, with 85% of non-traditional students achieving entry to degree study.

Tutors/mentors: (In each of five schools): groups of up to eight student volunteers who had studied at that school and used the university's summer school for special entry as a means of gaining entry to university.

Aims for tutors/mentors: Let other students (and teachers) know that they had gained entry to a degree place without formal qualifications, and that it was not only possible, but life-transforming. (Programme started as an informal initiative by students themselves.)

Tutees/mentees: Sixth-year pupils from five target schools where progression to university is not the norm. Sixth-year groups vary in size from around 30 to over 100.

Aims for tutees/mentees: Raise awareness of special entry scheme and encourage aspirations for HE by example. Raise awareness of the personal/ academic obstacles and how mentors coped. Develop study skills as one of the key coping strategies for gaining and sustaining entry to HE (essay writing, exam technique, time management).

Subject/substance of work: Workshops with access students from same school.

Date of start of scheme: 1993.

Duration of each cycle: Varies by school. Around twice a term, often as part of personal and social guidance curriculum.

Type and length of training: Own experience of coming into HE through access from the same school – awareness of personal, emotional, financial and academic problems, and ways in which they can be met.

Outcome measures: (Quantitative and qualitative): (1) number of access applicants from target schools; (2) questionnaires/interviews with staff and students identifying perceived benefits of programme in (a) encouraging consideration of HE, (b) developing study skills to support academic performance to achieve/sustain this.

Source and nature of finance: Not directly funded. Funding from BP and others for Aberdeen University special entry summer school means some support for outreach activities. Voluntary basis due to benefits and goodwill generated across institutions.

Report(s) available: Yes. Available at no cost but sae appreciated.

Materials Available: 'Coping with College/University', 'Exam Technique', 'Writing Essays in Exams', 'Vorsprung Durch Technik' (How Study Skills Can Give You An Advantage).

Person to contact: Jenny Ure.

Address: Centre for Continuing Education, University of Aberdeen, Regent Building, Regent Walk, Aberdeen AB9 1FX.

Telephone: 01224 273667   **Fax**: 01224 272478

   Email: ade015/j.ure@abdn.ac.uk%

Title of scheme: UK: Summer Schools for Special Entry to Higher Education in Scotland – A Paul Hamlyn Project

Overall purpose of scheme: To encourage greater participation in university study of students from social class III, IV and V; to assist access to higher education for disadvantaged students; and to increase participation in science and engineering. The Paul Hamlyn Foundation has funded a two-year project to assist in the development of Scottish summer school initiatives for special entry to higher education. The funding supports developments in cooperation between the existing special entry schemes and in the stimulation of new schools.

Tutors/mentors: Ten mentors per summer school. Each institution has at least 20 tutors who work on school-based initiatives.

Aims for tutors/mentors: Tutor – as above, purpose to encourage greater participation – demystify university, ease social/cultural changes. Mentors – to ease transition to university.

Tutees/mentees: Tutees – nearly all secondary schools in Scotland. Mentees – all students on summer schools – approximately 1,000.

Aims for tutees/mentees: To be encouraged to take part in HE.

Subject/substance of work: Academic and personal development courses to enable them to enter university, irrespective of their normal entry qualifications.

Date of start of scheme: Project started in 1993. Summer schools have been ongoing since 1978.

Duration of each cycle: Summer schools are three to ten weeks' long. School-based projects last all year.

Type and length of training: Two days' team work and individual counselling.

Outcome measures: Successful entry to HE and staying in HE for one year.

Source and nature of finance: Paul Hamlyn Project. Summer schools and school-based projects are funded by region and universities.

Report(s) available: Yes (sae).

Person to contact: Dr Sheila Watt, Educational Studies.

Address: Dundee University, Dundee, Tayside, Scotland DD1 4HN.

Telephone: 01382 344819   **Fax**: 01382 344105

   Email: swatt@dundee.ac.uk

Short notes on a variety of schemes

Title of scheme: USA: Hosts (Help One Student to Succeed)

Overall purpose of scheme: 'Hosts' is a structured mentoring programme that uses community, business and school mentors to improve reading, writing, vocabulary, study skills, high-level thinking, maths and life skills (goal-setting, decision-making, etc.) of the most at-risk, discouraged learners. The Hosts software system designs individualised lesson plans structured to match the students' age, reading level, learning style and assessed needs.

Tutors/mentors: Mentors are older students, college students, senior citizens (retired), business community, parents and other community organisations. We have over 60,000 mentors currently involved in over 800 programmes.

Aims for tutors/mentors: To be an advocate, guide and role model for students. To become an advocate for the schools and education in general.

Tutees/mentees: Our protégés (tutees/mentees) are students ages 5–18 who are the most at-risk of dropping-out of school; the bottom 40% of the youth population.

Aims for tutees/mentees: To accelerate student learning and build self-esteem – thus breaking the cycle of student failure.

Subject/substance of work: Reading, writing, vocabulary, study skills, high-level thinking, life skills and success-oriented strategies (goal-setting, decision-making, listening, etc.). Also maths skills.

Date of start of scheme: 1971.

Duration of each cycle: One school year (nine months in the US).

Type and length of training: Four and a half days for teachers who operate the programme and one day total for mentors and student protégés.

Outcome measures: Attendance, drop-out rates, discipline problems, school grades, test scores, behavioural observations, portfolios, teacher, student and parent feedback.

Source and nature of finance: Federal government and state government 'compensatory' funds.

Report(s) available: Yes. There is extensive research on the effectiveness of this USA national mentoring model.

Person to contact: Dr Jerry Willbur, President.

Address: Hosts, 8,000 NE Parkway Drive, Suite 201, Vancouver, WA 98662–6459.

Telephone: 360 260 1995   **Fax**: 360 260 1783

Students as tutors and mentors

Title of scheme: UK: Tyneside Students into Schools Project

Overall purpose of scheme: To raise awareness of higher education by pupils in Tyneside schools. To help raise the aspirations of young people towards higher levels of attainment, leading to further or higher education. To broaden the experience of university students.

Tutors/mentors: Undergraduate students from a wide range of academic disciplines and ages from the universities of Newcastle and Northumbria; but mainly science and engineering. Number – 670.

Aims for tutors/mentors: Satisfactory placements leading to development of transferable skills valued by employers.

Tutees/mentees: 90 schools/colleges from primary through to further education; all subjects but focus on maths, science and technology. (Numbers estimated at 670 x 40.)

Aims for tutees/mentees: Demystifying student stereotypes (especially in inner-urban schools), helping to make informed choices, raising self-esteem and broadening horizons.

Subject/substance of work: Standard ten half-day visits model, with students generally on their own or in pairs, working with classroom teachers.

Date of start of scheme: September 1993.

Duration of each cycle: Either October–March (voluntary) or October–February, ten visits (full-module accreditation) or October–January/March–May (half-module) or others.

Type and length of training: Two by two hours at start of session/cycle.

Outcome measures: Numbers of placements (and nature); qualitative feedback on process and tutoring (reliability and contribution of tutor); gains (changes in pupil attitude to education).

Source and nature of finance: Tyneside TEC, CSV (Fishmongers Company, Sir James Knott Trust), Universities of Newcastle and Northumbria, travel concessions (local PTE).

Report(s) available: Various at a variety of levels – depends on what people are interested in.

Person to contact: Jim Wood.

Address: Joseph Cowen House, St. Thomas Street, Newcastle NE1 TRU.

Telephone: 0191 2228677   **Fax**: 0191 2228170

  Email: J.M.Wood@ncl.ac.uk

REFERENCES AND FURTHER READING

AAM (1993) *Museums, Adults, and the Humanities* (Washington, DC: American Association of Museums)

Ahwireng-Obeng, F. (1995) Personal communication (Ghana)

Allen, M. (1988) *The Goals of Universities* (Philadelphia: The Society for Research into Higher Education and Open University Press)

Allen, V.L. (1983) 'Reactions to help in peer tutoring: roles and social identities', in A. Nadler, J.D. Fisher & B.M. DePaulo (eds) *New directions in helping*, 3 (pp. 213–232). (New York: Academic Press)

Allen, V.L. & Feldman, R.S. (1973) 'Learning through tutoring: low-achieving children as tutors', *Journal of Experimental Education*, 42, 1–5.

Allen, V.L. & Feldman, R.S. (1974) 'Tutor attributions and attitudes as a function of tutee performance', *Journal of Applied Social Psychology*, 4, 311–320.

Allen, V.L. & Feldman, R.S. (1976) 'Studies on the role of tutor', in V.L. Allen (ed.) *Children as teachers: theory and research on tutoring* (pp. 113–129). (New York: Academic Press)

Allwright, D. (1982) *The Importance of Interaction in Classroom Language Learning* (TESOL Convention Hawaii)

Amir, Y. (1976) 'The role of intergroup contact in change of prejudice and ethnic relations', in P.A. Katz (ed.) *Towards the elimination of racism* (pp. 245–308) (New York: Pergamon)

Anderson, E. (1990) *Streetwise: Race, Class, and Change in an Urban Community* (Chicago: University of Chicago Press)

ASTC (1990) *What research says about learning science in museums*, Volumes 1 and 2 (Washington DC: Association of Science and Technology Centres)

Astin, A.W. (1977) *Four critical years: Effects of college on beliefs, attitudes, and knowledge* (San Francisco: Jossey-Bass)

Astin, A.W. (1984) 'Student involvement: A developmental theory for higher education', *Journal of College Student Personnel*, 25, pp. 287–300

Atkinson, P. & Delamont, S. (1986) 'Bread and bad dreams or bread and circuses? A critique of "case study" research in education', in *Controversies in Classroom Research* (Chichester, UK: Wiley)

Attar, R. (1976) *PERACH: One-to-one tutorial project.* (Rehovot: The Weizmann Institute of Science)

Bacon, C.S. (1992) 'Pre-service teachers and at-risk students', unpublished paper, Indiana (ED351308)

Bandura, A. (1977) *Social learning theory* (Englewood Cliffs, NJ: Prentice Hall)

Bar-Eli, N. & Raviv, A. (1982) 'Underachievers as tutors', *Journal of Educational Research*, **75**, 139–143

Baum, H.S. (1992) 'Mentoring: narcissistic fantasies and oedipal realities', *Human Relations*, **45**, 3, 223–245

Bausell, R.B., Moody, W.B. & Walzl, F.N. (1972) 'A factorial study of tutoring versus classroom instruction', *American Educational Research Journal*, **9**, 592–597

Beady, C.H. & Hansell, S. (1981) 'Teacher race and expectations for student achievement', *American Educational Research Journal*, **18**, 191–206

Beardon, T. (1990) 'Cambridge STIMULUS', in Goodlad & Hirst (ibid.) Chapter 5

Beardon, L.A., Flinn, A., Green, L., Hughes, J. & Sims, R. (1991) *Tutoring Resource Pack* (London, BP Educational Service)

Beeby, C.E. (1966) *The Quality of Education in Developing Countries* (Harvard: Harvard University Press)

Behrendorff, M. & Marriott, P. (1993) 'Computer assisted training of student leaders for tutorials', in J. Jones, (ed.) *Peer Tutoring: Learning by Teaching.* Proceedings of the Conference at University of Auckland, Auckland, NZ

Benard, B. (1990) *The Case for Peers* (Portland, Oregon, Northwest Regional Educational Laboratory)

Berk, L.E. (1991) *Child Development* (Boston: Allyn and Bacon)

Berkowitz, L. (1972) 'Social norms, feelings and other factors affecting helping and altruism', in L. Berkowitz (ed.) *Advances in experimental social psychology*, Volume 6 (pp. 63–108) (New York: Academic Press)

Berkowitz, L. & Connor, W.H. (1966) 'Success, failure and social responsibility', *Journal of Personality and Social Psychology*, **4**, 664–669

Berkowitz, L. & Daniels, L.R. (1964) 'Affecting the salience of the social responsibility norm', *Journal of Abnormal and Social Psychology*, **68**, 275–281

Berkowitz, L. & Lutterman, K. (1968) 'The traditionally socially responsible personality', *Public Opinion Quarterly*, **31**, 169–185

Berger, P. (1963) *Invitation to sociology: a humanistic perspective* (New York: Anchor Books)

Bierman, K.L. & Furman, W. (1981) 'Effects of role and assignment rationale on attitudes formed during tutoring', *Journal of Educational Psychology*, **73**, 33–40.

Biggs, J.B. & Collis, K.F. (1982) *Evaluating the Quality of Learning: The SOLO Taxonomy* (New York: Academic Press)

References and further reading

Bines, H. (1992) 'Issues in course design', in H. Bines, & D. Watson, *Developing Professional Education* (Buckingham: Open University Press)

Bizman, A. & Amir, Y. (1984) 'Integration and attitudes', in Y. Amir & S. Sharan (eds) *School Desegregation* (pp. 155–188) (Hillsdale, NJ: Lawrence Erlbaum Associates)

Bloom, B. (1984) 'The search for methods as effective as one-to-one tutoring', *Educational Leadership*, 4–17

Bloom, S. (1975) *Peer and cross-age tutoring in the schools: an individualized supplement to group instruction* (Washington, DC: National Institute of Education (DHEW)) (ERIC Reproduction Service No. ED 118 543)

Bogdan, R.C. & Biklen, S.K. (1992) *Qualitative Research for Education* (Boston: Allyn and Bacon)

Borg, W.R. & Gall, M.D. (1979) *Educational Research* (New York: Longman)

Boud, D. & Felletti, G. (1991) *The Challenge of Problem Based Learning* (London: Kogan Page)

Bowden, J.A. & Masters, G.N. (1992) *Implications for Higher Education of a Competency-Based Approach to Education and Training: Interim Report* (Melbourne: DEET)

Boyd, E.M. & Fales, A.W. (1983) 'Reflective learning: key to learning from experience', *Journal of Humanistic Psychology*, **23**, 2, 99–117

Boyer, P. (1978) *Urban Masses and Moral Order in America, 1820–1920* (Cambridge, Mass.: Harvard University Press)

Bradbard, M.R. & Endsley, R.C. (1982) 'How can teachers develop young children's curiosity?', in J. Brown (ed.) *Curriculum Planning for Young Children* (Washington, DC: National Association for the Education of Young Children)

Brass, D.J. (1985) 'Men's and women's networks: a study of interaction patterns and influence in an organisation', *Academy of Management Journal*, **28**, 327–343

Brislin, R.W. (1981) *Cross-cultural encounters: Face-to-face interaction* (London: Pergamon Press)

Brock-Utne, B. (1980) 'What is educational action research?', *Classroom Action Research Network*, Bulletin No. **4**, Summer (pp.10–15) (Cambridge: C. A. R. N Publications)

Bronowski, J. (1973) *The Ascent of Man* (Australia: Angus & Robertson)

Brooks, D.M. & Hawke, G. (1985) 'Effective and ineffective session-opening teacher activity and task structures' in R. Tharp and R. Gallimore (1988) *Rousing Minds to Life* (Cambridge: Cambridge University Press)

Brown, J.S., Collins, A. & Duguid, P. (1989) 'Situated cognition and the culture of learning', *Educational Researcher*, **18**, 1, 32–42

Brown, R. (1965) *Social Psychology* (New York: Free Press)

Bruner, J. (1994) 'Four ways to make meaning', paper presentation to the annual meeting of the American Educational Research Association, New Orleans, LA

Burgess, R.G. (ed.) (1985) *Strategies of Educational Research: Qualitative Methods* (London: Falmer Press)

Burke, J.W. (ed.) (1989) *Competency-based Education and Training* (London: Falmer Press)

Butler, S.R. (1991) 'Reading program – remedial, integrated and innovative', *Annals of Dyslexia* **41**, 119–127

Cahalan, M. & Farris, E. (1990) *College Sponsored Tutoring and Mentoring Programs For Disadvantaged Elementary and Secondary Students*, Higher Education Surveys – Report No. 12. (Washington DC: US Department of Education. Office of Planning, Budget & Evaluation) (ED323884)

Cairns, M. (1993) 'Wits Mission Statement Project', unpublished (University of the Witwatersrand, Johannesburg)

Calderhead, J. (1989) 'Reflective teaching and teacher education', *Teaching and Teacher Education*, **5**, 1, 43–51

Cameron, L. & Jesser, P. (1992) 'Mentoring can add extra value to the training dollar', *HR Monthly: The Australian Human Resources Magazine*, April, 14–15

Campbell, I. (1995) *Student Tutoring and Pupil Aspirations* (CSV/BT Research, University of Birmingham)

Carre, C. & Ovens, C. (1994) *Science 7–11: Developing Primary Teaching Skills* (London: Routledge)

Carter, R. (1985) 'A taxonomy of objectives for professional education', *Studies in Higher Education*, **10**, 2, 135–149

Carter, R. (1994) 'Report of Task Group No. 9', unpublished (University of the Witwatersrand, Johannesburg)

Casey, M. Beth (1990) 'A planning and problem-solving preschool model: the methodology of being a good learner', *Early Childhood Research Quarterly*, **5**, 53–67

Cassidy, D.J. & Myers, B.K. (1993) 'Mentoring inservice training for child care workers', *Child and Youth Care Forum*, **22**, 5, 387–398

Cave, G. & Quint, J. (1990) *Career Beginnings Impact Evaluation: Findings from a Program for Disadvantaged High School Students* (New York: MDRC)

Chaiklin, S. & Lave, J. (1993) *Understanding Practice Perspectives on activity and context* (Cambridge: Cambridge University Press)

Challoner, J. (1994) *The Explorers' Book* (London: Science Museum)

Chen, M. & Goldring, E. (1992) 'The impact of classroom diversity on teachers' perspectives of their schools as workplaces', paper presented at the annual meeting of the University Council of Educational Administration, Minneapolis

Christie, P. (1995) Personal communication (South Africa)

Clawson, J.G. (1979) 'Superior-subordinate relationships for managerial development', unpublished doctoral dissertation, School of Business, Harvard University

Cloward, R.A. (1967) 'Studies in tutoring', *Journal of Experimental Education*, **36**, 1, 14–25

Cohen, J. (1986) 'Theoretical considerations of peer tutoring', *Psychology in the Schools*, **23**, 175–186

Cohen, P.A., Kulik, J.A. & Kulik, C.C. (1982) 'Educational outcomes of tutoring: a meta-analysis of findings', *American Educational Research Journal*, **19**, 237–248

Coleman, J.S. *et al.* (1974) *Youth: Transition to Adulthood* Report of the Panel on Youth (Chicago: University of Chicago Press)

Collier, G. (ed.) (1983) *The Management of Peer Group Learning: Syndicate Methods in Higher Education* (Guildford: Society for Research into Higher Education)

Collins, N. & Ronaldson, A. (1994) 'SI addressing needs', *Illumine*, November, p. 1 (Port Elizabeth: Information Service on Higher Education)

Collins, A., Brown, J.S. & Hollum, A. (1991) 'Cognitive apprenticeship: making thinking visible', *American Educator*, Winter 1991, **6**, 11, 38–46

Colmen, J.G. (1965) 'Volunteerism: a constructive outlet for youthful energy', *Journal of Marriage and the Family*, **27**, 171–175

Combs, A.W. (1972) 'Some basic concepts for teacher education', *Journal of Teacher Education*, **22**, 286–90

Committee on Women in Science, Engineering & Technology (1994) *The Rising Tide* The Cabinet Office (London: HMSO)

Cornwall, M.G. (1979) *Students as Teachers: Peer Teaching in Higher Education* (COWO University of Amsterdam)

Cross, M. (1995) Personal communication (Mozambique)

CSV (1994a) *CSV Learning Together Annual Review 1993–4:* Student Tutoring Scheme (London: Community Service Volunteers)

CSV (1994b) *It All Adds Up: Student Tutoring and Financial Literacy* (London : Community Service Volunteers)

Cullen, J. (1991) 'Young children's learning strategies: continuities and discontinuities', *International Journal of Early Childhood* 1, 23, 44–58

Curle, A. (1963) *Educational Strategy for Developing Societies* (London: Tavistock Publications)

Curle, A. (1964) 'Education, politics and development', *Comparative Education Review* 8, 33

Daniels, L.D. & Berkowitz, L. (1963) 'Liking and response to dependency relationships', *Human Relations*, **16**, 141–148

Davies, J.S. & Marquis, C. (1979) 'Interaction and Independence: getting the mix right', *Teaching at a Distance*, **14**, 29–44

Davis, D., Snapiri, T. & Golan, P. (1984) *A survey of tutoring activities in Israel and associated evaluation studies*, Publication No. 96. Jerusalem: Research Institute for Innovation in Education, The Hebrew University of Jerusalem, School of Education.

Devin-Sheehan, L., Feldman, R.S. & Allen, V.L. (1976) 'Research on children tutoring children: a critical review', *Review of Educational Research*, **46**, 355–385

Dewey, J. (1938) *Experience and Education* (New York: Collier)

DfE (1994) *Statistical Bulletin 11/94* (London: Department for Education)

Diamond, C.T.P. (1991) *Teacher Education as Transformation* (Philadelphia: Open University)

Dickson, A. (1972) *Each One, Teach One* (London: Frontier)

Dinsdale, C. (ed.) (1994) *It All Adds Up* (London: Community Service Volunteers/NatWest)

Donaldson, M. (1978) *Children's Minds* (London: Fontana)

Donaldson, M. (1992) *Human Minds, An Exploration* (Harmondsworth: Penguin Books Ltd)

Doring, A. (1994) 'Teacher training in England: is the profession being undermined?', *Unicorn*, **20**, 3, 46–53

Dovidio, J.F. (1984) 'Helping behavior and altruism: an empirical and conceptual overview', in L. Berkowitz (ed.) *Advances in Experimental Social Psychology*, Volume 17 (pp. 361–427). (Orlando, Florida: Academic Press)

Duffy, G.G., Roehler, L.R., Meloth, M.S. & Vavrus, L.G. (1986) 'Conceptualising instructional explanation', in R. Tharp & R. Gallimore, (1988) *Rousing Minds to Life* (Cambridge: Cambridge University Press)

Dugger, C. (1995) 'For young, a guiding hand out of the ghetto', *The New York Times*, 9 March.

Duin, A.H., Lammers, E., Mason, L.D. & Graves, M.F. (1994) 'Responding to ninth-grade students via telecommunications: college mentor strategies and development over time', *Research in the Teaching of English*, **28**, 2, 117–153

Duneier, M. (1992) *Slim's Table: Race, Respectability, and Masculinity* (Chicago: University of Chicago Press).

Dzvimbo, P. (1995) Personal communication (Zimbabwe)

Eisenberg, T., Fresko, B. & Carmeli, M. (1980a) *A Tutorial Project For Disadvantaged Children: An evaluation of the PERACH project* (Rehovot, Israel: Perach, Weizmann Institute of Science)

Eisenberg, T., Fresko, B. & Carmeli, M. (1980b) *PERACH: A tutorial project for disadvantaged children* (Rehovot, Israel: The Weizmann Institute of Science)

Eisenberg, T., Fresko, B. & Carmeli, M. (1981) 'An assessment of cognitive change in socially disadvantaged children as a result of a one-to-one tutoring program', *Journal of Educational Research*, **74**, 5 311–314

Eisenberg, T., Fresko, B. & Carmeli, M. (1982) 'Affective changes in socially disadvantaged children as a result of one-to-one tutoring', *Studies in Educational Evaluation* **8**, 2, 141–151

Eisenberg, T., Fresko, B. & Carmeli, M. (1983a) 'A follow-up study of disadvantaged children two years after being tutored', *Journal of Educational Research*, **76**, 5, 302–306

Eisenberg, T., Fresko, B. & Carmeli, M. (1983b) *The effect at different grade levels of one and two years of tutoring* (Rehovot, Israel: Perach, Weizmann Institute of Science)

References and further reading

English, L.D. (1988) *Young children's competence in solving novel combinatorial problems* (Department of Education: University of Queensland)

Entwistle, N. (1987) 'A model of the teaching learning process', in J.T.E. Richardson, *et al.* (eds) *Student Learning: Research in Education and Cognitive Psychology*, Chapter 2 (Milton Keynes: SRHE & Open University Press)

ERIC Office of Educational Research and Improvement (1988) *ERIC Database: College students who tutor elementary and secondary students* (Washington DC: US Department of Education)

Even, E. (1984) 'Change in student teachers' personality in PERACH project', paper presented at the 1st International Conference on Education in the 90s: Equality, Equity and Excellence in Education, Tel-Aviv, 16–19 December

Fagenson, E.A. (1989) 'The mentor advantage: perceived career/job experiences of proteges versus non-proteges', *Journal of Organisational Behaviour*, **10**, 309–320

Falk, H. & Dierking, L. (1992) *The Museum Experience* (Washington DC: Whalesback)

Farren, C., Gray, J.R. & Kay, B. (1984) 'Mentoring: A boon to career development', *Personnel*, Nov-Dec, 19–24

Fasko, D. & Flint, W.W. (1990) 'Enhancing self-esteem of at-risk high school students', unpublished report, Kentucky (ED348593)

Fischetti, J., Maloy, R. & Heffley, J. (1989) 'Undergraduates tutoring in secondary schools: collaborative opportunities for teacher education', *Action in Teacher Education* **10**, 4, 9–14

Fitts, W.H. (1965) *Manual for Tennessee self concept scale* (Los Angeles: Western Psychological Services)

Flanagan, D. (1976) *Can students be teachers too?* (ERIC reprint, E.D. 121723)

Flaxman, E., Ascher, C. & Harrington, C. (1988) *Youth Mentoring Programs and Practices* (New York: Institute for Urban and Minority Education)

Fleer, M. (1992) 'From Piaget to Vygotsky, moving into a new era in education', in B. Lambert (ed.) *Changing Faces, the early childhood profession in Australia* (Watson: Australian Early Childhood Association)

Flippo, R.F. *et al.* (1993) 'Literacy, multicultural and sociocultural considerations: student literacy corps and the community', paper presented at the annual meeting of the International Reading Association, San Antonio, Texas, 26–30 April (ED 356466)

Freedman, M. (1993) *The Kindness of Strangers: Adult Mentors, Urban Youth, and the New Voluntarism* (San Francisco: Jossey-Bass)

Fresko, B. (1988) 'Reward salience, assessment of success and critical attitudes among tutors', *Journal of Educational Research*, **81**, 341–346

Fresko, B. & Carmeli, M. (1990) 'PERACH: A nation-wide student tutorial project', in S. Goodlad & B. Hirst (eds) *Explorations in Peer Tutoring* (pp. 73–81) (Oxford: Basil Blackwell)

Fresko, B. & Chen, M. (1989) 'Ethnic similarity, tutor expertise and tutor satisfaction', *American Educational Research Journal*, **26**, 1, 122–140

Fresko, B. & Eisenberg, T. (1985) 'The effects of two years of tutoring on mathematics and reading achievement', *Journal of Experimental Education*, **53**, 4, 193–201

Fretz, B.R. (1979) 'College students as paraprofessionals with children and the aged', *American Journal of Community Psychology*, **7**, 357–360

Freund, L.S. (1990) 'Maternal regulation of children's problem-solving behaviour and its impact on children's performance', *Child Development*, **61**, 113–126

Fullan, M. (1991) *The New Meaning of Educational Change* (London: Cassell Educational)

Fuchs, L.S., Fuchs, D., Bentz, J., Phillips, N.B. & Hamlett, C.L. (1994) 'The nature of student interactions during peer tutoring with and without prior training and experience', *American Educational Research Journal*, **31**, 1, 75–103, Spring

Gadsby, M. (1993) *The Birmingham Connection: Student tutoring scheme* (London: Community Service Volunteers)

Gadsby, M. (1994) *The Birmingham Connection* (CSV Learning Together Report) (London: Community Service Volunteers)

Gartner, A. & Riessman, F. (1993) *Peer Tutoring: A New Model* (New York: Peer Research Laboratory)

Gerdes, P. (1994) Personal communication (Mozambique)

George, P. (1992) 'Models of professional education', unpublished paper referred to in H. Bines, 'Issues in Course Design' in H. Bines, and D. Watson, *Developing Professional Education* (Buckingham: Open University Press)

Gerth, H. & Mills, C.W. (1967) 'Institutions and persons', in J.G. Manis & B.N. Meltzer (eds) *Symbolic Interaction* (pp. 185–188). (Boston: Allyn & Bacon)

Gipe, J.P. & Richards, J.C. (1990) 'Promoting reflection about reading instruction through journaling', *Journal of Reading Education*, **15**, 3, 6–13

Gipe, J.P. & Richards, J.C. (1992) 'Reflective thinking and growth in novices' teaching abilities', *Journal of Educational Research*, **86**, 1, 52–57

Glaser, B. (1978) *Theoretical Sensitivity: Advances in methodology in grounded theory* (Mill Valley, Calif.: Sociology Press)

Glazer, J.S. & Wughalter, E. (1991) 'MENTOR in education: attracting minority students to teaching careers', *Mentoring International* **5**, 1–2, 15–20

Glenny, G. & Hickling, E. (1992) 'Designing the practicum in teacher education', in H. Bines and D. Watson, *Developing Professional Education* (Buckingham: Open University Press)

Goldman, R. *et al.* (1975) 'Small groups and the introductory course in American politics', *Teaching Political Science*, **3**, 1, 37–62.

Goldschmid, M.L. & Shore, B.M. (1974) 'The learning cell: a field test of an educational innovation', in W.A. Verreck (ed.) *Methodological Problems in Research and Development in Higher Education* (Amsterdam: Swets and Zeitlinger)

References and further reading

Goodlad, S. (1979) *Learning by teaching* (London: Community Service Volunteers)

Goodlad, S. (ed.) (1982) *Study Service: An examination of community service as a method of study in higher education* (Windsor: NFER-Nelson)

Goodlad, S. (ed.) (1984) *Education for the Professions: Quis Custodiet?* (Windsor: SRHE & NFER-Nelson)

Goodlad, S. (1985) 'Putting science into context', *Educational Research* **27**, 1, 61–67

Goodlad, S. (1995a) 'Students as tutors and mentors', keynote address, IC/BP International Conference, London, April

Goodlad, S. (1995b) *The Quest for Quality: Sixteen forms of heresy in higher education* (Buckingham: SRHE & Open University Press)

Goodlad, S. & Hirst, B. (1989) Peer tutoring: a guide to learning by teaching (London: Kogan Page)

Goodlad, S. & Hirst, B. (eds) (1990) *Explorations in peer tutoring* (Oxford: Basil Blackwell)

Goodlad, S., Abidi, A., Anslow, P. & Harris, J. (1979) 'The Pimlico Connection: undergraduates as tutors in schools', *Studies in Higher Education* **4**, 2, 191–201

Gore, J. (1987) 'Reflecting on reflective teaching', *Journal of Teacher Education*, **38**, 2, 33–39

Gregory, L. & Berley-Mellits, B. (1988) *An Evaluation of the City University of New York/New York City Board of Education Collaborative Programs* (Philadelphia: Public/Private Ventures)

Grimmett, P. (1988) 'The nature of reflection and Schon's conception in perspective', in P. Grimmett and G. Erickson (eds) *Reflection in Teacher Education* (pp. 5–15) (New York: Teachers College Press)

Gurteen, S.H. (1882) *Handbook of Charity Organization* (Buffalo, New York: Published by the author)

Habershaw, S., Habershaw, T. & Gibbs, G. (1993) *53 Interesting Things to do in your Lectures and Tutorials* (New South Wales: St Clair Press)

Hakim, C. (1987) *Research Design – Strategies and choices in the design of social research* (London: Allen and Unwin)

Hall, C. (1993) Private communication. University of Victoria (Wellington, New Zealand)

Hamilton, S. (1990) *Apprenticeship for Adulthood* (New York: Free Press)

Hammersley, M. (1990) *Classroom Ethnography* (Milton Keynes: Open University Press)

Harlen, W. (ed.) (1985) *Primary Science Taking the Plunge* (London: Heinemann Educational)

Hayson, J. (1994) *Science Sense* (Toronto: Ontario Institute for Studies in Education)

Healy, J.M. (1990) *Endangered Minds: Why children don't think and what we can do about it* (New York: Simon and Schuster)

319

Hedin, D. (1987) 'Students as teachers: a tool for improving school climate and productivity', *Social Policy*, **17**, 42–47

Henderson, J.G. (1992) *Reflective Teaching: Becoming an Inquiring Educator* (New York: Macmillan)

Hennig, M. & Jardim, A. (1977) *The Managerial Woman* (New York: Doubleday/Anchor Books)

Henze, R.C. (1992) *Informal Teaching and Learning: A study of everyday cognition in a Greek community* (Hillsdale, NJ: Lawrence Erlbaum Associates, Inc.)

Hill, S. & Topping, K.J. (1995) *Cognitive and Transferable Skill Gains for Student Tutors* (CSV/BT Research, Dundee University.) (See Chapter 11 of this book)

Hobfoll, S.E. (1980a) 'Interracial commitment and involvement in undergraduate tutors in an inner-city preschool', *Journal of Community Psychology*, **8**, 80–87

Hobfoll, S.E. (1980b) 'Personal characteristics of the college volunteer', *American Journal of Community Psychology*, **8**, 503–506

Hoetker, J. & Ahlbrand, W. (1969) 'The persistance of recitation', in R. Tharp & R. Gallimore (1988) *Rousing Minds to Life* (Cambridge: Cambridge University Press)

Holmberg, B. (1980) *Essentials of Distance Education* (A course on distance education) (Hagen: Fernuniversitat, ZIFF)

Holmes Group (1986) 'Tomorrow's teachers', referred to in Penelope L. Peterson (1988) 'Teachers' and students' cognitional knowledge for classroom teaching and learning', *Educational Researcher*, June/July, **5**, 14

Hughes, J. (1991–2) *The Pimlico Connection: Students Tutoring in Schools*, 17th Annual Report (London: Imperial College of Science, Technology & Medicine)

Hughes, J. (1993) 'Can Student Tutoring Raise Pupils Aspirations?', dissertation, King's College, London

Hughes, J. (1993a) *The Pimlico Connection: Students Tutoring in Schools*. 18th Annual Report 1992–3 (London: Imperial College of Science, Technology and Medicine)

Hughes, J. (1993b) 'The effectiveness of student tutoring to raise pupils' aspirations', paper presented at the second Scottish conference on student tutoring, Glasgow 30 April

Hughes, J. (1993c) 'Student tutors as interpreters in the Science Museum', unpublished paper

Huisman, C. *et al.* (1992) *Student Mentoring Program 1989–1992: Evaluation Report* (Portland, Oregon: Oregon Community Foundation) (ED356701)

Hunt, D.M. & Michael, C. (1983) 'Mentorship: a career training and development tool', *Academy of Management Review*, **8**, 473–485

Inbar, D., Resh, N. & Adler, C. (1984) 'Integration and school variables', in Y. Amir & S. Sharan (eds) *School Desegregation* (pp. 119–132) (Hillsdale, NJ: Lawrence Erlbaum Associates)

References and further reading

Isango, M. (1995) Personal communication (Zaire)

Jacobi, M. (1991) 'Mentoring and undergraduate success: a literature review', *Review of Educational Research*, Winter, **61**, 4, 505–532

Jeannerat, J., Connor, T., Horwitz, K. & Kearns, M. (1994) 'Student tutor report', Department of Social Anthropology, Wits, South Africa (unpublished)

Jenkins, Sir Brian (1992) 'RSA lecture on learning together', Royal Society of Arts, 11 November

Johnston, S. (1994) 'Experience is the best teacher: or is it? An analysis of the role of experience in learning to teach', *Journal of Teacher Education*, **5**, 3, 199–208

Jones, J. (1989) *Effect of Student Tutors on School Students' Attitudes and Aspirations*: report to the Department of Education (Auckland: Higher Education Research Office)

Jones, J. (1990) 'Tutoring as field-based learning: some New Zealand developments', in Goodlad & Hirst (ibid.) Chapter 6

Jones, J. (1993a) 'University students as tutors in secondary schools', in proceedings of a conference on peer tutoring at the University of Auckland, New Zealand, 19–21 August, (Higher Education Research Office and University of Auckland)

Jones, J. (ed.) (1993b) *Peer Tutoring: Learning by Teaching*. Proceedings of Auckland Conference on Peer Tutoring, August (see references to papers by Arneman, Hay, Howse, Johnston, Leveson, Loh, Loo and Miles)

Jones, J. & Jones, A. (1987) 'Spreading the word: university students in school classrooms', paper presented at the 13th Annual HERDSA Conference, Perth, Australia.

Jones, J. & Bates, J. (1987) *University Students as Tutors in Secondary Schools* (Auckland: Higher Education Research Office, University of Auckland)

Jones, J. & Jones, J. (1989) 'Spreading the word: university students in school classrooms', in D. Norman (ed.) *Research and Development in Higher Education*, **10**, 202–214 (Sydney: HERDSA)

Juel, C. (1991) 'Cross-age tutoring between student athletes and at-risk children', *The Reading Teacher*, **45**, 3, 178–186

Juler, P. (1992) *Distance Teaching and Learning*, UDE604, University of South Australia.

Kagan, D.M. (1992) 'Professional growth among preservice and beginning teachers', *Review of Educational Research*, **62**, 2, 129–169

Kanter, R.M. (1977) *Men and Women of the Corporation* (New York: Basic Books)

Karungu, P. (1995) Personal communication (Kenya)

Katz, D. & Kahn, R.L. (1976) *The social psychology of organizations* (New York: John Wiley & Sons)

Kelly, G.A. (1955) *The Psychology of Personal Constructs* (New York: W.W. Norton)

Kilborn, W. (1993) *Final report and recommendations for the text book evaluation. Mathematics*, INDE Research Report Studies No. 4

Kirsten, J.M. (1994) *'Building a new UPE: The contexts of institutional transformation'*, address delivered on the occasion of his inauguration as fourth Vice-Chancellor and Principal of the University of Port Elizabeth (University of Port Elizabeth Publication Series)

Klaus, R. (1981) 'Formalized mentor relationships for management and development programs in federal government', *Public Administration Review*, July-August, 489–496

Klosterman, R. (1970) 'The effectiveness of a diagnostically structured reading program', *The Reading Teacher*, **24**, 159–62

Knowles, J.G. (1993) 'Life-history accounts as mirrors: a practical avenue for the conceptualization of reflection in teacher education', in J. Calderhead & P. Gates (eds) *Conceptualizing Reflection in Teacher Education* (London: Falmer Press)

Kotler, P. (1994) *Marketing Management* (Englewood Cliffs, NJ: Prentice Hall)

Kram, K.E. (1980) *'Mentoring processes at work: developmental relationships in managerial careers'* dissertation, Yale University

Kram, K.E. (1985) *Mentoring at work: developmental relationships in organisational life* (Glenview Illinois, Scott Foresman)

Kram, K.E. (1986) 'Mentoring in the workplace', in D.T. Hall and associates *Career Development in Organisations* (San Francisco: Jossey-Bass)

Kram, K.E. & Isabella, L.A., (1985) 'Mentoring alternatives: the role of peer relationships in career development', *Academy of Management Journal*, **28**, 110–132

Kuyper, J. (1993) *Volunteer Program Administration* (New York: American Council for the Arts)

Kwapong, A.A. (1993) 'Keynote address: round table on teacher education for science, mathematics and technical/vocational subjects', Teacher Education in Science, Mathematics and Technical/Vocational Subjects, Commonwealth of Learning, Vancouver

Larwood, L. & Blackmore, J. (1978) 'Sex discrimination in manager selection: testing predictions of the vertical dyad linkage model', *Sex Roles*, **4**, 359–367

Lave, R. & Wenger, E. (1991) *Situated learning legitimate peripheral participation* (Cambridge: Cambridge University Press)

Lean, E. (1983) 'Cross-gender mentoring – downright upright and good for productivity', *Training and Development Journal*, **37**, 5, 60–65

Lee, S., Bryant, S., Noonan, N. & Plionis, E. (1987) 'Keeping youth in school: a public-private collaboration', *Children Today*, **4**, 15–21

Levin, H.M., Glass, G.V. & Meister, G.R. (1987) 'Cost-effectiveness of computer-assisted instruction', *Evaluation Review*, **7**, 1, February, 50–72

Levin, R. (1995) Personal communication (Swaziland)

Levinson, D.J. (1977) 'The mid-life transition: a period in adult psychological development', *Psychiatry*, **40**, May

References and further reading

Levinson, D.J., Darrow, C.N., Klein, E.B., Levinson, M.H. & McKee, B. (1978) *The Seasons of a Man's Life* (New York: A.A. Knopf)

Liederman, D. (1990) 'We need a corps of inner-city youth workers', *The New York Times*, 19 September

Loevinger, J. (1976) *Ego Development: Conceptions and Theories* (San Francisco: Jossey-Bass)

Lubove, R. (1965) *The Professional Altruist: The Emergence of Social Work as a Career, 1880–1930* (Cambridge, Mass.: Harvard University Press)

MacDonald, B. & Walker, R. (1977) 'Case-study and the social philosophy of educational research', in *Beyond the Numbers Game* – a reader by Hamilton, Jenkins, King, MacDonald and Parlett (eds) (London: Macmillan Education)

MacDougall, G. (1993) *Student Tutoring in Tayside*. Report on the Student Tutoring Programme 1992/3 (Dundee: Tayside Regional Council)

Mackinnon, A. (1987) 'Detecting reflection-in-action among preservice teachers', *Teacher and Teacher Education*, 3, 2, 135–145

McPartland, J. & Nettles, S. (1991) 'Using community adults as advocates for mentors for at-risk middle school students: A two-year evaluation of project RAISE', *American Journal of Education*, August.

McWilliam, E. (1992) 'Student talk/expert talk: reconceptualising contemporary teacher education needs', in J. Knight, L. Bartlett & E. McWilliam (eds) *Unfinished business: reshaping the teacher education industry for the 1990s* (Rockhampton: University of Central Queensland)

Makgoba, M.W. (1995) Personal communication (South Africa)

Marton, F. & Saljo, R. (1976a) 'On qualitative differences in learning: outcome and process', *British Journal of Educational Psychology*, 46, 4–11

Marton, F. & Saljo, R. (1976b) 'On qualitative differences in learning: II. Outcomes as a function of the learner's conception of the task', *British Journal of Educational Psychology*, 46, 115–127

Maslow, A.H. (1968) *Toward a Psychology of Being* (New York: Van Nostrand)

Massengill, D. & DiMarco, N. (1979) 'Sex-role stereotypes and requisite management characteristics: a current replication', *Sex Roles*, 5, 561–570

Mevarech, Z. (1985) 'The effects of cooperative mastery learning strategies on mathematical achievement', *Journal of Educational Research*, 78, 372–377

Mezirow, J. (1981) 'A critical theory of adult learning and education', *Adult Education*, 32, 3–24

Miles, M.B. & Huberman, A.M. (1994) *Qualitative Data Analysis* (Thousand Oaks, Calif.: Sage Publications)

Moore, M.G. (1989) 'Three types of interaction' (editorial), *American Journal of Distance Education*, 3, 2, 1–8

Morgan, A. (1991) 'Classroom processes: a case study of course production', in *Windows: Research and Evaluation on a Distance Education Course*, UDE 606, Research in Distance Education, University of South Australia

Mulaik, S.A., James, L.R., Van Alstine, J., Bennett, N., Lind, S. & Stilwell, C.D.

(1989) 'Evaluation of goodness-of-fit indices for structural equation models', *Psychological Bulletin*, **105**, 430–445

National Conference of Charities amd Correction (1887) *Proceedings* (Boston: National Conference)

Neugarten, B.L. (1975) 'Adult personality: toward the psychology of the life cycle', in W.C. Sae (ed.) *Human Life Cycle* (New York: Jason-Aronson)

Newble, D. & Clarke, R.M. (1986) 'The approaches to learning of students in a traditional and in an innovative problem based medical school', *Medical Education*, **20**, 267–273

Newman, D., Griffen, P. & Cole, M. (1989) *The Construction Zone: Working for cognitive change in school* (Cambridge: Cambridge University Press)

Noe, R. (1988) 'Women and mentors: a review and research agenda', *Academy of Management Review*, **13**, 65–78

Noe, R.A. (1987) 'An exploratory investigation of the antecedents and consequences of mentoring', unpublished manuscript, University of Minnesota, Industrial Relations Centre

Novak, J.D & Gowin, D.B. (1984) *Learning How To Learn* (New York: Cambridge University Press)

Oakland Museum, The (1976) *A personal training program for docents* (California: Oakland Museum)

O'Leary, V.E. (1974) 'Some attitudinal barriers to occupational aspirations in women', *Psychological Bulletin*, **81**, 809–826

Osgood, C.E., Suci, G.J. & Tannenbaum, P.H. (1957) *The measurement of meaning* (Urbana, Illinois: University of Illinois Press)

Otter, S. (1992) *Learning Outcomes in Higher Education* (London: Unit for the Development of Adult Continuing Education)

Palinscar, A. & Brown, A. (1984) 'Reciprocal teaching of comprehension fostering and comprehension monitoring activities', *Cognition and Instruction*, **2**, 117–175

Palme, M. (1994) 'The child's right to education: understanding school failure and drop out in primary education in Mozambique', *Educational and Child Psychology*, **11**, 4, 45–54.

Parlett, M. & Hamilton, D. (1977) 'Evaluation as illumination: a new approach to the study of innovative programmes', in *Beyond the Numbers Game* – a reader in educational evaluation by Hamilton, Jenkins, King, MacDonald and Parlett (eds) (London: Macmillan Education)

Pascarella, E.T. & Terenzini, P.T. (1977) 'Patterns of student-faculty information interaction beyond the classroom and voluntary freshman attrition', *Journal of Higher Education*, **48**, 540–552

Pask, G. (1976) 'Conversational techniques in the study and practice of education', *British Journal of Educational Psychology*, **46**, 12–25

Paul, R.H. (1990) *Open learning and open management – leadership and integrity in distance education* (New York: Kogan Page)

References and further reading

PERACH Central Office (1984) *PERACH 1974–1984: Ten years of tutoring* (Rehovot, Israel: The Weizmann Institute of Science)

Peres, Y. (1977) *Ethnic relations in Israel* (Tel-Aviv: Sefriat Hapoelim) (in Hebrew)

Personal Skills Unit (1993) *A conceptual model of transferable personal skills* (Sheffield: University of Sheffield)

Phillips-Jones, L. (1983) 'Establishing a formalized mentoring program', *Training and Development Journal*, **21**, 38–42

Pietig, J. (1994) 'Celebrating twenty-five years of AESA from foundations to scaffolding and beyond', AESA Presidential address 1993, *Educational Studies*, **25**, 1, 1–23

Potter, J. & Daniel, A. (eds) (1994) *CSV Learning Together Annual Review 1993–1994* (London: Community Service Volunteers)

Potter, J. & Porter, J. (1992) *TUTORING: Students as Tutors in School* (London: BP International Ltd)

Powell, J.V., Weisenbaker, J. & Conner, R. (1987) 'Effects of intergenerational tutoring and related variables on reading and mathematics achievement of low socioeconomic children', *Journal of Experimental Education* **55**, 4, 206–211

Pride, A. and Slater-Simmons, E. (1985) *Help in the Classroom: Getting the best from your student tutor* (London: Community Service Volunteers)

Prillaman, D. & Richardson, R. (1989) 'The William and Mary mentorship model: college students as a resource for the gifted', *Roeper Review*, **12**, 2 114–118

Putnam, R.D. (1995) 'Bowling alone, revisited', *The Responsive Community*, **5**, 2, 18–33

Race Relations Survey (1987/88) South African Institute of Race Relations, Johannesburg, South Africa

Race Relations Survey (1993/4) South African Institute of Race Relations, Johannesburg, South Africa

Rajput, S.J. (1993) 'Teacher training and the context of science education at the elementary stage', *Teacher Education in Science, Mathematics and Technical/ Vocational Subjects*, Commonwealth of Learning, Vancouver, 1993

Ramsden, P. (1992) *Learning to teach in higher education* (London: Routledge)

Raupp, C.D. & Cohen, D.C. (1992) 'A thousand points of light'. Illuminate The Psychology Curriculum: Volunteering as a learning experience, *Teaching of Psychology* **19**, 1, 25–30

Reisner, E.R., Petry, C.A. & Armitage, M. (1990) *A review of programs involving college students as tutors or mentors in grades K-12* (Volumes I and II) (Washington DC: Policy Studies Institute) Department of Education

Rennie, J. (1989) 'Business and schools: a dynamic duo', *Personnel*, **66**, 11, 40–44, November

Reykowiski, J. (1982) 'Motivation of prosocial behavior', in V.J. Derlega & J. Grzelak (eds) *Cooperation and helping behavior: theories and research* (pp. 355–375). (New York: Academic Press)

Rhodes, E.M. & Garibaldi, A.M. (1990) 'Teacher cadets answer the call', *Momentum* **20**, 4, 36–38

Rhodes, J., Ebert, L. & Fischer, K. (1992) 'Natural mentors: An overlooked resource in the social networks of adolescent mothers', *American Journal of Community Psychology,* 445–461

Richert, A. (1992) 'Voice and power in teaching and learning to teach', in L. Valli (ed.) *Reflective Teacher Education: Cases and Critiques* (pp. 187–197) (Albany: State University of New York)

Richmond, M. (1899) *Friendly Visiting Among the Poor: A Handbook for Charity Workers* (Montclair, NJ: Patterson Smith)

Riley, S. & Wrench, D. (1985) 'Mentoring among women lawyers', *Journal of Applied Social Psychology,* **15**, 374–386

Roberts, D. (1984) 'Ways and means of reducing early student drop-out', *Distance Education,* **5**, 1

Robinson, J.P. & Shaver, P.R. (1973) *Measures of social psychological attitudes* (Revised edition) (Ann Arbor, Michigan: Institute for Social Research, University of Michigan)

Roche, G.R. (1979) 'Much ado about mentors', *Harvard Business Review,* **57**, 1, 14–31

Rogoff, B. & Lave, J. (eds) (1984) *Everyday Cognition: It's Development in Social Context* (Cambridge, Mass.: Harvard University Press)

Rogoff, B., Mosier, C., Mistry, J. & Goncu, A. (1993) 'Toddlers guided participation with their caregivers in cultural activity', in E.A. Foreman, N. Minick & C. Addison Stone *Contexts for Learning* (New York: Oxford University Press)

Rosen, B., Templeton, M.E. & Kirchline, K. (1981) 'First few years on the job: women in management', *Business Horizons,* **24**, 12, 26–29

Ross, S.M. *et al.* (1989) 'The apple classroom of tomorrow programme with at-risk students', in proceedings of selected research papers presented at the annual meeting of the Association for Educational Communicators and Technology, Dallas Texas, 1–5 February (ED308837)

Rowntree, D. (1992) *Exploring Open and Distance Learning* (London: Kogan Page)

Rynes, S. & Rosen, B. (1983) 'A comparison of male and female reactions to career advancement opportunities', *Journal of Vocational Behaviour,* **22**, 105–116

Sandler, I.N., Reich, J.W. & Doctolero, J. (1979) 'Utilization of college students to improve inner-city school children's academic behavior', *Journal of School Psychology,* **17**, 3, 283–290

Sarbin, T.R. (1976) 'Cross-age tutoring and social identity', in V.L. Allen (ed.) *Children as teachers: theory and research on tutoring* (pp. 27–40) (New York: Academic Press)

Saunders, D. (1992) 'Peer tutoring in higher education', *Studies in Higher Education,* **17**, 2, 211–218

References and further reading

Sawyerr, G.F.A. (1988) 'A fragment on the socio-cultural role of the university in Commonwealth Africa: What can we do for our countries?' (London: Association of Commonwealth Universities)

School of Computing and Information Studies (1990) *A Study of Personal Transferable Skills Teaching in Higher Education in the UK, Final Report* (Birmingham: University of Central England)

Schor, J.B. (1991) *The Overworked American: The Unexpected Decline of Leisure* (New York: Basic Books)

Schwartz, G. (1977) 'College students as contingency managers for adolescents in a program to develop reading skills', *Journal of Applied Behavior Analysis*, **10**, 645–655

Schwartz, S.H. & Howard, J.A. (1982) 'Helping and cooperation: a self-based motivational model', in V.J. Derlega & J. Grzelak (eds) *Cooperation and helping behavior: theories and research* (pp. 327–353) (New York: Academic Press)

Sewart, D. (1978) *Continuity of concern for students in a system of learning at a distance* (Hagen: Fernuniversitat (ZIFF))

Sewart, D. (1981) 'Distance teaching: A contradiction in terms', *Teaching at a Distance*, **19**, 8–18

Shapiro, E.C., Haseltine, F.P. & Rowe, M.P. (1978) 'Moving up: role models, mentors, and the "Patron System"', *Sloan Management Review*, **19**, 3, 51–58

Sharpley, A.M., Irvine, J.W. & Sharpley, C.F. (1983) 'An examination of the effectiveness of a cross-age tutoring program in mathematics for elementary school children', *American Educational Research Journal*, **20**, 103–111

Siegel, I.E. & Saunders, R. (1979) 'An inquiry into inquiry: question asking as an instructional model', in L.G. Katz (ed.) *Current topics in early childhood education*, 2. (Norwood, NJ: Ablex)

Siegler, R.S. and Crowley, K. (1991) 'The microgenetic method: a direct means of studying cognitive development', *American Psychologist* **46**, 6, 606–620

Simons, H. (1977) 'Case studies of innovation', in *Beyond the Numbers Game – a reader in educational evaluation* by Hamilton, Jenkins, King, MacDonald & Parlett (eds) (London: Macmillan Education)

Singh, A. (1992) A contribution to 'The University in the Twenty-First Century' symposium papers, *MINERVA*, **XXX**, 2, Summer, 230–234

Slade, C. (1995) 'Higher order thinking in institutions of higher learning', *Unicorn* **21**, 1, 37–47

Slavin, R. (1990) 'Research on cooperative learning: consensus and controversy', *Educational Leadership*, 512–554

Soffair, E. (1986) 'Tutorial programs – the importance of tutor-tutee similarity', MA thesis submitted at Tel-Aviv University, Department of Psychology

Sommerfeld, M. (1992) 'Asked to dream, students beat the odds', *Education Week*, 8 April

Stanwyck, D.J. & Anson, C.A. (1989) *The Adopt-A-Student Evaluation Project:*

Final Report (Atlanta: Department of Educational Foundations, Georgia State University)

Staub, E. (1974) 'Helping a distressed person: social, personality and stimulus determinants', in L. Berkowitz (ed.) *Advances in Experimental Social Psychology*, Volume 7 (pp. 294–341) (New York: Academic Press)

Stedman, H.J. (1990) 'Museums and universities: partners in continuing education', in J.W. Solinger (ed.) *Museums and Universities: New paths for continuing education* (New York: Macmillan Publishers)

Stenhouse, L. (1988) 'Case study methods', in *Educational Research, Methodology and Measurement*: An International Handbook edited by John P. Keeves (Oxford: Pergamon Press)

Stewart, L.P. & Gudykunst, W.B. (1982) 'Differential factors influencing the hierarchical level and number of promotions of males and females within an organisation', *Academy of Management Journal* **25**, 586–597

Stewart, M.E. & Palcic, R.A. (1992) 'Writing to learn mathematics: the writer-audience relationship', paper presented at the annual meeting of the Conference on College Composition and Communication, Cincinnati, Ohio, 19–21 March (ED347549)

Stewart, M.F. (1990) 'Peer tutoring: what's in it for you?', *School Science Review* **71**, 257, 140–142

Storr, A. (1963) *The integrity of the personality* (Baltimore: Penguin Books)

Strauss, J.P., Plekker, S.J. & Strauss, J.W.W. (1991) *Education and Manpower development*, Report No. 12. August. (Bloemfontein, SA: Research Institute for Education Planning)

Stuart, P. (1992) 'What does the glass ceiling cost you?', *Personnel Journal*, November, 70–80

Swartz, N. (1995) Personal communication (South Africa)

Taft, R. (1988) 'Ethnographic research methods', in *Educational Research, Methodologies and Measurement*: An International Handbook edited by John P. Keeves (Oxford: Pergamon Press)

Tann, S. (1993) 'Eliciting student teachers' personal theories', in J. Calderhead and P. Gates (eds) *Conceptualizing Reflection in Teacher Education* (London: Falmer Press)

Taylor, R. (1990) 'South Africa's open universities challenging apartheid?', *Higher Education Review*, **23**, 3, 5–17

Terenzini, P.T. & Wright, T.M. (1987) 'Influences on students' academic growth during four years of college', *Research in Higher Education*, **26**, 161–179

Tharp, R. & Gallimore, R. (1988) *Rousing Minds to Life* (Cambridge: Cambridge University Press)

Tierney, J. & Branch, A. (1992) *College Students as Mentors for At-Risk Youth: A study of Six Campus Partners in Learning Programs* (Philadelphia: Public/Private Ventures)

Tinto, V. (1975) 'Dropout from higher education: a theoretical synthesis of recent research', *Review of Educational Research*, **45**, 89–125

References and further reading

Tobias, P.V. (1983) 'Apartheid and medical education: the training of black doctors in South Africa', *International Journal of Health Services*, **13**, 134

Topping, K.J. (1988) *The Peer Tutoring Handbook* (London: Croom Helm)

Topping, K.J. (1995) 'The effectiveness of peer tutoring in higher and further education: a typology and review of the literature' (in press)

Topping, K.J. & Hill, S. (1995) 'University and college students as tutors for schoolchildren: a typology and review of evaluation research' (in press)

Topping, K. & Whiteley, M. (1988) 'Sex differences in the effectiveness of peer tutoring', *The Paired Reading Bulletin*, **4**, 16–23

Topping, K. & Whiteley, M. (1990) 'Participant evaluation of parent-tutored and peer-tutored projects in reading', *Educational Research*, **32**, 14–27

Tough, J. (1973) *Focus on meaning: talking to some purpose with young children* (London: George Allen and Unwin)

Tracey, T.J. & Sedlacek, W.E. (1985) 'The relationship of noncognitive variables to academic success: a longitudinal comparison by race', *Journal of College Student Personnel*, **26**, 405–410

Trawick-Smith, J. (1994) *Interactions in the Classroom: Facilitating Play in the Early Years* (New York: Merrill College Publishing Company)

Tremper, C. & Kostin, G. (1993) *No Surprise: Controlling Risks in Volunteer Programs* (Washington, DC: Non-Profit Risk Management Center)

Tudge, J. & Caruso, D. (1988) 'Cooperative Problem Solving in the Classroom: Enhancing Young Children's Cognitive Development', *Young Children*, November 46–52

Turkel, S.B. & Abramson, T. (1986) 'Peer tutoring and mentoring as a drop-out prevention strategy', *Clearing House*, **60**, 2, 68–71

Tyler, J.L., Gruber, D. & McMullan, B.J. (1987) *An evaluation of the City University of New York/New York City Board of Education Collaborative Programs* (Philadelphia PA: Public/Private Ventures)

Valenzuela-Smith, M. (1983) 'The effectiveness of a tutoring program for junior high Latino students' (San Francisco: University of San Francisco) (ED237307)

Walker, R. (1986) 'The conduct of educational case studies', in M. Hammersley (ed.) *Controversies in Classroom Research* (Chichester, UK: Wiley)

Ward, W.E.F. (1959) *Educating Young Nations* (London: Allen and Unwin)

Werner, E.E. & Smith, R.S. (1982) *Vulnerable but Invincible: A Study of Resilient Children* (New York: McGraw-Hill)

Wertsche, J.V. (1985) *Vygotsky and the social formation of mind* (Cambridge, Mass.: Harvard University Press)

White, R. (1992) 'Implications of recent research on learning for curriculum and assessment', *Journal of Curriculum Studies*, **24**, 153–164

Wildman, T.M., Magliaro, S.G., Niles, R.A. & Niles, J.A. (1992) 'Teacher mentoring: an analysis of roles, activities and conditions', *Journal of Teacher Education*, **43**; 3, May–June, 205–213

Williams, T. & Kornblum, W. (1985) *Growing Up Poor* (New York: Lexington Books)

Wood, D.J., Bruner, J.S. & Ross, G. (1976) 'The role of play tutoring in problem solving', *Journal of Child Psychology and Psychiatry*, **17**, 89–100

Wrightsman, L.S. (1991) 'Research methodologies for assessing mentoring', presented at the annual conference of the American Psychological Association, Los Angeles (ERIC Document Reproduction Service No. ED 209 339)

Wunsch, M.A. (1994) 'Developing mentoring programs: major themes and issues', *New Directions for teaching and learning*, **57**, Spring, 27–34

Yogev, A. & Ronen, R. (1982) 'Cross-age tutoring: effects on tutors' attributes', *Journal of Educational Research*, **75**, 261–268

Zey, M.G. (1985) 'Mentor programs: making the right moves', *Personnel Journal* **64**, 2, 53–57

Zey, J. (1988) 'A mentor for all reasons', *Personnel Journal*, January, 45–51

Index of People and Places

331